PRAISE FOR *THE ORG*

"The writing is compelling, the research is rigorous and the topic could hardly be more relevant to us all—*The Org* is a must-read."
Tim Harford, author of *The Undercover Economist Strikes Back*

"If you despair at endless meetings and interfering managers - you need to read *The Org* . . . a charming and deeply researched field guide to what makes organisations tick, and why they sometimes drive us crazy."
Oliver Burkeman, Guardian columnist and author of *The Antidote*

"a compelling new book . . . The book offers telling insight on a topic that has ebbed and flowed across the world over the last 30 years, as governments of all stripes have set out to privatize state-owned enterprises and outsource services – what does the private sector do better than government, and what does it do worse?"
Eduardo Porter, *The New York Times*

"*The Org* makes the world of work comprehensible to anyone who's been driven to cynicism by the dysfunction of nearly any organization. And with examples from McDonald's to the Methodist Church, it may even make life inside the org a little more fun."
Richard Florida, author of Rise of the Creative Class; professor, University of Toronto and NYU; and senior editor, *Atlantic*

"For many of us who are seeking a framework for understanding the confusing an̲d̲ ̲r̲a̲... ̲ supply chains and trade, *The Org* pro̲v̲i̲d̲e̲... ̲ ...nceptual lens."

...M... ...ze in Economics
...of *The Next Convergence*

ABOUT THE AUTHORS

Ray Fisman is the Lambert Family Professor of Social Enterprise and codirector of the Social Enterprise Program at the Columbia Business School. Ray received his PhD in business economics from Harvard University and worked as a consultant in the Africa Division of the World Bank for a year before moving to Columbia in 1999. His work has been covered widely in the popular press, from Maureen Dowd's column in the New York Times to Al Jazeera to the Shanghai Daily. He also writes a monthly column for Slate magazine. His first book, Economic Gangsters (with Ted Miguel), was published to great critical acclaim by Princeton University Press in 2008.

Tim Sullivan is the editorial director of Harvard Business Review Press. He has been a senior editor at Princeton University Press, where he worked on the social sciences lists, including the best academic economics list in the world; a senior editor at Portfolio, the business imprint at Penguin; and an executive editor at Basic Books.

THE
ORG

How the Office Really Works

RAY FISMAN and TIM SULLIVAN

JOHN MURRAY

First published in Great Britain in 2014 by John Murray (Publishers)
An Hachette UK Company

First published in the US in 2013 by Twelve.

1

A CIP catalogue record for this title is available from the British Library

ISBN 978 1 84854 996 8

Printed and bound in Great Britain by Clays Ltd, St Ives plc

John Murray policy is to use papers that are natural, renewable and
recyclable products and made from wood grown in sustainable forests.
The logging and manufacturing processes are expected to conform
to the environmental regulations of the country of origin.

John Murray (Publishers)
338 Euston Road
London NW1 3BH

www.hodder.co.uk

To my mother and father   —Ray

To my mother   —Tim

CONTENTS

THE
ORG

Introduction

A Machine for Getting Stuff Done

ACCORDING TO A NATIONAL TIME USE SURVEY, in 2008 the average employed American parent between the ages of twenty-five and fifty-four spent more than a third of the day, nearly nine hours, at work and in "related activities." We spend as much time at work as we do eating and sleeping, combined. More time with our coworkers than with our loved ones.

In fact, we spend so much time with our coworkers that some of them serve as substitutes for our loved ones. Consider the idea of the "work spouse," someone with whom you have a platonic relationship, but one of such intimacy that it replicates your marriage, perhaps even doing it one better by not involving domestic and financial tensions. In one survey, 65 percent of respondents said they had an "office husband" or "office wife."

This is just the most recent data point in a worldwide trend of more work. Since the early 1980s the amount of time we work has been on an upward trajectory, and with the advent of e-mail and smartphones, the invasion of our home lives by work is nearly complete: you can take the worker out of the office, but you can't take the office out of the worker.[1]

Despite the hours logged at the office, or maybe because of them, most employees struggle to make sense of their work lives. Many give up trying: office life can seem just too nonsensical to bother. So we descend into cynicism, offering up sarcastic commentary and office jokes that follow a few well-worn premises: clueless managers who have no idea what their direct reports do, failure to communicate objectives, failure to *have* real objectives, a blatant disregard for data and evidence, perverse incentives and personal fiefdoms, rote behavior in the face of new challenges, meaningless memos sent down from on high, the disconnect between HR proclamations and the experience of the average cubicle dweller. The list, as they say, goes on.

It's not that you couldn't make this stuff up, but you don't have to. Ask a friend. Stop a random commuter. Read a strip from Scott Adams's *Dilbert*, a cartoon built largely on readers' suggestions from their own experiences. Office life is so full of absurdities that our reality provides rich fodder for satirists to return to again and again.

But when satire pales in the face of reality, what are we left with? That's the kind of existential question that modern organizations inspire.

While this existential dread moves many to cynicism, it moves others toward action. In her book *Escape from Cubicle Nation*, for instance, Pamela Slim, a career and marketing blogger, advises readers on how to escape "corporate prison" to become thriving entrepreneurs (with no more pesky organizational headaches to deal with, of course). Slim isn't the only one: the bookstore shelves are filled with other similarly aspirational volumes.

But before you rail against the system or dive in to fix it, it might just pay to figure out how things got to be the way they are in the first place. That's where this book comes in. We're offering a description of how and why orgs do what they do—how the parts fit together, how the rules get made, and what happens when you change the rules or move things around. We aim to shed light on the anxiety and confusion that can accompany life in cubicle nation, to show how the path from one-room-workshop-cum-homestead to world-bestriding behemoth is pockmarked with daunting trade-offs and compromise, to demonstrate the logic of office life.

Then, armed with a clearer understanding of how orgs work, you can descend into better-informed cynicism.

The Least Possible Dysfunction

We're not organizational mechanics. There are lots of those around—experts who'll tell you how to fix your organization, which tactical levers to pull, exactly what steps to take to get employees to be more productive, more devoted, more engaged, more trustworthy. Nor are we here to tell you that everything you know about orgs is wrong. It's not.

Instead, we aim to explain the inner workings of the org, drawing on the tools of organizational economics. For decades, economists—people who we might think would have something to say about work—treated the workplace or organization ("the firm," as economists call it) as a black box. In economists' models of the world, stuff went in (inputs) and product came out (outputs). These inputs and outputs might be given more descriptive labels: "labor," "capital," and perhaps even "technology" went into the production of "widgets" (a placeholder for any manufacturing item).[2] Then firms marketed the outputs, consumers bought them, and economists measured it all with demand curves to determine how many widgets would get made. And there you have the manufacturing economy of the mid-twentieth century. What actually happened within the black box of the organization—be it a giant *Fortune* 500 company or a small entrepreneurial shop—was largely beyond the scope of the economics profession.

But then along came organizational economics. While it has deeper historical roots, org econ really matured starting in the mid-1980s (at about the same time, coincidentally, that our work hours were slowly increasing). Organizational economists build mathematical models that aspire to make sense of why organizations look the way they do, how they function, and how they might improve: page after page of algebra impenetrable to the very subjects whose experiences the economists are trying to describe. But lying behind the Greek symbols and esoteric economic jargon are a set of logical principles that can help us make sense of our experiences. Economics doesn't provide a complete view of the org—psychology, sociology, and other disciplines have lots to say as well—but it is very good at showing us the logical structure, the architecture of our organizational lives.

When economists look at the firm, they don't see the dysfunction—or at least that's not *all* they see. Rather, they recognize a set of compromises that result from trade-offs among many competing interests and objectives. From these compromises comes the seeming dysfunction of our work lives—the cost side of all those cost-benefit trade-offs. Organizational economics can help explain why the highly imperfect office of today may nonetheless represent the least dysfunctional of all possible worlds, however depressing the idea of "least dysfunctional" may be.

It's All about Trade-Offs

Consider the case, for instance, of Mr. X, a former member of the user experience design team for American Airlines. In the spring of 2009, Dustin Curtis, a user interface designer himself and a regular blogger, went on an extended rant about AA's terrible website, written in the form of an open letter to the airline, complete with examples of what a better-designed website might look like (which Curtis said he threw together in just a couple of hours). Curtis's web pages were far, far better, at least from the customer's perspective, than those of American Airlines. Curtis ended his letter by asking the company to "imagine what you could do with a full, totally competent design team."

AA's Mr. X sent Curtis an e-mail, which Curtis, with Mr. X's permission, posted to his website, omitting some identifying features (such as Mr. X's real name). "You're right...You're so very right. And yet," began Mr. X's e-mail, before launching into a description of the various trade-offs the AA.com design team had to confront. "The problem with the design of AA.com," Mr. X explained, "lies less in our competency (or lack thereof, as you pointed out in your post) and more with the culture and processes employed here at American Airlines."

Mr. X went on to note that the group running the AA.com website consisted of two hundred people spread out among different groups, including "QA [Quality Assurance], product planning, business analysis, code development, site operations, project planning, and user experience," plus many, many others with a vested interest in how the site works and what it does. And while new features have to go through the UX (user experience) team, the experts on how customers will experience the site, numerous others have the ability to "push" content onto

AA.com without any interference or suggestions from anybody else.

"Simply doing a home page redesign" is not the issue, Mr. X explained—that's a "piece of cake." Rather, it's the competing interests that pose the problem. As Mr. X put it, "AA.com is a huge corporate undertaking with a lot of tentacles that reach into a lot of interests." He ended his missive on an optimistic note: "Even a large organization can effect change," he wrote. "It just takes a different approach than the methods found in smaller shops. But it'll happen because it has to, and we know that. And we'll keep on keepin' on, even if most of us really and truly would prefer to throw it all away and start over."

Mr. X's optimism was unwarranted. AA tracked him down by searching company e-mail data from the UX group and fired him, ostensibly because he had revealed proprietary information. Three years later, the AA.com website is better than it was, thanks in part to Mr. X's erstwhile colleagues' efforts, but not good enough to save the company—American declared bankruptcy in late 2011.[3]

Curtis—or Mr. X, apparently, had he been organizationally unfettered—could have made a superior website than American Airlines had, at least as measured in terms of aesthetics and usability. In fact, Curtis's proposed redesign of the AA interface that he showcased on his website as part of his open letter is a work of clarity, simplicity, and appeal. But Curtis most assuredly could not fly anyone from point A to point B, or negotiate fuel prices, or arrange international flight schedules, or deal with labor disputes, or maintain jet engines. Luckily, Curtis doesn't seem to want to—but if he did, he'd have to build an organization that looks an awful lot like American Airlines.

Principal, Meet Agent

The challenges many organizations face are the outgrowth of a pretty simple problem: How do you get people to do what you want them to do? Over the millennia, smart bosses have learned that when it comes to motivating workers, you get what you pay for. It's all about incentives. Getting the trade-offs right in designing these incentives—and figuring out what it is that you're actually paying for—is the art and science that lies behind every successful boss and organization. Owners and managers create *high-powered incentives* (pay for performance) to push employees to work harder, but this might, for instance, motivate employees to push toxic loans out the door as fast as they can (hello, mortgage crisis).

If you're the owner or manager of an enterprise and you can't watch over everyone all the time, how do you make sure your managers are making as much money as possible, and passing it on to you? If you're one of those managers, how do you make sure that your workers are doing what they're supposed to? That anxiety travels down through every level of the organization, through every department. More work, less skimming.

Economists call this *the principal-agent problem*: how to align the interests of those who want things to get done and those who do the work. This starts with the owners of the corporation (the principals), who want to generate profits, and the CEO (the agent) they hire to make money on their behalf. The CEO, in turn, needs to motivate his agents—the division managers—and so on, resulting in a cascade of principal-agent relationships that follow the org chart all the way down to the store manager and her sales clerks.

The most obvious way of motivating employees is to pay them.

Soon after Henry Ford installed the first conveyor-belt-based assembly line in the car factory in his Highland Park, Michigan, plant, he discovered that even as his line workers became familiar with the process and more experienced at their jobs, their productivity remained about the same. Why? Because they hated the boring, repetitive work.

Ford's innovative solution shook the world. He first introduced the $5.00 day in January 1912, a radical and, to his business peers, disturbing solution. Ford recognized that the $2.30 daily wage that Highland Park workers earned before the pay hike was only as good as other manufacturing jobs in nearby plants, yet the assembly-line work was even more mind numbing. By more than doubling the pay to five dollars for an eight-hour shift, Ford inspired his men to work with zeal through the daily grind, regardless of boredom or unpleasantness. The money was just too good to pass up. In fact, Ford later commented, "The payment of five dollars a day for an eight-hour day was one of the finest cost-cutting moves we ever made." Ford saw increased productivity and better retention rates among trained workers (although retention fell by 1916 as other firms' wages caught up with Ford's).

Ford had discovered what economists call *efficiency wages*: the enormous motivation that comes from above-market wages coupled with the threat of dismissal. He also recognized the need for monitoring a labor force given such a generous salary. Ford thus did his best to weed out those lacking the moral fiber to resist the temptations that would inevitably accompany such stratospheric pay: drink and related sources of moral turpitude. He hired up to two hundred detectives (called the Sociological Department) to spy on every aspect of his workers' private lives.

Who watched the watchers? The detectives of the Sociological Department were making pretty good money as well. Who would ensure that they pursued "thrift, cleanliness, sobriety, family values, and good morals in general," as line workers were expected to? Here's another of the trade-offs that every organization faces. Departments and positions to monitor workers proliferate. Soon you have an organization that looks like the old Fabergé shampoo commercial, where a woman, so thrilled with the shampoo, tells two friends about it, and they tell two friends, and *they* tell two friends, "and so on, and so on..." while her image multiplies relentlessly on the screen.[4]

Anyone who has ever had to fill out a travel and entertainment expense report is familiar with the wages of monitoring. The T&E is a way for the employee to request reimbursement from the company for business-related costs: flying to a meeting, taking a client out to dinner, paying for a taxi to an event uptown. In one popular version—different companies have different methods of tracking expenses—the employee covers the costs and then fills out a form (or has an assistant fill it out) to get his money back. There is much photocopying and compiling of receipts and explaining of various transactions and who was there and what was discussed and the looking up of cost centers. By the time you get your reimbursement, it feels a little like the company has built a $10,000 fortress of checks and balances to secure a $20 bill.

Robots: The Perfect Employees?

As far as Ford was concerned, the perfect employee would probably have been a robot. Robots don't drink or slack off, they take no breaks, they don't treat clients to expensive dinners, and they require no monitoring—just some upkeep costs. (Of course, then you need a labor force of robot upkeepers, and you're back to incentives and monitoring. But we digress.) The problem is that robots don't innovate. They just perform the same routine time after time, tirelessly. Robots didn't invent the internal combustion engine. Or Gmail.

Gmail sprang from the fact that Google doesn't hire mindless automatons. It hires very smart people to solve very difficult engineering problems and then allows them to play with a pretty substantial portion of their time—20 percent, or one day a week—banking on the fact that they'll produce something interesting or, more to the point, profitable. In other words, Google bucked the trend of monitoring their employees' every move. And it paid off: about 50 percent of new Google products, including AdSense and Gmail, got their start through the policy of granting employees time for independent creative work.[5]

But even Google gets what it pays for, good or bad (or both). Clearly, Google spends lots of time, money, and effort to hire smart, creative engineers who relish the challenges that Google's business presents. And it pays to keep them, and to keep them happy. Google's campuses are lush places to work. Their fabled amenities—setting the standard for Silicon Valley companies, which were already pretty generous—include restaurants, snack rooms, massage salons, $500 toward takeout food when employees have a new baby, gyms, language courses, laundry facilities, shuttle buses, and motorized scooters. Quite apart from production efficiencies sacrificed in the name of innovation, innovative people are expensive.

Google's engineers are getting ever more expensive in large part because every other tech company in Silicon Valley is trying to hire them away. And despite all the perks, Google does lose employees. The allure is mostly money: The skilled engineer who can get into a promising, yet still privately held tech company early on will probably get at least some compensation in the form of stock options, which stand a good chance of being worth lots of money later on. For instance, Facebook's current valuation, despite its lackluster IPO, sits at around $40 billion. Even a tiny fraction of that amount is a huge payday.

When Facebook first went after Google's talent, Google let the engineers go without making counteroffers. If the engineers were going to be so mercenary as to leave the greatest company in the world, they were welcome to. But this kind of defection really hurt the company, damaging productivity and derailing projects. So, in an effort to stanch the bleeding, Google started to make significant counteroffers. But even these didn't always work. In the fall of 2010, for instance, it allegedly lost a well-paid engineer to Facebook despite a counteroffer that included a 15 percent raise and a $500,000 bonus. In a recent salvo, Google offered one key engineer, who had a string of successes at Yahoo and Apple, $3.5 million in restricted stock. (The engineer stayed but leaked his bonus information to the press and was identified and fired.)[6]

Problem easily, if expensively, solved: you just need deep pockets to play the game.

But that's not the end of the story. Remember, you get what you pay for. While Google was paying for, and getting, retention, it was also setting up clear signals to its entire staff: if you want a big raise, get a Facebook offer and we'll counter. Google was also paying for trolling and disloyalty.[7]

A Machine for Getting Stuff Done

The impulse to create an org represents the best of our optimistic nature: a bunch of like-minded individuals decide to get together to accomplish a shared goal. But designing organizations is hard, and we end up with a gap between expectations ("We're going to be awesome and get stuff done!") and reality ("I can't believe this place gets anything done!"). Yet at some basic level the org really is a machine for getting stuff done—stuff that we can't get done on our own or pay others to take care of on our behalf. Amid the trade-offs and dysfunction, though, it can quickly stop feeling that way. By better understanding the nature of the org, you should be able to bridge, and perhaps even shrink, the disheartening gap between expectations and reality.

CHAPTER 1

The Outsider

SCOTT URBAN LEADS A MONKISH EXISTENCE. A single bed and a small desk sit in one corner of his studio apartment; a pair of old bicycles in another. In the center of his room stands a CNC router, an ungainly piece of woodworking equipment that Scott uses to transform solid blocks of exotic wood into rough-hewn eyeglass frames. He finishes the frames by hand, using tools that hang from one wall of his apartment to complete the painstaking process of producing custom-order artisanal eyewear. The apartment, the tools, a Web presence, and Scott himself comprise the totality of his business, Urban Spectacles.

Scott's handiwork doesn't come cheap. When *Wired* magazine featured his "Roasted Rack of Lamb" specs, the accompanying caption described them as "perfect for the entrepreneur inking a deal with Google." But if you think $1,000 is a hefty price tag for eyeglasses (lenses extra), Scott would argue that you've got the wrong frame of reference. Scott sees himself as a craftsman and artist, a hero in our made-in-China age where low-cost production rules the marketplace for eyewear and everything else. (In a video that was once posted on Scott's website, a voiceover repeats the mantra "When I think about the current state of eyewear, it makes me want to kick something," as Scott kicks ever-larger objects, from a Nerf football up to a wooden chair.)

For Scott, the price comparison isn't with other eyeglass frames. Instead, as with any artisan, he argues that you should consider the value of his craft and think about glasses as functional art. A single pair of glasses can easily take him half a year from conception to completion, and the annual production of Urban Spectacles totals no more than a few dozen pairs.

Scott didn't plan to design and sell high-end frames for a living. He worked construction jobs during summer vacations and learned a bit here and there about machine tools and woodworking. After college, he took a nine-to-five job at a company that organized art fairs, staying up late into the night to complete his own woodworking projects. He made his first pair of specs after shattering his glasses while learning to break-dance (another project). The busted frames were vintage '60s-era plastic, inherited from his father, and he named the wooden replica that he created Dadda. The design is still available in the Urban Spectacles catalogue.

As he started selling his specs at craft fairs and as enthusiasts began spreading the word, Scott spent more and more time with his router, shaping wood, and less and less time organizing art fairs, until, eventually, he didn't work for anyone else at all.

Scott has achieved what remains an unfulfilled ambition for so many—to be able to focus full time on his craft. He can indulge his creative side, even as he struggles to make ends meet. His gallery of artistic oddities includes "beyecycle" specs (from old bike parts), "beergoggles" (from old beer bottles), and an "Elton J. Head" design, with each lens peering out of a piano carved out of ebony, bone, and crystal. Urban Spectacles has appeared on Al Jazeera news and Fashion Week runways in New York and Rio. They've adorned the rotund face of celebrity chef Graham Elliot during the third season of Fox's *MasterChef*, and they've been featured on the trend-spotting site coolhuntings.com and showcased in design spreads in everything from *EyeCare Professional* to *House Beautiful* to the aforementioned *Wired* piece.[1]

Success. On his own terms and in a gloriously boss-free way. Since leaving his art fair job, Scott has existed in the pristine simplicity of a one-person org. Interns join him during summer break from art school, but he doesn't manage anyone and no one manages him. His customers serve as his bosses, after a fashion, but there's enough demand for his work that Scott can "fire" them if they become troublesome. He leads a flexible and free, if solitary, existence.

Yet all is not well in Scott's organizational and artistic Utopia. As he basks in his combination of organizational minimalism and artistic freedom, he's barely keeping his head above water, financially speaking. If $1,000 seems a lot to spend on glasses, when multiplied by only thirty or forty frames a year, it adds up to a meager annual income, particularly after you've subtracted $10,000 for supplies and another $10,000 to $12,000 for Scott's other "necessities," which he lists as "rent, food, utilities, and beer." He's barely scraping by.

Scott certainly has room to grow. The wait for a pair of his frames speaks to the mismatch between the demand for his products and Scott's ability to satisfy it. That people are willing to wait months for a pair of Urban Spectacles is a good sign that he could either make more or charge more. There's also other evidence that the market—or at least a certain segment of it—is hungry for his work. For instance, Barneys, the upscale department store in New York City, began selling Takahiro Miyashita's quince wood frames for $2,665 a pair shortly after Urban Spectacles made its New York media debut.[2] The specs on display at Barneys are, in Scott's view, a clearly inferior product, a rip-off, in fact, of one of his designs.

Why not make the leap to a bigger org? It's something Scott has thought about over the years. He could produce a line of machine-made, non-custom frames that would come off the shelf at your neighborhood optician, much as Oscar de la Renta sells fifty-dollar sundresses on Amazon while continuing to show intricately embroidered evening gowns at Paris Fashion Week.

There are other good reasons to expand. Without an accounting or packaging or marketing department, Scott ends up dealing with all sorts of administrative tasks he'd like to avoid—the kind of nonsense that artisans who work in large, faceless design shops are spared, even as they have to put up with other organizational nonsense and constraints.

Why choose to stay small? When Scott peers through his Urban Spectacles at corporate America, what does he see that he's so scared of? His fears—many of them well founded—can be best understood if we look at the life and times of another start-up venture that began not in a basement, but in a single-car garage on Addison Avenue in Palo Alto, California. The garage served as the workshop of two guys, Bill and Dave, and now it and the house on Addison are landmarked by the California government as "the birthplace of Silicon Valley."

The Birth and Death of the HP Way

Like Scott, in the beginning Bill and Dave—they christened their company with their surnames, Hewlett and Packard—thrived on the creative and technical challenges of their work. Early custom jobs from the late 1930s and early 1940s included prototypes of a harmonica tuner, and an "exerciser" that used electrical pulses to activate muscle tissue (tested on the "accommodating" wife of the entrepreneur who commissioned the product). And like Scott Urban, in the early days, Bill and Dave did just about everything themselves. The Stanford-trained engineers designed, built, and packaged their products. They also set prices, wrote ad copy, and swept the factory floor.[3] Unlike Scott, however, as demand took off for their first successful product, a radio oscillator, they hired an assistant to help with the sweeping, packaging, and other odd jobs.

At the same time, Bill and Dave shared many of Scott's fears and apprehensions about growing beyond a two-person partnership. From the beginning, they worked to maintain the intimacy and culture of a garage start-up that, in the words of one HP biographer, "could perpetually produce near-miracles of invention, quality, and adaptability." They referred to employees as family and set out to keep management from interfering with "the natural desire of employees to do their jobs well." It was called management by objectives—providing guidelines for what needs to get done and trusting the judgment and wisdom of lower level employees to do the "right" thing.[4]

This management style, later christened the HP Way, focused on the people who made up the company rather than on the products. "The essence of the idea, radical at the time," Peter Burrows wrote in *BusinessWeek*, "was that employees' brainpower

was the company's most important resource." The HP Way included a profit-sharing plan that helped align the employees with
the company's goals. That, combined with the fact that friends
and employees called the founders by their first names, gave HP
a human focus and feel, and it consistently ranked high in any
best-place-to-work poll.[5]

Bill and Dave grew their start-up into a corporation that employed a hundred thousand people by 1992. That year, the *New
York Times* reported that "a malaise had settled over the company, in part because of too much bureaucracy." Even under
the founders, the HP Way had started to slip and eventually
succumbed to the weight of the growing organizational super-
structure. It just wasn't (and isn't) possible to run something that
size without some checks and balances.[6]

By 2011, HP no longer came close even to its 1992-era self,
let alone to the ideal embodied by the HP Way. It had become
the eleventh-largest company in America, with more than three
hundred thousand employees. Building the HP empire may have
required the conscious decision to leave the HP Way behind to
deal with the realities of a workforce that could no longer be
monitored and motivated by "management by objectives," investors eager for a higher return on their HP shareholdings, and
the financial controls needed to keep tabs on a far-flung corporate empire.

To get the employees' view on this shift at HP, you can browse
the feedback posted on glassdoor.com, a website that gives insiders a chance to vent anonymously about present and past
employers. Average feedback on HP is 2.5 out of 5.0, putting it
18th from the bottom out of 112 computer hardware companies
with glassdoor ratings.

The summary reviews of the "most helpful" listings in April

2011 leave no ambiguity about employee sentiment at HP: "Employees treated as numbers." "It's a paycheck but that's about it." "Behind the times that the market wants." "Disappointing." "A toxic environment." The strongest endorsement on the first page of comments is damning in its faint praise: "Ok for new employees not good long term." The details that follow belie everything that Bill, Dave, and the garage on Addison Avenue represented, and speak to the challenges of upholding the HP Way in the Hewlett-Packard of the twenty-first century: "Leaders are not authentic, they don't engender trust." "Complete lack of employee engagement." "Lack of innovation and innovators."

As a Reuters article put it in 2010, "Bill Hewlett and Dave Packard would not be amused."[7]

Despite the loving restoration of the HP garage and continued lip service to the HP Way, today's Hewlett-Packard seems to be all about profits, more or less. These days, employee-friendly practices such as telecommuting, flextime, freedom to pursue independent projects, and airtight job security need to pass the "market test." Do they boost productivity enough to justify their expense? When profits and employees' interests come in conflict, profits win out, as in 2005, when the new CEO handed out thousands of pink slips, to the glee of Wall Street investors. *InformationWeek* magazine ran an opinion piece called, "In Praise of [HP CEO] Mark Hurd's 9,000 Layoffs" in 2010.[8]

After his investor-cheered downsizing, Hurd resigned when an investigation into a sexual harassment claim revealed inconsistencies in his travel and expense account, sending the stock price tumbling nearly 10 percent. The HP board was widely criticized, even as it struggled to find a successor. When it did, its choice was Leo Apotheker, an outsider who was fired eleven months later after suggesting that HP get out of its core business of producing computer hardware. And the newest HP savior, CEO Meg Whitman, announced another round of layoffs in 2012, this time totaling twenty-seven thousand jobs.

This is what scares the crap out of Scott Urban.

Why Orgs?

If orgs are so terrifying, and not just to Scott, then why do we have them in the first place? It's easy to say "to get more done," but there's so much evidence of malfunction that it's far from obvious that this is the case.

Before we can answer that question, we have to take a brief excursion to beautiful downtown eighteenth-century Edinburgh, capital of Scotland and birthplace of Adam Smith and the idea of the market. Smith's greatest contribution to economics, or at least the one he's best remembered for, was his inspired description of the magic of prices in directing traffic in the apparent chaos of a market economy. He likened prices that govern the market to an "invisible hand" that guides each person to make decisions that lead to the same outcome as would occur if affairs were directed by an all-knowing, all-powerful planner with the best interests of society in mind.

To be concrete about what Adam Smith had in mind with his invisible-hand metaphor, think of your last trip to the grocery store, a decidedly market-based transaction. You wander up and down the aisles placing items in your cart based on a combination of clearly marked prices and what you'd like to eat for dinner. There's relatively little experimentation involved: people try new things from time to time, but mostly this involves shifts among brands, a switch from, say, one make of peanut butter or jelly that's not so different from the old one. Grocery shopping involves little uncertainty over what you're getting and, at least in most countries, no ambiguity over what you'll pay. In markets, prices "decide" how peanut butter, jelly, and everything else gets distributed.

What led Smith to his conclusion was a reckoning of how prices get set in a well-functioning market. Smith talked about pin factories, brewers, and bakers, but let's return to our grocery store. A sixteen-ounce jar of Skippy costs $3.99, and at that price, many thousands of consumers put jars of Skippy in their shopping baskets each day. Skippy is owned by Unilever, a company that is happy to supply the world with peanut butter at this price. (Unilever's profits overall were close to $7 billion in 2009.) The market for peanut butter "clears": there's no excess of peanut butter or dissatisfied consumers in search of more. If the price were higher, Unilever would accumulate unsold jars and would eventually be forced to sell at a discount. If prices were any lower, global peanut butter shortages would spur price increases.

Smith's deeper insight on the invisible hand is that this all works for society's best interest. Suppose that tastes switched to more jelly, less peanut butter. Inventories of unsold peanut butter would build up amid grape jelly shortages. Smucker's would ramp up production, Unilever would downsize, and order would soon be restored with each sandwich containing the new ideal peanut-butter-to-jelly ratio. The magic of the market is that billions of individual decisions work to produce the "right" mix of peanut butter, jelly, and everything else in the economy.

Captivated by these insights, economists occupied themselves with filling in the gaps created by Smith's model of the market.[9] The organization in the meantime remained a black box, with inputs such as glass jars and peanuts going in one end and fully formed consumer products such as peanut butter coming out the other.

This may be in part because what goes on inside organizations seemed so very simple by comparison to the intricacies of the market. In organizations, people, not prices, do the deciding. The one who gets to decide is called the boss. Often, rules "decide"— how much you get paid, whether you need to show up for work at eight or at nine, when to take breaks and for how long. But who sets (and changes) the rules? The boss, of course.

But anyone who has ever experienced the tangled mess of reporting relationships, rules, and exceptions that govern any modern organization may see things a little differently from the economists' black box. A *Fortune* 500 CEO certainly doesn't have the time to make every little decision himself, so some things are necessarily left to underlings. In fact, the CEO has to decide which decisions will be his, and which will be left to his deputies. They in turn need to decide what gets handed off to lower-level managers, and so on, down the line. Just deciding who decides can become a complicated mess. If, by the time we get down to line workers, there's not much deciding left to be done, that's because there are so many rules governing those line workers' lives. Someone has to make up those rules, which means yet more complicated decisions for one of the bosses. The problem isn't that the inside of the org was (and is) too simple, but rather that it was too complicated for the models that earlier economists used to understand the world.

So, figuring out what it is that any given org should do—how it decides what to make and what to buy—or even why it exists is something that classical economic theory never really confronted. Yet, after 150 years of ignoring the complicated inner life of the org, economics discovered it in the person of a twenty-

one-year-old British exchange student on a traveling scholarship
to America, where he'd come to look inside the black boxes of
Ford, U.S. Steel, and other giants of American industry. Ronald
Coase is the person who'll help us answer the question "Why
orgs?"

Ronald's Big Adventure

Coase was born into the org-less world of economics in 1910 to
parents whom he described as, while literate, much more interested in sports than academics. His father was the county lawn
bowling champion. Coase himself was more cerebrally inclined.
He recalls playing chess games with himself as a child, moving
each side in turn. He read widely, borrowing "indiscriminately
from the local library." At age eleven, he was taken to see a doctor
of phrenology (a pseudoscience already on the wane by 1920),
who assessed Coase's intellectual prospects based on the shape
of his skull. (Looking at his picture, we see nothing dispositive
about the shape of his head.)

After a physical inspection and engaging Coase in conversation, the phrenologist came up with a verdict: "You are in
possession of much intelligence, and you know it, though you
may be inclined to underrate your abilities." He recommended
that Coase study commercial banking or accountancy, and suggested horticulture and poultry-rearing as appropriate hobbies.

In the end, Coase came to study economics and commerce
quite by accident, or rather by process of elimination. He never
picked up Latin (a requirement for an arts degree) and found
that "mathematics was not to my taste," which closed the door
to any further study in science. The only option remaining at

the Killburn Grammar School was commerce, a course of study he continued at the London School of Economics in 1929, after passing his matriculation exams (which he took as clear evidence of the low standards for higher education in Britain at the time).

Perhaps fortunately, Coase never attended any formal lectures on economics at the LSE. He focused instead on a course of study relevant to the up-and-coming English businessman of the day: taking classes such as commercial law, the organization of transport, and "the economic development of the overseas dominions, India, and the tropical dependencies." His introduction to modern economics came through Arnold Plant, a business manager turned professor, and the LSE's first instructor in the emerging field of business administration.

Plant, a trained economist, revealed to Coase the glories of the invisible hand. While acknowledging the existence of businessmen—after all, he had started his own career as a manager in an engineering firm—Plant thought of them as largely subservient to the market demands of their customers. Plant also disabused Coase of his early socialist leanings, convincing him of the evils of special-interest-driven government monopolies and "the benefits which flow from an economy directed by the price system." Plant's theory of managers amounted to a set of mechanical cogs and gears driving the activities within the black box.

Coase passed his university examinations after two years, and, needing to bide his time for one more year to fulfill the required three years of study, resolved to travel to America to understand why industries and the companies within them were organized as they were. Armed with letters of introduction to various businessmen from a senior official at the Bank of England, he arrived in America in the fall of 1931.

Coase observed the vast General Electric generator plant in

Schenectady, traveled to Detroit to see how Ford and General Motors made automobiles, and stopped in at the steelworks in Gary, Indiana, before heading to Chicago to the headquarters of the Sears, Roebuck and Company. He talked with managers, purchasing agents, accountants, sometimes even the boss. He read widely and indiscriminately, absorbing trade journals, Federal Trade Commission reports, and even the yellow pages, where he was "fascinated to find so many specialist firms operating within what we thought of as a single industry, as well as such interesting combinations of activities as those represented by coal and ice companies."

With an understanding of business organization that came from direct observation and a close reading of the Chicago phone book, Coase returned to London in 1932 to explain why coal and ice were sold by the same company, why some chemical companies sold their own output directly to end users while others handed it off to middlemen, and why some companies grew to the vast scale he had observed in America while others remained mom-and-pop shops.

It took five years to refine these ideas into the 1937 essay that helped Coase win a Nobel Prize sixty years later. "The Nature of the Firm" begins with a gentle rebuke of his fellow economists for taking so long to try to explain what goes on inside firms: "Economists in building up a theory have often omitted to examine the foundations on which it is erected." To understand what goes on between firms and their customers, you have to understand what companies themselves are up to, rather than thinking of them—quoting an earlier economist, Dennis Robertson—as "islands of conscious power in this ocean of unconscious co-operation like lumps of butter coagulating in a pail of buttermilk." (Farm life was a powerful influence for many early economists. You think a lot about markets when the family farm hinges on prices and output. In fact, many leading economists grew up in farm country, including John Kenneth Galbraith, Google chief economist Hal Varian, and Nobel laureate Vernon Smith.)

How does society "decide" what stays within the organization—and so falls under the purview of the boss—and what is bought and sold on the market? The answer, from an economist's perspective, is whatever maximizes efficiency. Competition for customers will favor whoever or whatever, org or market, does the most with the scarce resources available. For a businessman, the choice between market and organization is survival of the cheapest. But making that calculation can be much harder than you might think.

Before the publication of "The Nature of the Firm," the economics profession's party line used technology to define the firm's boundaries: an artisanal producer of wooden spectacles such as Scott Urban must painstakingly perform each operation by hand. If he doubled the size of his firm by hiring an employee, the two of them together wouldn't produce any more than double the number of wooden specs. By contrast, the steel foundries and car factories that Coase visited in his post-college tour of industrial America required enormous machines and an army of workers to keep the wheels of industry turning. You can't line up ten foundries side by side and hope to produce as much steel as one giant foundry that's ten times bigger. There are economies of scale in steel production, but not in artisanal eyewear.

Yet this doesn't help us answer the question of why Scott Urban should contract out for the lenses for his glasses, or why a fashion label might want to buy Urban Spectacles outright, taking away Scott's autonomy but giving him a steady paycheck.

And it doesn't explain why companies are forever buying new operations to cut out the middleman of the market, only to spin them off a few years later in the name of focus.

One reason organizations make such diverse choices, and why companies veer from cost-saving in-house production to cost-cutting outsourcing, is that there are arguments both ways. Why should Scott limit himself to frames, giving up margins and profits to companies that mine for sand and metal, or to the middlemen who sell him lenses and screws? Yet the logic of the invisible hand is impeccable: the gospel of Adam Smith was that it's the market that is most efficient and hence, from an economic point of view, right.

Coase's explanation for when and why organizations outdo the efficiency of markets was his fundamental contribution to economics. His argument started with the self-evident proposition that GE and Ford would own iron mines to build turbine generators and automobiles if it were cheaper than buying inputs on the open market from U.S. Steel. Scott Urban might get into the lens business if he could do it cheaper than the cost of buying them from his lens guy, Donny Q. The Nobel committee didn't cut Coase a $1 million check for that obvious insight but rather for his arguments about what drives the costs of market transactions versus those that happen inside an org. His framework gives us a way to figure out which is going to be cheaper, the market or the org.

In the pristine world of Adam Smith's invisible hand, there's little cost to relying on market prices. Everyone shows up at the local market, prices are announced, sellers trade their wares for customers' cash, and we get all the PB&J, lenses, and sheet metal we might want. That's essentially how many raw materials markets work in practice: makers of copper, wheat, and pork bellies "meet" at the Chicago Mercantile Exchange, where prices are announced and contracts signed for the exchange of goods.[10] It's also not too far from a description of the market for wood that supplies Scott Urban with the raw material for his eyeglass frames. A wood merchant serves as intermediary between lumber companies and Scott, setting prices and facilitating the trade of wood for cash.

But what Smith's account is missing, among other things, is the real cost of doing business on the open market. These factors—what Coase labeled "transaction costs"—find no place in the mathematical models that the followers of Adam Smith developed to explain the superiority of the market's invisible hand to the controlling hand of bosses. But they lie at the heart of Coase's theory of the firm. Once you acknowledge just how expensive it can be to transact in the market, you can begin to see why, economically speaking, you might want to bring a bunch of jobs under the umbrella of a single organization.

In his twenty-page essay, Coase gave a rough sense of the transaction costs he had in mind. The cost of using the market includes the price you pay for what you're buying—say, $399.99 for an iPhone—but there are other costs, too: the cost of discovering what these prices are, including the time spent shopping around for the lowest-priced retailer, for instance. And that's assuming that all iPhones are created equal. (If you believe the Internet has cut these search costs to zero, think again. You still pay a different price for lots of books on Amazon versus BN.com, and a study of airfares found that the Internet hasn't really changed the extent of price differences among airlines flying the same routes. These price differences persist because—Google and Expedia notwithstanding—it's still sufficiently time-consuming to find and purchase the lowest-cost book or flight available.)[11]

Apple's success has spawned an assortment of knockoffs, so surveying the market for an iPhone-like device involves not just searching retailers for the lowest price, but also experimenting with various Android and Microsoft offerings to see what best suits your purposes. Firms face the same costs of market transactions in searching out products and learning about prices. Scott Urban has a range of possible CNC routers to choose from. GM can buy its fuel pumps from Mitsubishi or Delphi, or experiment with one of the up-and-coming Chinese manufacturers. Apple is always on the lookout for cheaper, better suppliers of iPhone components. And for companies buying container loads of fuel pumps or semiconductors, figuring out the "price" of the product is much more complicated.

For the casual iPhone purchaser, sticker prices are at least more or less fixed, once you discover them—just like the cost of PB&J at the grocery store. And an iPhone is an iPhone is an iPhone. The "contract" between buyer and seller is simply an exchange of product for money, with a bit of after-market service thrown in. The occasional miserable customer service experience notwithstanding, you get what you expected to pay for.

A contract between Apple and its myriad suppliers, by contrast, is likely to be a thousand-page affair filled with stipulations and contingencies outlining the responsibilities of each party. It's too expensive for Apple to constantly resurvey the outsourcing landscape to find new suppliers, and also expensive for suppliers to constantly find new work to fill their factories. The contract aims to give a steady flow of work and income for Apple's suppliers and a stable supply of iPhones for Apple. How much work does Apple promise each month? And what defect rate does its supplier guarantee in turn? What happens to the price paid by Apple if the price of lithium doubles? Or gets cut in half? And with every change in supplier, Apple would have to go through an internal overhaul as well, retraining its workers and adjusting its supply chain to accommodate the new partner.

All of a sudden, doing business on the open market is a lot more expensive than just the purchase price.

Coase's conception of the market involved a lot more friction and discord than Adam Smith's original vision. It gives us a more complete understanding of why orgs exist and why we don't trade for everything on the open market, and a way of thinking about how orgs make decisions about drawing their boundaries. Those high costs of transacting business on the market drive people to organize. And Coase's main insight—that the cost of an in-house transaction needs to be compared with the cost of a market trans-action—has served as the basic building block for the modern economic theory of what organizations do.

The Cost of Transacting Business

If Coase proved that it can be exceptionally and unexpectedly expensive to trade on the market, why not bring *everything* in house? Why don't we all work for one big org? Coase offered an answer to this question, too, drawing on his view of the then-flourishing Soviet Union, which provided one of the many sources of inspiration for his thinking about the trade-offs be-tween markets and orgs.

For the seventy-five years following the Bolshevik Revolution of 1917, Russians got to experience what it was like to live in one big firm. According to Lenin, the Soviet economy would be run as a giant factory, making it the largest firm in human history. We all know how that turned out.

But at the time Coase was forming his theories, no one knew that the Soviet system would collapse on itself. The horrors of Stalinist gulags did not yet exist. And while Soviet Russia built its industrial state in the 1930s on the backs of eighteen-hour workdays, with a proletariat slaving to meet production quotas (lest they endanger their meager food allotments), very few of the details seeped out to the rest of the world. Many world leaders (and economists) were impressed by the Soviet "one-firm" approach and the Soviets' successes in large-scale, capital-intensive industrialization. Partly as a result, many of the economists and thinkers whom Coase encountered in his travels and studies were captivated by the idea of a state directed by a set of enlightened planners who would design and run the economy like a finely tuned Swiss watch. And who might these planners be? The economists, of course.

The Soviet one-firm approach was also an economic disaster. Overseen by Kremlin-based planners and bosses, it produced a fine fleet of nuclear missiles but was unable to fill store shelves with bread or shoes, despite the willingness of Russians to pay for such basic necessities. If the single-firm model would fare any better in the relatively unfettered capitalism of the United States, we'd all be laboring for a bloated conglomerate that could undercut any stand-alone firm that tried to compete with it. Instead, as Coase noted from his reading of American yellow pages, we see orgs of every size and flavor jostling for market share.

Coase realized that you need to think about how market and organization costs grow with each additional batch of product. As production scales up, market costs don't change much. Prices "tell" each firm in the production line, from extractors of iron ore to molders of plastic casings, what to produce and how much.

Prices also "tell" the industry whether it should be growing or shrinking. That's the beauty and elegance of the invisible hand.

But, Coase discovered, expanding the business within a single org isn't simply a matter of self-replication. More product means more employees to manage, and more managers to manage them. Eventually the limits of human cognition come into play, and there's only so much the boss can keep his eye on. You end up with organizational costs that are too high, and things spill back out into the market.

Put those two arguments together and you have the org and the market living together in economic harmony. As companies boost production or expand across product lines, work stays in the org up to the point where escalating costs of management and coordination outstrip the costs and headaches of dealing with outside suppliers. Then the market takes over. This balancing act was Coase's big insight.

"The Nature of the Firm" provides an economic rationale for why orgs exist and why we don't trade for everything on the open market, and a nice rule of thumb for how orgs make decisions about drawing their boundaries. As with many great ideas, the arguments put forth in "The Nature of the Firm" can seem completely obvious—but only after the fact. Perhaps the theory appears so straightforward because it's a framework for understanding a world of organizations that we're already familiar with but probably haven't stopped to think about. People on both sides of the Iron Curtain have suffered at the hands of Politburo-like planners at the Department of Motor Vehicles or its equivalent, and have witnessed the bureaucracy wrought by multilayered corporate hierarchies. No imagination is required to picture bureaucratic costs spiraling out of control.

Coase gave economists a much-needed look inside the black

boxes that trade with one another amid markets that were far less perfect than economists had previously realized. Yet few paid any attention to Coase's paper for several decades after its quiet appearance in the British journal *Economica* in 1937.[12] (It was Coase's second publication in the journal. His 1935 study, "Bacon Production and the Pig-Cycle in Great Britain," hasn't had quite the same lasting influence.) But a new generation of economists, guided by Coase's fundamental insights, took up the mantle decades later. Starting in the mid-1970s, these scholars began devising theories of what managers do, how organizations are organized, and why in-house production costs inexorably spiral out of control, to color in the details of Coase's broad outline.

As for Scott Urban, despite the inefficiencies of his approach to making eyeglass frames, he doesn't have any real interest in expanding. For him, the object is perfecting his craft, not maximizing efficiency. Working in isolation doesn't seem to be an issue. When told of communal "hacker spaces" popping up around the country, where like-minded techies, knitters, and artisans get together to work on their projects, he replied, "Nice idea, but not really my style. I'm more into hermit spaces." For him, working alone or with an intern is enough; he has only an idle outsider's interest in theories of the org. But for most of us, Coase's insights and the work that flowed from them can help make sense of the organizations that define so much of our existence.

CHAPTER 2

Designing the Job

ON OCTOBER 29, 1999, Peter Moskos sat in the office of the acting commissioner of the Baltimore City Police Department facing a life-altering choice: sign up for training with Baltimore City Police recruit class 99-5 or return to the Harvard sociology department a failure.

Moskos was a sociologist, born and bred. His father, Charles, a renowned military sociologist, was best known as the originator of President Clinton's "Don't Ask, Don't Tell" policy. After graduating magna cum laude from Princeton with a degree in sociology, Peter Moskos enrolled in Harvard's prestigious PhD program (rejection rate: 95 percent) and planned to study policing. Moskos wanted to follow in the footsteps of other sociologists by immersing himself in the lives of his subjects—in his case, the police officers who fought the war on drugs.[1]

Police departments routinely let Boy Scouts, Junior Police Rangers, and Hollywood stars ride along. But Moskos is no Boy Scout, and he's certainly no Matt Damon. No one Moskos approached with his proposal would give him the time of day. And

why would they have? What commissioner would let some potentially uber-liberal Ivy League do-gooder sociologist into his
department to pick at old scabs, dig up trash, and document well-
hidden skeletons in the department's closet?

But after months of frustration, Moskos finally got a lucky
break in Charm City.

A ranking police officer, a friend of Peter's father, whispered in
the ear of Baltimore's police commissioner, Thomas Frazier, who
knew he was on his way out. A mayoral election was just around
the corner, and all the leading candidates save one were on the
record saying that the police department needed new leadership.
A commissioner who knew he'd be gone in a matter of months
didn't need to give much thought to the wreckage Moskos's visit
might leave behind. Frazier allowed Moskos to observe recruit
class 99-5 during their time at the police academy and then to
follow them out onto the streets.

Still, Frazier's replacement, Ronald L. Daniel—who would be
stuck with any fallout from Moskos's work—didn't have quite so
laissez-faire an attitude.[2] Once informed of the situation, Daniel
ordered Moskos into his office but didn't send him packing outright. Instead, he offered Moskos a choice. He could stay, Daniel
said, only if he passed the hiring requirements of the department
and was willing to become a real police officer. No ride-alongs,
no observer status, no sitting back while others did the work.
Moskos would get an almost unprecedented look inside the department if he took the full-time job, but he'd also have to put
his life at risk policing the city's crime-ridden Eastern District.

Commissioner Daniel presumably felt sure—without knowing
anything about the Harvard grad student sitting before him—
that Moskos would accept the offer only if he weren't the type to
make trouble for the department. The job of policing is largely

one of enforcement, sometimes of the heavy-handed variety, something that a soft-on-crime, bleeding-heart Harvard academic never could have abided. Observing is one thing; participating is something else altogether. It's much easier to criticize from a distance than as an insider. Seeing how Moskos reacted to the offer, we can suppose, allowed Daniel to gauge the sociologist's true intentions, to assess whether he would align himself with his fellow officers or with his fellow graduate students. In agreeing to police the Eastern District, Moskos provided the commissioner with a credible assurance that he wouldn't stir up too much trouble.

If Moskos's interview with Daniel seems decidedly atypical, his path to the Baltimore PD was a variation on how orgs pick the people who will populate them, a challenge that every manager faces: making sure the right person gets selected for the job at hand.

Jobs that stay inside the org are the hard ones: hard to measure, hard to define, and hard to do. If they were easy, we'd hire contractors to do them for us, and the market, with prices working their magic, would work just fine at getting the job done. Inside the org, the boss struggles to keep tabs on what is—or perhaps, more to the point, isn't—getting done. Managers and supervisors can't be everywhere at once, and the moment one of them wanders out of sight, everyone can return to their hallway chats, idle Web surfing, and games of Angry Birds.

And so the architects of the org face a monumental set of challenges: to ensure that jobs that are neither observable nor rewardable nonetheless get done. This begins, as Peter Moskos found out, before we even gain entry into the org, at the point of hiring. The org has to define the job, pick the right person, and figure out how to get that person to do the work.

The Baltimore City Police Department has the unenviable charge of cleaning up the streets of a city that's a perennial front-runner for top spot in virtually every class of violent crime statistic—it's affectionately nicknamed "Bodymore, Murdaland," and is the setting for HBO's celebrated crime drama *The Wire*—and to do so amid the larger municipal dysfunction of failed schools, a failed economy, and the worst drug problem in America. That makes it a great model for explaining the difficulties that orgs face in getting employees to do their jobs, and for allowing one to appreciate the near-miracle that anything ever gets done there at all. To get a view into the logic and workings of cubicle nation, we consider the particularly messy job of policing the Eastern District on the midnight-to-8:00-a.m. shift. The lessons from Moskos's experience on the Baltimore City police force—from his hiring, to his job assignments, to how his sergeant monitored and evaluated his performance—can teach us a lot about the decidedly imperfect workplaces where most of us spend our lives.[3]

The Multitasking Police Officer

Most people think of multitasking as a symptom of the information age, the irresistible distractions of smartphones, e-mail, real-time stock quotes, and the Web being such that we can't stay on task for more than seconds at a time. But when economists speak of *multitasking*, they're talking about jobs that have multiple components to them—that is, just about any job at all. This presents a challenge to motivating and evaluating employees. Those on the receiving end of performance evaluations will devote themselves to the tasks that are evaluated while ignoring those that aren't. If what gets measured is what gets managed, then what gets managed is what gets done.

Pay customer service reps for the number of calls handled rather than an hourly rate, and queries will be dispatched with efficiency. Compensate snowplow drivers for inches of snow cleared instead of by the hour—as Boston began doing in 2009—and they'll miraculously start plowing faster. Unfortunately, however, performance in customer service and snowplowing aren't about just speed; they also have an element of quality. Service reps paid per call may leave behind legions of angry customers whose complaints were received with abrupt (if speedy) indifference. And plowmen motivated by pay-per-inch contracts may speed their trucks through slick, snow-covered streets with rash abandon, ignoring black ice and other hard-to-clear road hazards.

Still, it's pretty easy to come up with controls to regulate quality through random spot-checks and audits with customer service reps or even plowmen. That's why so many customer service calls start with the notice "This call may be monitored or recorded for quality assurance and training purposes."

Yet, like police officers, most of us juggle many more balls than do snowplow drivers or customer service reps—which is what makes it so hard for the police department to figure out what to tell policemen to do, let alone motivate them to do it.

Suppose you want to pay cops to solve crimes—or, even better, to prevent crimes from happening in the first place. The FBI's Uniform Crime Reports (UCR) provides a useful classification system to get started. The FBI divides crimes into Part I and Part II offenses. Part I crimes are further subdivided into property and violent crimes. Each of these has four separate offense classes— aggravated assault, forcible rape, murder, and robbery are classified as violent, while arson, burglary, larceny/theft, and motor vehicle theft are classified as property crimes. Burglary has three further subdivisions.

On it goes, and that's before we even get to the twenty or so offenses in Part II, which range from the seemingly innocuous—vagrancy and loitering, for example—to crimes with tragic consequences for thousands. (Bernie Madoff's multibillion-dollar investment fraud, which bilked thousands of individuals and charities of their savings, was a Part II offense.)

If you included every UCR crime stat in calculating a police officer's bonus, accounting for each one of them via some complex calculation, any given officer would probably be just as unmotivated as with no performance pay at all, and a whole lot more confused about how to spend his time.

You could stick with crimes that really mattered. If police were paid to get homicide rates down, there would surely be fewer murders in Charm City—you almost always get what you pay for.[4] The unfortunate corollary to this, however, is that you *don't* get what you *don't* pay for. If low-value burglary were left off the list of remunerated felony arrests, burglars would make out like bandits. If the chosen threshold for a burglary to make it onto the list were $1,000, thieves would soon figure out that the cops won't bother coming after them if they limit their loot to $999.

Burglary need not even be omitted to create incentive mayhem. If different crimes warranted different rewards, finding the "right" mix of compensation rates for catching thieves versus murderers versus loiterers would be impossible. If all crimes are rewarded equally, police will go after the low-hanging fruit such as parking violations and shoplifters, despite the much higher social cost of murders and billion-dollar frauds. Getting incentives wrong could literally be deadly. And who gets rewarded if the job's well done? The individual detective who breaks the case? The beat cop who noticed something suspicious? The forensic technician who dug up the critical piece of DNA evidence?

Despite its precision, or maybe because of it, this is *not* a good way of figuring out what the typical police officer should do, or how to pay him.

Keeping It Simple

These complications might go some way toward explaining the reward structure that filtered down for Baltimore's patrolmen, summarized by one of the officers in Moskos's district: "Sarge really likes arrests, and I give them to him…If I see a white junkie coming here to cop [buy drugs], I'll stop them. Conspiracy to possess. Loitering." That's straightforward: Sarge likes arrests; cops arrest people. End of story.

Keeping things simple has its own set of deficiencies. It's not that there's anything *wrong* with making arrests for loitering (except a potential violation of civil liberties and damaging relations with the public). As Moskos notes, it's a good way of clearing the streets of dealers and junkies, at least temporarily. But it also means that lots of cops will look for the lowest-cost way of boosting arrest stats, regardless of whether it's the best way of making the Eastern District a better, safer place to live. Sarge never said that he likes only *good* arrests, after all, and the Baltimore officers aren't rewarded for successful prosecutions, just the arrest itself. So, as with telemarketers paid by the call, if Sarge likes arrests, he risks getting quantity at the expense of quality.

That said, at least cops in the Eastern District are arresting *somebody*. And so the police force may be best off keeping it simple—it's a trade-off. The same goes for a sales force paid for generating revenues. They may be tempted to give their customers discounts to make sales without concern for the impact on the company's bottom line.

To illustrate the double-edged sword of arrest incentives, Moskos recounts the example of a fellow officer who decided to set a record for monthly arrests. His plan: lock people up for violating bicycle regulations. At night, all bikes need a light. The officer would stop cyclists in breach of the bike light rule (which was most of them), ask for ID, and pull out his pad to write a citation. Most riders, though, were biking without ID, and since all offenses become arrestable without identification, the officer's little scheme netted twenty-six arrests in a single month. A record. His sergeant was thrilled, telling Moskos, "Look, I don't know what his motivations are. But I think it's good. He's locking people up, which is more than half the people in this squad." Why was the sergeant so happy? His boss, the lieutenant, also got kudos for arrests on his shift, and in the sergeant's words, "As long as the lieutenant likes them, I'm all for it." And why did the lieutenant like them? Probably because the major did. And so on. Ultimately, we can surmise, the mayor could then say, "We arrested lots of people in the Eastern District. We're doing our jobs to keep the streets safe," which, when the streets aren't particularly safe, also helps to deflect the blame.

Police officers in the Eastern District certainly got the message. Moskos wrote, "There are 70,000 arrests a year in the city of Baltimore. When I policed, 20,000 of those happened in the district I policed. The population of the Eastern District is less than 45,000. That's a lot of lockups." Nearly one for every two residents. The department paid for arrests, and it got them.

This may seem nonsensical, even counterproductive, yet arresting light-less bikers had its purpose. While it might not seem among the Eastern District's most pressing problems, many cyclists out in the middle of the night without identification were up to no good. By locking up twenty-six cyclists, the record-setting officer also took some drugs off the street.

The pitfalls of arrest quotas come into sharper relief with Moskos's account of the trade-offs faced by a cop chasing down a drug suspect. During Moskos's time in uniform, drug charges in Baltimore couldn't be prosecuted unless an officer maintained constant sight of the drugs, a fact well-known to suspects, who will often throw down their drugs when fleeing. The pursuing officer will have to choose between keeping an eye on the drugs and actually arresting the suspect. While found drugs are critical to prosecution, police are judged on arrest statistics, not conviction rates. Officers generally follow the suspect rather than pausing to scoop up the evidence, all the while knowing that the prosecution will fail as a result. But the arrest will still be good.

Eventually, at least in Baltimore, the misalignment of arrest quotas with the overall goal of keeping the peace caused the arrangement to break down. When the Baltimore murder count reached new heights in June 2007, then-commissioner Leonard Hamm was held accountable for the lack of progress in lowering crime rates—despite the astronomical arrest rate—and forced to resign. Of course, we never observe what crime rates would have been like with a different approach. For all the system's shortcomings, it's possible that focusing on monthly arrest counts was the best approach for dealing with Baltimore's crime problem in the world of multitasking, hard-to-monitor police officers.[5]

Police Teamwork

If individual cops have so many tasks that providing clear and compelling incentives borders on the impossible, why not divide up the job into its constituent parts and assign each part to individual police officers? Some aspects of law enforcement do work this way. Homicide detectives solve murders. Period. Given their relatively narrow and focused mandate—they don't handle calls to break up domestic disputes or patrol the streets—the department can more effectively use crime solving as measured by arrest and prosecution to motivate and evaluate specialized units such as Homicide and Narcotics. (The idea that you can judge the quality of these detectives' work by the prosecution and conviction rates has some merit, since the District Attorney's Office will pursue only those cases it feels assured of winning, which requires careful police work.)

Taking this observation to its logical extreme, why not separate policing into its individual measurable components, and outsource the entire enterprise to the market? We do just that with some types of policing. The job of retrieving indicted criminals who flee to Mexico when out on bail, for example, is handled by independent contractors. Often the bail is posted by bondsmen who set up shop near the courthouse. They get their money back only when the accused is returned to face trial. The outcome is a single, easily measured objective: Does the parolee show up for his day in court? The level of compensation is equally straightforward: a fraction of the bond posted. And thus the job of recovering those who jump bail is largely handled by a thriving market of bounty hunters who contract with bail bondsmen on a fee-per-fugitive basis.

Similarly, private security firms protect wealthy homeowners from break-ins, as the ubiquitous Chubb and ADT signs posted on well-manicured lawns in upscale neighborhoods indicate. The company's job is to keep the home and its inhabitants safe.

Neither bounty hunter nor private security firm provides a reliable model for keeping the peace. The cinematic depiction of a bounty hunter as a lone black-clad cowboy riding into town in search of his prey is not a bad approximation of reality. Bounty hunters work alone or in small teams. And while the likes of Chubb and ADT work in teams guarding the mansions of Beverly Hills, they're focused on protecting only the homes of their customers. Chubb doesn't care if, by scaring off would-be thieves from a Chubb-secured home, it simply diverts them to the house across the street.

(What might life be like with ADT as the only cop in town? Ask the residents of Obion, Kentucky, what happens when only those who pay seventy-five dollars in protection money to nearby South Fulton get help in case of a fire. One Obion family, the Cranicks, chose not to pay, and when their house caught fire, firefighters stood by until the flames spread to the field of an unlucky neighbor, who then had a fire on his property despite having paid the protection fee. As for the Cranicks, they were completely out of luck. "'I thought they'd come out and put it out, even if you hadn't paid your $75, but I was wrong,' said Gene Cranick." While Cranick offered to pay the firefighters on the spot whatever it would cost to save his house, they demurred.)[6]

Policing an entire community—in contrast to chasing fugitives or protecting individual homes—involves teamwork across districts in a city and across divisions within a department. A homicide detective relies on beat cops on the lookout for suspects and suspicious activity, and the diligent analysis of forensic technicians. Beat cops, while often patrolling solo, provide one another with rapid-response backup. Dispatchers direct patrol officers based on incoming calls. All three squads of Baltimore's Eastern District are on the same frequency, and assist others as necessary. If individual incentives were too strong, officers might spend too much time hunting down arrest opportunities at the expense of supporting fellow officers.

Unlike with a bounty hunter, the effectiveness of one police officer depends on the goodwill and assistance of his colleagues. In some ways, it's a variant on the multitasking problem. An ad sales rep can selflessly devote herself to developing tools that can be used by the entire sales force, or just concentrate on closing deals. A lawyer can work on his own cases or take the time to provide advice to fellow partners at his firm. A detective can "take one for the team" by accepting the hard-to-solve cases, or take it easy by angling for the easy conviction. If employees—whether salesmen or cops—are paid based on their own annual sales figures or murder cases closed, they're motivated to look out for themselves rather than the common good.

In game theory, this is known as the Prisoners' Dilemma and it captures succinctly the challenges of team production. In the classic formulation, the police arrest two suspects, partners in crime, and try to elicit a confession from each suspect separately, offering them both the same deal: if one testifies against the other while the other remains silent, the confessor goes free and the silent one suffers the full force of the law, let's say ten years. If both remain silent, they receive much lighter sentences of only a few months. And if each betrays the other, both receive a yearlong sentence. Do you betray your partner or cooperate with him and remain silent, even though he won't know you're cooperating when he makes his decision? You choose.

The dilemma is that if each prisoner cares only about serving the least amount of jail time, the "rational" choice leads both players to confession and betrayal, because you get less prison time that way, even though each would do better if they both stayed silent. If his partner confesses, the other prisoner gets a year instead of a decade of jail time by confessing himself; if the partner stays silent, the other prisoner can still save himself a few months in prison by giving a confession and going free. No matter what the other does, each partner is better off confessing.

The same challenge exists in team production: how to ensure that each "prisoner"—that is, employee—is looking out for the group. There's no simple solution to the Prisoners' Dilemma. You can try to change the game so jobs are set up to require only one individual's effort; you can put a team in the same work space so its members can police one another; and perhaps you can foster a sense of solidarity and mutual trust within the group. But these are all halfway measures that inevitably leave team performance as less than the sum of its potential.

Regardless, it's often worth it to team up to get things done. In the early 1970s, for example, Swedish automakers Saab and Volvo both began experimenting with building car components in four-to-seven-person teams.[7] The companies' motivations weren't to implement Scandinavian-style socialism within the firms but rather to improve quality and even increase worker output. In manufacturing, team production makes it easier for workers to help one another out if one team member falls behind on a task or to shift manpower around when bottlenecks arise. It also makes the job of an autoworker more pleasant and less monotonous than the traditional assembly-line method used since Henry Ford's day.[8]

But when production is done in teams, performance needs to

be graded for groups rather than individuals. The net effect is familiar to anyone who has ever suffered through a group assignment at work or at school. Among a bunch of coworkers, there will inevitably be at least one free rider who figures that others will do the work and he'll get the credit. A free rider doesn't mind the risk of a lower grade if it allows him to slack off completely.

So, like so much else in the life of organizations, it's a tradeoff: the camaraderie, mutual support, and stimulation of group production versus the assembly line, where laggards are easily exposed and fired. GM, after its ill-fated foray into team production with the Saturn brand, has decided that the soul-destroying yet highly motivating efficiency of the assembly line works best. The Swedes and many Japanese automakers still favor team production. (A *Time* magazine article from 1972 reported that GM's earlier approach to lowering absenteeism wasn't team production but more individual incentives: free mugs to line workers with good attendance records. And of course we know that everyone's in it for the free mugs.)[9]

Unlike auto production, policing can't be grouped or ungrouped at will. If it could, it might veer from one management fad to the next, trying to keep the peace with teams of beat cops one year and bounty hunters the next. But as it is, the entire force needs to work as a collective to keep the city safe, and in a way, individual incentive pay is accordingly set to respond to the effectiveness of these combined efforts. That is to say, each cop has little individual incentive to do much of anything.

And maybe that's just as well given that, as it turns out, so much of policing, like so much office work, can't be evaluated or rewarded at all.

Hidden Policing

The objectives of policing are a lot murkier than those of a for-profit company, which are, at least to a first approximation, to make money. The stated mission of the Baltimore City police force is to "protect and preserve life, protect property, understand and serve the needs of the city's neighborhoods, and to improve the quality of life of our community."

There's a lot involved in keeping the peace. Lowering the murder rate, clearing 911 calls, and reducing the supply of crack cocaine may contribute to the broader objectives of policing, but so do many other, hard-to-observe and harder-to-quantify aspects of the job. For instance, after politely settling down a group of young men sitting on a front stoop drinking malt liquor and blasting a boom box (only one of them carrying ID) Moskos's partner commented that it "pisses me off...now they respect me more...because I wasn't a dick. Would I be doing a better job if I locked them up? But I don't get any credit for good policing."

Moskos's partner's idea of "good policing" highlights once again the problem of motivating a multitasking police officer, but with a twist. The officer himself is aggravated by the fact that so much of what police do can't be measured at all. Moskos's partner was clearly doing his job, but in no quantifiable way. It's hard to measure something that never happens. From the perspective of a commissioner guided by monthly crime reports, the lack of criminal activity might be the result of good policing as defined by the patrolman. After all, clearing the corner probably meant one less call to 911—but fewer emergency calls to 911 might also be a consequence of a rainy night, or a cold snap that kept would-be criminals indoors, or improved economic conditions in the district.[10] Who's to say the cop didn't sit in his warm patrol car under a bridge somewhere, as even Moskos admits that he himself occasionally did?

The fact that so much of policing is invisible to a desk-bound sergeant leaves each individual officer with enormous discretion that can be used in lots of ways: to slack off, to boost his stats, or to keep the peace. Even in the high-crime Eastern District, most cops patrol solo, so there isn't even another officer to bear witness to good (or bad) behavior. On any given shift, an officer can decide to focus on traffic citations, bike arrests, or busting drug corners. He can let off minor offenders with a warning, or place them under arrest.

One of Moskos's fellow officers described the way he flaunted this power in dealing with loiterers: "Sometimes I'll flip a quarter. Tails, he goes to jail, and heads, he doesn't. They'll be going, 'Heads! Yeeeah!'" Does anyone ever complain when the coin comes up tails? Apparently not—everyone knows that for minor arrests, they're at the policeman's mercy, and better not to endanger a system where you have at least a fifty-fifty chance of going free rather than none at all.

Whereas arrests for minor crimes are all a matter of discretion, catching violent felons also involves a lot of luck. An officer can't set out on a shift with the intention of bringing in an armed robber or a murderer. He has to stumble upon one. And absent an obvious suspect, the case then just gets handed over to a detective.

If so much of good policing is invisible—such as defusing a potentially dangerous confrontation—and making arrests involves a mixture of luck and stretching police discretion to stop and frisk errant cyclists and loiterers, why build a system based on arrest quotas? Because it's still the best you've got. Given the group work involved in peacekeeping, you can't reward individual officers for the dog that fails to bark. It encourages them to push criminals and crimes onto someone else's shift or into another precinct. It may be better to have a lot of bad arrests than no arrests at all.

What saves the system from complete collapse is that many police care about more than just juking, or inflating, their stats. After a few years, many officers get tired of policing "cowboy style" and come to see arrests as a sign of failed policing. If they were doing the job right, there wouldn't be so much crime in the first place. Among the cops who don't put up decent arrest stats, some are surely lazy and others burned out, but many are probably excellent police. You just can't see it in the numbers.

Good thing, then, that while arrests are encouraged and rewarded via promotion and overtime pay, the incentives are pretty weak. If you just stay out of trouble and make an arrest now and then, no one gives you too hard a time. The older cops who have left their cowboy policing days behind them do just fine. If this weren't the case, there might not be any excellent police in Baltimore at all.

Designing the Job

It's a little funny to think about how to design incentives to make sure a job gets done before thinking about how to design the job itself. The list of possible ways the police commissioner can organize policing is nearly infinite—emergency response teams versus foot patrols, partnered versus solo patrols, rotating cops through different units or keeping them focused on the same job day in and day out. For any member of the force, the right incentives will depend on what the boss has set forth as his job.

If there's an overarching principle that guides job design, it's to minimize exactly the sort of incentive problems we've described as bedeviling the Baltimore police and almost any other org. The objective isn't to make the problems go away, but to reduce the extent to which incentives misfire.

Ill-conceived job descriptions can wreak havoc on incentives. Imagine a bank loan officer at now-defunct Washington Mutual whose job it was to outcompete other lenders in selling mortgages. If you wanted to give him clear, simple incentives, pay him a commission on each dollar lent. Just as rewards-per-arrest encourage a focus on arresting loiterers over murderers, pay-per-loan incentives motivate loan officers to push more loans out the door, regardless of the odds the borrower will later default. Unfortunately, it's tricky to punish a loan officer for bad mortgages, since default may appear far in the future, by which time there's a good chance that officer has moved on to another job at another company. Quantity is easy to measure, but quality shows itself only years down the line.

That's why WaMu had, like other mortgage brokers, a loan approval department to vet the quality of proposed loans. It's stupidly obvious that combining the tasks of loan selling and loan approval is a bad idea. The jobs have contradictory incentives: selling at all costs versus monitoring the quality of each sale. They also have differing degrees of observability. It's easy to count loans but hard to measure approval quality to calculate an annual bonus. A sensible assignment of tasks and incentives would be to split the job of selling mortgages off from that of approving them, and to provide high-powered selling incentives while putting approvers on fixed salaries. In fact, mortgage selling is so straightforward, why not just have it done through the market by dedicated mortgage brokers? This was more or less the system that developed at WaMu, which had its loans sold both by internal, commission-based loan officers and by independent brokers who also worked on a fee-for-loan arrangement.

The problems at WaMu and elsewhere in the loan business—now known as the subprime meltdown of 2007—weren't the result of bundling opposing incentives. Rather, the problem was that incentives for brokers, approval departments, and everyone else were so out of kilter that they may as well have all been one massive selling department, hell-bent on pushing whatever loan product generated the highest commissions. Loan sellers were paid based on the interest rates they could push onto borrowers—the higher the better—subject to loan approval. Those in the processing department tasked with vetting loans weren't asleep at the wheel; they were doing what they had been told to do, which was to approve as many loans as possible. What if you didn't do as you were told? Keysha Cooper, a senior underwriter at WaMu, told the *New York Times* of being put on probation for thirty days for refusing to sign off on what she felt was a fraudulent loan. The loan was "restructured" and approved by her supervisor, only to go into default a few months later.[11]

David Kreps, a Stanford economist, and his colleague at Yale, James Baron, draw the distinction between "star" and "guardian" tasks, which should be combined only if completely unavoidable, yet are often lumped together. In WaMu's case, the guardians were the loan approvers and risk managers, who, as former WaMu risk manager Dale George put it in an interview with ABC News, are like the brakes on a car. WaMu executives "took the brakes off and drove over a cliff."[12] George's brethren in safety, audit, and compliance departments are similarly given the unglamorous job of guarding against the catastrophic decisions of others.

Star performers, by contrast, do their jobs best when they're swinging for the fences, not worrying about risk. If you're hiring R&D scientists, better to have gamblers than worrywarts. The billions in profits from one blockbuster drug will cover the cost of thousands lost from failures, and then some. The last thing you want is researchers obsessing over every disappointment.

Any org has to have both stars and guardians, carefully balanced. When the guardians become too powerful, innovation grinds to a bureaucratic halt. When stars hold sway, sooner or later we end up with something like the financial crisis. Police officers who may have an impulse to jack up crime statistics, plant guns or drugs, or beat up suspects need internal affairs and officers to manage them. Oil drillers who are paid to get profitable wells up and running need safety-control departments. Financial wizards scheming up exotic new derivatives need a chief risk officer. That's why we'll always have oppressive bureaucrats, and free-thinking entrepreneurs oppressed by them. And that's okay.

Sometimes, as counterintuitive as it may seem, the opposite is true: jobs work even better when seemingly disparate tasks are bundled together. In a stroke of incentive design genius, cofounder of the travel search engine Kayak.com, Paul English, turned the multitasking problem on its head by forcing his software engineers to answer customer service calls. Why would you have software engineers who earn $150,000 a year waste their time listening to customer complaints when the same task could be outsourced to minimum-wage labor in Arizona or, even better, to a dollar-an-hour customer service agency based in India? And why would you want to force your customers to talk to software engineers, a group not exactly known for its warm and fuzzy demeanor?

Unlike the competing interests of most tasks, writing software code and listening to customers complain about the code you've written are mutually reinforcing, in large part because software engineers hate dealing with ornery customers. Says English, "If you make the engineers answer e-mails and phone calls from the customers, the second or third time they get the same question, they'll actually stop what they're doing and fix the code. Then we don't have those questions anymore."

English further amplified the bug-fixing incentives of his engineering staff by purchasing a big red phone with a loud and grating ring that was loathed by all. When employees complained, English told them, "There's a really simple solution: Answer the friggin' phone and do whatever it takes to make that customer happy. Then hang up, unplug the phone, walk it down to the other end of the office, and plug it in down there" for the next programmer in the customer service queue to deal with an incoming call.

While it might be unpalatable to the highly trained yet introverted software engineer, fielding service calls forces them to hear direct feedback on product defects and shortcomings, providing a sort of mini-focus group on what future designs should look like. (English himself claims to love hearing customer complaints for exactly this reason.)[13]

These are all essentially better and more sophisticated ways of making it possible to monitor and motivate workers. Yet they all can be undermined by a sufficiently determined workforce. The camaraderie of teamwork cuts both ways. Workers meant to monitor one another can instead collude as a group against management—punching one another's time cards, covering breaks, working together to embezzle funds or doctor expense accounts.

Inevitably, there will be times and situations in most jobs

where it's easy enough to sleep on the job, choose between easier or harder customers to deal with, and generally pick between what's good for the org and what's easy for the individual. Which is why companies expend so much time and effort trying to find people who will do right by the org when there aren't any incentives or monitoring at all.

Finding That Special Someone

For most of the second half of the twentieth century, selling encyclopedias door to door was a respectable, if not terribly exciting job for young, fresh-faced college graduates. In the business's early days, salesmen literally went door to door with samples, hawking their product. By the 1990s, a customer service agent would canvas a neighborhood to find likely customers, and the company would dispatch a salesman to close the sale by building the "four walls of the deal": constructing an argument for spending $800 on a five-hundred-pound, twelve-volume shelf-filler that was so airtight that the customer could see no way out. The salesmen worked on commission.[14]

If Encyclopædia Britannica picked a dud salesman, no big deal—sales in his area would be slow for a bit, but soon enough he'd figure out he wasn't any good at the job (and hence not earning any commission) and there would be a parting of ways. New salesmen were lining up every day.

But when a Silicon Valley firm hires a software engineer or the blue-chip consulting firm McKinsey takes on a junior consultant—or Baltimore hires a police officer—it invests in training and nurturing a salaried employee. Once inside the org, employees enjoy perks well beyond standard health benefits and

pension plans. And Silicon Valley tech companies, Google included, offer remarkable perks.[15]

All those perks are intended to make sure that new hires choose
to stay (and work late). After all, both companies are largely the
sum of their hiring decisions. Much of Google's original search
algorithm was developed by Craig Silverstein, Google Employee
Number One, whom founders Sergey Brin and Larry Page hired
out of their Stanford PhD class. Many of the company's most
successful innovations, from Gmail on, came bubbling up from
engaged and motivated engineers. As for McKinsey, the consulting firm doesn't actually offer anything to its clients beyond the
brainpower of its seven-thousand-strong army of consultants, so
each and every one had better be among the best.

Not surprisingly, then, both Google and McKinsey have invested intensively in developing the secret sauce that will get
the right people on their payrolls. The companies are entirely
forthcoming about the general process: the questions asked, the
sequence of steps from telephone through in-person interviews,
how long it takes them to make a decision. McKinsey even hands
out lots of information on the brain teasers and case studies
that confront applicants during interviews: How do you persuade
consumers to pay for bottled water? How many golf balls in the
world are aloft at 12:00 noon EST? Why is a manhole cover
round? They're looking for college and business school graduates with basic business sense and high IQs. Google focuses more
on programming skills. While they don't post sample questions
online, plenty have filtered out via Internet chat rooms. Recent
postings from interviewees: "Write a 'C' program to turn ON the
655th bit of an input data stream arriving through an input port"
and "How many cans of paint would it take to cover an entire
747?" They are looking for excellent programmers with high IQs.

As important as IQ and analytics: Is an applicant conscientious? Emotionally stable? If McKinsey's people are what make McKinsey what it is, the company had better be able to divine these attributes from its interview notes. If evidence from experiments by social psychologists is any indication, though, neither McKinsey's nor Google's interviews are likely to provide this glimpse into applicants' souls. A study from 2002 found that there's very little correlation between interviewers' ratings of conscientiousness and emotional stability and self-ratings given by applicants prior to the interview. It's a lot harder to ferret out emotions than analytics. Applicants tell the interviewer what he wants to hear. For cans of paint or golf balls in the air, there's no incentive to lie. But any interviewer so lacking in originality as to ask an applicant about his greatest weakness will likely get a response such as "I'm too conscientious."

Some companies claim to have congeniality tests for job applicants. Commerce Bank is one. After screening résumés and conducting telephone interviews, prospective candidates are invited for an in-person interview. The candidates think they've arrived for a rigorous cross-examination, but Commerce really just wants to watch them *wait* for the interview. Like McKinsey, Commerce is a customer-service-oriented org, and it's discovered that the tellers who provide the best customer experience are those who smile when they're at rest—it shows an easygoing attitude and generally friendly outlook. So, as candidates wait, the receptionist watches their expressions and, barring any disaster during the actual interview, Commerce hires those who pass its "smile test." The smile test is followed by congeniality training that ensures "service with a smile" at all Commerce Bank branches.[16]

Yet, to state the obvious, a smile test has its limits. For one thing, readers of this book now know to smile during a Commerce Bank interview. And the psychological profiles that organizations such as McKinsey and Google are looking for involve more than just a smile. So, in addition to the regular screening and interviewing process, they try to figure out ways to have prospective employees signal that they truly are worthy of filling one of their coveted openings.

Buying the Signal

It currently costs a little under $120,000 in tuition and fees to attend Harvard Business School (HBS), a sum that does not include the cost of forgone earnings.[17] Those taking a cynical view on the value of an HBS degree might refer to it as "a $120,000 signal" that doesn't do anything beyond proving that you're willing to devote two years of your life to learning how to answer questions such as those on how to market bottled water in the case-style discussions that McKinsey seems to value so much. Attending HBS is an effective signal that you have the skills and inclination to be a fine management consultant. (McKinsey is HBS's top recruiter; Google hires there as well.)

Just paying McKinsey $120,000 for a shot at a junior analyst position wouldn't do the trick, even if anyone were so inclined. The HBS experience demonstrates to McKinsey (or whomever) that not only did you get through the business school's strict entrance guidelines—the admissions rate for 2010 was only 12 percent—but you also had the wherewithal to survive a demanding, case-based course of study.

Others get more creative in looking for the right signal. Zappos, the Internet shoe company, is legendary for its extreme customer service. They've set a record with one service call that lasted more than eight hours. (We could debate whether that's a good thing or not.) One oft-repeated gem of company lore tells of a service rep who, on finding out that a customer hadn't sent back her order as planned because her mom had died suddenly, arranged for UPS pickup of the shoes and sent a bouquet of white lilies, roses, and carnations to the customer-in-mourning. Zappos CEO, Tony Hsieh, endlessly repeats his mantra that Zappos is a customer service company that happens to sell shoes.

New recruits are oriented—perhaps *indoctrinated* is a better word—in a 160-hour customer loyalty training program, at full pay. After just a week of immersion in the Zappos way, they're offered $2,000 to quit ("the Offer," as it's known in the company's mythology), plus the week's salary they've already earned. Why pay people you've vetted and chosen to work for the org to quit? The Zappos way involves commitment to doing whatever it takes to make the customer happy. This can involve sending flowers or engaging in marathon chitchat sessions with needy clients. It's not for everyone. Making "the Offer" ensures that any new hire who doubts his commitment to service will self-select out of the new job, which is what about 10 percent of customer loyalty trainees do. But as far as Zappos is concerned, having a company comprised of people who turned down $2,000 to leave is worth a whole lot more.[18]

This Hurts Me More Than It Hurts You

Zappos wants a few good service reps who will put their hearts and souls into satisfying customer wants, Commerce Bank wants people who pass their smile test, and McKinsey and Google are looking for perseverance and a high IQ. What Baltimore's police commissioner needs is cops who will aggressively chase down potentially armed and dangerous suspects when the opportunity arises, rather than spending their nights asleep in donut shop parking lots. The temptation for a quiet life of lazy days and a generous pension can easily get in the way, particularly given the combination of limited rewards and precious little oversight. The commissioner needs people who, presented with the choice between sleeping and policing, will police.

The Baltimore City Police Department's version of the smile test is the willingness of recruits to put up with the quasi-military regime of the police academy. According to Moskos, days are filled with jogging while chanting cadence, uniform inspection, nearly pointless classes on the rules governing police behavior, saluting, punishments built around demerits and push-ups, complete with drill sergeants who yell for fun—plus a trip to the morgue. If you enjoy playing with guns and learning about how best to deploy a nightstick to immobilize a suspect, *and* you're willing to put up with all that "bullshit," as one instructor (and we're sure many recruits) called the course of study, then you're showing the department that, deep down in your heart, you really want to clean up the streets.

The department needs this signal of recruits' budding desires because catching criminals can be more punishment than reward. A suspect may turn out to be unarmed and innocent, but with the Eastern District awash in guns and drugs, a cop who wants to live to see his pension can't make such assumptions. And cops who are perceived as overly aggressive may find themselves suspended, their pensions in peril. (According to Moskos, the difference between good policing and police brutality isn't necessarily evident to the uninformed viewer of video footage of an arrest, so even a cop who's doing his job carefully risks investigation and censure.)

In a world of discretionary policing, a commissioner with the community's best interests at heart might want to enlist cadets who get inherent enjoyment from chasing down and apprehending criminals, and to nurture a culture of aggressiveness once they're enrolled. They'll uphold the law—and do so aggressively—for the sheer pleasure of it, just as Commerce Bank's tellers will provide great customer service because it's in their nature.

Unfortunately, there's also a decent chance that the type of person who collars perps for fun also could be the kind of cop who goes a little (or a lot) too far in upholding the law and meting out his own form of justice.

In fact, the older cops on Baltimore's payroll spoke with a certain degree of nostalgia about an old and very unofficial practice they called "beat and release." Moskos writes, "By the time I hit the streets, crimes 'abated by beating' [that is, possible crimes that police handled by beating the suspect] were already history. Word undoubtedly came from up high that extra-legal alternatives to incarceration are not to be considered in this modern age... [I]n the old days, a smack-talking tough guy might have gotten a lump on the head... Rumor has it that back in the old days a wife-beater might get beaten himself. Now, with ineffective and discretion-reducing mandatory arrest laws for domestic violence, any sign of injury means somebody is going to jail. End of story."

Policing has changed in Baltimore, as it's changed around the country, partly as a result of a system called CompStat, a data-driven approach using GIS computer systems and statistical techniques to map, identify, and respond to crime problems—

the ultimate management tool for directing officers' efforts. CompStat was pioneered by the New York City police force under William Bratton in the mid-1990s, and many departments, including Baltimore's, have since adopted it. The data-driven focus on getting crime numbers down, and arrest rates up, is what accounts, at least in part, for the obsession with arrests that has made its way down the chain of command. In the words of Moskos's sergeant, "This is CompStat bullshit. It's all numbers. The major goes downtown and gets grilled if they see a zero in any category. So now we can't put zeros down for anything… If I get yelled at, then I'm going to be pissed."

To make sure he makes his numbers, the major pressures the sarge to boost the stats, who then bullies his beat cops to make arrests, who may in turn resort to questionable methods to meet their quotas. On the ultimate receiving end of this chain of command is the alleged criminal, who finds himself in custody for perhaps nothing more than being in the wrong place at the wrong time. From the criminal's perspective, this may or may not be better than taking some lumps.

Citizen complaints could serve as the ultimate check on police misbehavior, in much the same way that customer feedback is used to keep servers friendly in a café and gate attendants cordial in the face of flight delays. (Cafés even have a devious technique that uses customers to keep employees honest. That promise of a free meal if you don't get a receipt? The register makes sure that employees aren't skimming from the till, and by demanding a receipt, you're ensuring that the employee uses the register.) But who is the customer equivalent for Baltimore cops?

While they serve primarily the law-abiding residents of the city, it's criminals and miscreants whom cops deal with most often and most directly. The same goes for the police department's bureaucratic brethren: child welfare agencies tasked with removing kids from neglectful homes, the IRS auditing potential tax evaders, TSA personnel charged with uncovering bombs and contraband. Their objective isn't "customer satisfaction guaranteed." Nor should it be. Perhaps this is why you rarely get service with a smile at the airport security checkpoint. Happy flyers are not what security is aiming for.

For orgs so at odds with their customers' interests, this takes away a critical monitoring mechanism. If the feedback of ornery airline customers might not line up with maximizing airline profits, the "customers" of the police force are almost by definition entirely opposed to the force's very existence. In this context, soliciting feedback from the "customer" borders on the absurd. It's hard to imagine the police department's special customer liaison asking, "On a scale of one to ten, how would you rank your arrest experience?"

The absurdity of criminals policing the cops was what struck Canice Prendergast, a University of Chicago economist, on reading a 2000 *New York Times* Magazine feature on the reform of the Los Angeles Police Department, almost ten years after LAPD officers were caught on videotape beating Rodney King, an unarmed black motorist, to near-unconsciousness. The tape made global headlines, and the acquittal of the officers sparked riots in South Central L.A. and resulted in national legislation giving the federal government the right to take control of out-of-control police departments.

The Rodney King episode had national reverberations in the way policing was done. Moskos cites it as a turning point in his colleagues' conduct. Beat and release was replaced with fears of reprimand and lost pensions. Handheld video recorders shifted police oversight back into the public domain. It was no longer a cop's word against that of an accused felon when the evidence was right there in front of the jury.

The *New York Times* Magazine article that caught Prendergast's interest described a post-1991 LAPD that had proved extremely resistant to any effort at monitoring or reform. L.A. had a famously aggressive department that clung to its right to use force with near impunity in fighting the city's gang and drug problems. L.A.'s cops, it seemed, did not fear the democratization of police oversight.[19]

In an effort to bring in accountability, the article explained, the new police chief, a thirty-five-year LAPD veteran by the name of Bernard Parks, issued an order in 1997 requiring an investigation of every citizen complaint against a police officer. Predictably, complaints flooded in, weighing down department staff with paperwork and alienating the rank and file from police leadership. Too bad, responded Parks—the new system was meant to serve the public, not the LAPD.

This was where Prendergast parted ways with Commissioner Parks. Los Angeles needed to recruit cops who were willing to chase down criminals, Prendergast reasoned, instead of marking time before their pensions kicked in—possibly even cops with a mean streak. Yet even aggressive officers will start to think twice when the fuzzy line between use of force and abuse of force shifts sufficiently in criminals' favor. To maintain their edge over their adversaries, cops *needed* to be able to act with a degree of impunity. So the department didn't just need to hire tough cops, in Prendergast's view; it also had to do its best to ignore complaints against them. Angelinos might not have liked police brutality, but it was a situation they may have had to accept as collateral damage in keeping the streets a bit safer.

Indeed, Angelinos sided with Prendergast, not Parks. A couple of years into the commissioner's tenure, an epic scandal broke in the department's anti-gang force, CRASH (Community Resources Against Street Hoodlums), in the division that policed the Ramparts housing projects. While questions remain surrounding the extent of police abuse, this much is apparent: some CRASH officers took full advantage of their near immunity from criticism or censure to plant firearms on suspected gang members to boost arrest numbers, beat up or shot others under false pretenses of self-defense, and even dealt drugs themselves. Gang members' complaints fell on deaf ears—as Prendergast's customer service theory of policing would have predicted.

The *Times* article reported that the response to the Ramparts scandal was muted among L.A. residents, especially among those living in Ramparts. Residents were more concerned with growing gang violence than police abuse, and viewed police brutality as a necessary part of keeping the gangs in check. Hiring brutal officers and ignoring complaints against them may sound like a terrible way to police a city. But it may be the best option available to the people of L.A., given the thorny task of monitoring and motivating policemen.

A Theory of Necessary Employee Disillusionment

You hire the best people you can, the ones who are most eager to do the job, be it policing or coding software. But you're not always going to get employees who work for the sheer enjoyment of it. And so you set up incentives and rewards, you monitor, and you measure. Ironically, those same incentives and measurement systems run the risk of driving your best workers—the ones who see their jobs as avocations and not just a way to mark time and get a paycheck, who truly believe in doing the job well without necessarily worrying about the incentives and rewards—to become the most frustrated by the lack of clear connection between management measures and job performance. Think of Moskos's partner clearing a stoop, making the neighborhood a better place, and doing it all without ever making an arrest. He's pissed off because his good policing goes unrecognized. And yet he's exactly the kind of police Baltimore is looking for.

This logic, taken to an extreme, could suggest that you know the org is working when your best employees are disgruntled and disillusioned. This is most emphatically not what we're suggesting.

But knowing that this is where the logic can take you should be a warning to those captivated by the idea of an org based on high-powered incentives and other rational economic principles. Orgs have to work very hard to balance incentives with an acknowledgment of the kind of intrinsic motivation that helped to get Hewlett-Packard off the ground. It's also a warning to employees that finding this balance is extraordinarily hard—and yet is a necessary cost of organizing.

CHAPTER 3

Putting Together the Organizational Puzzle

AT HIS FAREWELL DINNER on July 17, 1505, a nineteen-year-old German named Martin told his gathered friends and relations, "This day you see me, and then, not ever again." Martin was facing the kind of crisis of late adolescence that wouldn't be out of place in contemporary America: he'd experienced an unpleasant situation at school (he compared it to hell and purgatory), been strong-armed by his father into studying for a legal career, been depressed over the recent death of two friends, and been scared into thinking deeply about his own mortality when he was nearly struck by lightning riding his horse home one stormy night.

Martin's next step, though, was entirely foreign to today's experience of teen angst. On that July evening, Martin was on the verge of becoming a cloistered Roman Catholic monk, pursuing a life of religious devotion and introspection in an Augustinian friary from whose confines he planned never to emerge.

Pope Leo X, Martin's nemesis in the drama that was to follow, surely wished that things had worked out that way.

For, just twelve years later, having left the monastery to become an ordained priest and teach theology at the University of Wittenberg, Martin—his last name was Luther—would present the Archbishop of Mainz and Magdeburg with a document containing the 95 Theses that would shatter the Catholic Church and all of Europe.[1]

Martin Luther's break with the church, and the rise of Protestantism, provides us with an opportunity to understand how organizations go about the business of organizing, starting from scratch. In rejecting the Catholic Church, Protestants of every denomination—from the Anglicans in England to the Calvinists in Geneva—had to decide how to set themselves up to achieve the goal they'd taken on: attracting members and saving their immortal souls. Would they turn into some massive anti-Catholic hierarchy? Or let each parish church choose a path on its own, thereby giving up any kind of central control over the direction the denomination would take? Or would they take some middle path, giving autonomy to each church, but creating a bureaucracy, complete with endless meetings and communication, to maintain quality control and ensure agreement on their chosen direction?

The Org's Great Balancing Act

Every org faces some version of these questions—rarely with the objective of saving souls but generally around coordinating all the different and necessary pieces of the org. How do you align each person, regardless of his job or function, to make sure he's contributing to whatever goal the org has taken for itself? And how do you combine these many roles under the larger umbrella of the org? Peter Moskos's Baltimore City Police Department had to keep the peace, and it did so with beat cops, detectives, sergeants, officers, internal affairs, K-9 divisions, SWAT teams, and a host of others, all motivated, tasked, monitored, and rewarded in different ways. In any org, this multiplicity of moving parts must fit together to achieve some larger objective—whether saving souls, keeping the peace, or making money.

If every aspect of the org needs to fit together, by the same token, every tweak to incentives and oversight requires the architects of the org to rethink its design. And any redesign demands an adjustment to incentives. A start-up that becomes a sprawling bureaucracy can no longer motivate programmers through stock options. A CEO who empowers his divisional managers to set their own agendas needs to ensure that they're motivated to do what's best for the business overall, lest an every-division-for-itself ethos tear the company apart. Bishops and other church leaders need to match how their ministers are motivated, financially and spiritually, and how the church is designed.

A military-like set of rigid rules and intense oversight are one solution. This was the Catholic Church circa 1516. Local parish priests, not terribly well educated, served the needs of their congregants while adhering to the central tenets of faith as outlined by church leadership. If a priest proved himself well suited to higher office in the church hierarchy (mostly by accident of birth, at least in the Middle Ages), there was also the opportunity for promotion. Parish priests weren't asked to exercise initiative, nor were they expected to volunteer any. (Luther showed initiative, and look at what happened there.)

Bishops and their staff monitored the priests, making sure they showed up to do their jobs in the pulpit and at the confessional, and that they remained doctrinally pure. Cardinals, monks, pardoners, vicars, deans, deacons, and so on down the ranks—each had a specific role to play to make the church run, and each was rewarded differently.

The church's rigid hierarchy was well suited to its oppressive oversight and blunt incentives, and vice versa. If it wasn't a recipe for a dynamic, inventive church, that wasn't the point anyway. The church had worked for centuries in serving the religious needs of the uneducated Catholic masses spread across a vast Christian empire, which needed to be managed in a slow-moving age that predated the printing press and long-distance communication.

Atop the Catholic hierarchy sat Pope Leo X. Born to the influential Medici family and made cardinal by age thirteen and pope in his late thirties, Leo spent his days admiring Roman art and music, banqueting, and pursuing—ahem—other earthly pleasures. He was prone to three-day-long orgiastic banquets and became obsessed with extracting enough money from the church's followers to line his own pockets and build St. Peter's Basilica in Rome as his legacy. This left little time to watch over the church bureaucracy, even if Leo had been qualified to do so. Compounding the effects of his neglect, Leo was the last in a line of inattentive popes who, distracted by the worldly temptations of Rome, had left the church rudderless and adrift.

Such financial profligacy and fiscal mismanagement drove the church into bankruptcy, compelling Leo to cross the line into selling off sin and salvation itself through the aggressive peddling of indulgences throughout Christendom. In return for a small contribution, the pardoner (a church-sanctioned marketing and sales professional) would guarantee that the church would intercede with God on your behalf or on behalf of a loved one, either to wipe away your sin or to open the gates of

Heaven for those stuck in purgatory.[2] It was this mercenary approach to religious fund-raising that spurred Martin Luther to write and post his 95 Theses. Which gets us back to the story of how Luther and his followers would set up their churches to compete with Leo for the hearts and minds of Christians the world over.

Accomplishing the Great Commission

We won't be able to explore the paths taken by every denomination in how they chose to organize, so we'll focus on one in particular, the United Methodist Church. Understanding how the Methodists put together the layers of their organization—at the local, diocesan, and national levels—and how this in turn fits with the tools they use to motivate and inspire their ministers, can help us appreciate the challenges faced by every org.

The Methodists' story can feel complicated at times. We'll discuss different kinds of compensation for different kinds of conversions, competing incentives from the local parish and the state-wide diocese. But that's because the Methodist Church is using every lever it's got to balance its need to let each parish manage its own affairs, while making sure that it doesn't stray too far from the interests of the Methodists' overall mission. Without the hierarchy and strict controls of the Catholic Church, the Methodists have had to come up with new systems for accomplishing the job of saving souls in their own unique way.

Two economists will help us to navigate the complex inner workings of the Methodist bureaucracy: Chris Parsons, the son of a Baptist preacher in Texas, and his thesis adviser, Jay Hartzell, whose stepdad was a Methodist pastor. Working with colleague

David Yermack of New York University, the pair compiled the financial and human resource archives from the Oklahoma diocese, where Hartzell's stepdad had risen to the number-three position in the church hierarchy. Those records, stretching back to 1961, gave the researchers a complete accounting of each minister's compensation as well as attendance at Sunday services and church expenditures. Based on these detailed records, Hartzell, Parsons, and Yermack were able to provide a statistical reckoning of how the Methodists confronted the tasks of organizing their church and motivating its ministers.

The Methodists take their cue from the Gospel of Matthew, where Jesus tells his followers, "Go therefore and make disciples of all nations, baptizing them in the name of the Father and of the Son and of the Holy Spirit, and teaching them to obey everything that I have commanded you to attract disciples." The Methodists have embraced this "Great Commission" and focus on finding new members, primarily through disciple-making in local churches.[3]

Like any org, the Methodists have to motivate their employees. It's just that, in this case, the employees in question happen to be ministers. It might seem a bit odd to think about how incentives affect men and women of the cloth. We don't expect them to be paid like investment bankers, precisely because they're motivated by otherworldly concerns. Serving God, and heavenly rewards in the Great Hereafter, should be enough to keep them focused on the church's mission.

But even the Bible recognizes that ministers might need some nonspiritual incentives. Consider these lines from the Apostle Paul's First Letter to the Corinthians: "If we have sown spiritual seed among you, is it too much if we reap a material harvest from you? If others have this right of support from you, shouldn't we have it all the more?" In other words, if Goldman Sachs bankers get paid based on profits they earn for the company, why shouldn't preachers get bonuses based on souls saved (and paying members recruited)?[4] Of course spiritual men and women respond to material incentives. They're only human, after all.

Some are more human than others, falling prey to the same temptations that gripped Pope Leo, albeit on a lesser scale. Self-serving preachers date back at least to the days of Judas, whom John the Evangelist accused of stealing from the disciples' collection box. With the advent of radio came radio evangelists, and characters such as Aimee Semple McPherson, founder of the International Church of the Foursquare Gospel, which raised a fortune to build a 5,000-seat house of worship, the Angelus Temple, and also a 4,400-square-foot Moorish Revival mansion for its leader. Television brought televangelists such as Jim and Tammy Faye Bakker, who used the wealth generated by their PTL (Praise the Lord) ministry to finance a home with gold-plated bathroom fixtures, a fifty-foot walk-in closet (and shopping sprees to fill it), not to mention the widely reported air-conditioned doghouse for Tammy's much-loved pooches. It all unraveled when Jim revealed an extramarital affair and went to prison for a Ponzi scheme around the financing of their Heritage USA theme park and condo development.[5]

From Judas to Jim and Tammy Faye—these are clearly extreme examples of the conflict between divine and secular incentives. The average preacher surely has at least some of each. But more to the point, there need not be, and ideally isn't direct conflict between the religious ends of the church and the financial objectives of its pastors.

The Complicated Business of Saving Souls

Recognizing that even the religious need some kind of compensation—if only to keep body and soul together—you might think that measuring a pastor's performance and paying him accordingly would be easy: a productive pastor is one with more baptisms and fewer lapsed congregants. If there's pay for preacher performance, attracting new congregants should add up to more pay and greater chance of promotion. If only it were that easy.

The Methodists aspire to more than just boosting the membership rolls. "We reach out to people and welcome them into the church" may be the church's top priority, but it's only the first of four bullet points in the Methodist mission statement. The rest involve cultivating the faith of existing disciples—to "deepen their relationship with God" and more broadly "nurture people in Christian living." A minister's job, it turns out, involves as much multitasking as any beat cop's or office worker's.

To get all of their varied and sometimes competing objectives accomplished, the Methodists have built an organization with a relatively tight structure and more centralized control over what it means to be a member of the church than competing denominations such as, say, the Baptists, whose churches have broad discretion over setting their own course. Yet the Methodists remain emphatically apart from Catholicism's command-and-control approach to faith and worship. They describe themselves as deliberately having "no single central office, no archbishop, no pope. This reflects the representative nature of the church's organization—which also provides a system of checks and balances...one of the most carefully organized and largest denominations in the world."[6]

In this limited religious hierarchy, each church reports to a bishop, who watches over all Methodist parishes within a state or region. Representatives from each region meet regularly to deal with larger, organization-wide questions. The church also explicitly involves laypersons in managing local church affairs, true to the spirit of Luther's populist revolt.

If the church rewarded pastors based solely on a headcount of parishioners, ministers might devote more time and effort to attracting new members, but at the expense of attending to the many needs of existing congregants. A minister's tasks in serving his parish range from the spiritual to the truly mundane. He is a performer, manager, and social worker all rolled into one. He must deliver engaging sermons, counsel congregants facing personal crises, and visit with the sick and others in need. At the same time, he must spend endless evenings attending committee meetings, write or at least oversee a church newsletter, and keep the collection box full (unfortunately, the church can't keep the lights on and the pews in good shape without cash on hand). Member retention may give some indication of how any one minister is doing on these many tasks, since dissatisfied churchgoers will eventually seek religious fulfillment elsewhere. But it's a blunt instrument for evaluating the care and compassion that pastors show in serving their congregations.

So while recruitment and retention statistics from each church can be counted and entered into a spreadsheet, and pay doled out accordingly, such figures provide a very limited view of each pastor's performance. The day-to-day work of a minister is taken up with duties that may have no direct impact on membership, and will go unnoticed by a less-than-all-seeing bishop trying to keep tabs on hundreds of parishes around the state.

This is why Methodist Church leaders in Oklahoma, as in the

rest of the world, delegate the job of setting pay to local pastor-parish relations committees (PPRCs), comprised of half a dozen or so congregants. Each committee has a range of responsibilities, from setting priorities for the church to making sure the parish is functioning effectively. It also evaluates the pastor's performance and cuts him a check accordingly, and can even fire him "if it should become evident that the best interests of the church and pastor will be served by a change of pastor."[7] This structure hands off the job of setting compensation to church members most capable of observing the effort and care with which the pastor tends his flock.

An average minister could expect to make around $35,000 in 2006, and a young seminary grad serving three rural communities as a roving preacher might barely clear a five-figure salary. So the few thousand dollars in one direction or another at the discretion of the PPRC can make a big difference to a pastor's take-home pay. Then there's the further carrot of career advancement. Promotion to a congregation of thousands in Tulsa or other urban areas in the state brings a higher pay grade, a fancier house, and greater prestige. Superstar pastors in big-city churches earn as much as a quarter of a million a year when you add in fringe benefits such as the free house and generous pension.

The PPRC members undoubtedly do their best to steward the local parish in carrying out the church's larger mission. But they're only human, after all, and subject to the frailties of human nature. The church recognizes as much. Immediate relatives of the pastor are barred from the committee, lest he try to stack it with allies.

Egregious nepotism aside, PPRC members might have other reasons to let local parish interests color their thinking on how the pastor is tending and growing his congregation. But that's okay, because, for the most part, their selfish interests happen to align quite well with those of the church. The Oklahoma bishop would like to add members and bring in more revenue, as would committee members watching over church finances. The bishop wants congregants to be happy, stay connected to the church, and become more active Methodists—and so does the PPRC. So most of the time, it works pretty well for the bishop to outsource to local committees the job of keeping tabs on local ministers.

Incentive Pay for Saving Souls

Parsons and Hartzell never questioned whether ministers working twelve-hour days for low five-figure salaries were motivated by something more than money. But they wanted to know whether the PPRC used financial rewards—incentive pay for saving souls—to prod their pastors to work that much harder to accomplish their calling. Had the church followed Paul's advice in his First Letter to the Corinthians?

Parsons and Hartzell are economists, not theologians, so when they set out to understand how the Methodist Church managed its pastoral affairs, it was through the lens of economic incentives and the statistical analysis of church data. They've produced two studies whose cold, dispassionate titles—"Human Capital and the Supply of Religion" and "Is Higher Calling Enough? Incentive Effects in the Church"—warm an economist's heart but rankle some in the Protestant community who see this research as casting aspersions on pastoral motivations.[8]

Theological opposition notwithstanding, it's hard to argue with the data: lo and behold, when they ran the numbers, Parsons and Hartzell found that minister pay was indeed sensitive to performance in disciple-making. Each new congregant translated into an additional fifteen dollars or so in compensation, and each one lost caused a comparable drop in pay. Even two jaded economists were surprised by just how sensitive the pay-for-performance relationship is for ministers. Methodist pastors keep about two cents for each extra dollar in the collection plate. This is in the same ballpark as the pay-for-performance sensitivity of *Fortune* 500 CEOs, who keep about three or four cents on each dollar of profit they create (although the number of dollars involved is of course much, much higher for CEOs).

Just looking at changes in membership is a rather crude indication of whether the pastor is doing his job, as many factors that affect congregants are outside his control. Births and deaths of disciples, for example, is a matter for the Great Manager in the Sky to decide. Methodists move into the church's neighborhood, others move out. Why should the minister take the blame (or get full credit) for what are essentially acts of God?

The ministers' paymasters are quite savvy in filtering out these gains and losses due to random chance—births and deaths and the growth or shrinkage of towns and villages have no effect on the salary of clergy. Instead, professions of faith—that is, conversions—and Methodists attracted from other parishes are worth about $25 apiece. This may not sound like much, but in a church of even relatively modest size, a few dozen members can be gained or lost in a year, resulting in a $1,000 bonus (or loss) for a pastor earning an annual salary of only $30,000.

But the pay-for-member incentives employed by PPRCs also raise the possibility of unpleasant conflict with the bishop, which presents itself most obviously in the new disciples recruited to fill the pews of a pastor's church. Both the bishop and local overseers will take an interest in converting nonbelievers. The mission of the church, after all, is partly a missionary one of saving souls by attracting them to the Christian faith. As dues-paying members, new Methodists will also help with church finances. It's good for the local church's bank balance, which keeps the bulk of member contributions, and it's good for the Oklahoma Methodist head office in Tulsa, which levies a tax on the earnings of its churches.

Their interests diverge, however, when it comes to attracting congregants from nearby Methodist parishes—"sheep stealing," in church jargon. No additional souls are saved, and the Oklahoma Methodists don't see any additional revenues at all. From the bishop's perspective, competition among his pastors for the fixed pie of Oklahoma Methodists is a zero sum game. For each local church, though, stolen sheep are as valuable—at least in financial terms—as new converts.

The bishop may not be averse to a little friendly competition. Ineffectual pastors *should* lose their parishioners to better ones, just as unproductive firms ought to lose market share to more efficient producers.[9] And a comparison of member recruitment across parishes can help the bishop and his conference decide which of Oklahoma's pastors should be rotated to other churches, or encouraged to leave the clergy altogether.

But competition also has a darker side. In his aptly titled book *Stealing Sheep*, preacher-author William Chadwick doesn't mince words in describing what competition has done to America's churches: "The McChurch has replaced the traditional home church and its relational values. Fast-food Christians pull up to ecclesiastical drive-through windows, order their McGroups, consume the experience and then drive off, discarding relationships like burger wrappers on the highway of life. Savvy...pastors quickly learned that significant growth can occur if a church learns how to market its burgers to capture the appetite of this roving crowd."[10]

Why is parish growth so much more easily accomplished by poaching from others' flocks? Stolen sheep come cheap. Chadwick explains that converting nonbelievers is hard work, with "the gospel presented in a fashion they can understand, and often this requires the building of...bridges to their world." Why reach out to new worlds when you can get many of the same benefits by raiding the flock across town?

Methodists at other congregations may also come with high benefits relative to the newly converted. Although church-shopping Methodists have shown a willingness to experiment with different services and communities, and hence may once again choose to move on to sample yet another churchly burger stand, they at least have a commitment to Methodism. New converts may just be sampling from the full menu of offerings in America's crowded religious marketplace. Having gone through the hand-holding and cultivation involved in introducing a fresh disciple to the Methodist Church, a minister risks losing the newly baptized to some other flavor of Christianity or perhaps to another religion entirely. Those in search of spiritual meaning may similarly travel among cities just as they do among religions, and so may be lost to geographic relocation as well. These itinerant souls may also not have the stable earning power to support the church financially.

Finally, as Hartzell and Parsons argue, if the local PPRC sees the parish losing congregants to a church across town, it may take it as a pretty damning indication of the quality of its own pastor. If he can't even keep his own flock happy, what hope is there of ever building the congregation? (Likewise, a pastor whose commitment and rhetorical talents lures nearby Methodists must be a great pastor, relatively speaking.)

By Hartzell and Parsons's statistical reckoning, attracting a new Methodist from a neighboring congregation is worth about thirty-five dollars in pastor pay, as compared to seventeen dollars for a "profession of faith" of a new Christian. The gap in the benefit between professions of faith and poaching Methodists is much smaller in rural congregations, where Methodists probably just come and go from the congregation when families move in or out of town, which can hardly be pinned on the pastor's talents.

The differences in pay-for-membership are even wider for losses from the congregation. The pastor's pay isn't at all sensitive to memberships lost to death—again, a matter of divine rather than earthly intervention. Nor is he punished for lapses of faith. Congregants who leave Protestant Christianity altogether likely have much bigger bones to pick with the Methodist Church than just the local leadership. But losses to other Methodist congregations come with the stern financial rebuke of fifty-five dollars in lower pay.

While higher pay for stealing sheep isn't quite what the Apostle Paul had in mind for church performance pay, it is, at least to economists, a natural side effect of the church's structure, which delegates authority to local interests that may not always align perfectly with the org's broader objectives. Pastors and their compensation committees are vulnerable to the same human frailties of those in any other org. If the incentives are strong enough, they may give in to the temptation of poaching others' flocks, and set pay in such a way as to encourage it.

The Cost of Stealing Sheep

It's impressive that the Methodists, perhaps without even meaning to, have done such a good job of aligning pay with the goal
of parish growth. But with these incentives, you might think that
Methodist ministers spent all their time chasing one another's
parishioners. Why does the bishop allow PPRCs to give in to
this temptation? Remember, the bishop is too busy running an
enormous consortium of hundreds of churches statewide, which
is why he has delegated the task of pay setting in the first place.
It's the same trade-off between limited time and attention and
the loss of control that afflicts any org as it grows beyond a single
church or factory.

But that doesn't mean he needs to give local compensation
committees the last word. While each committee may have a
clear sense of what's going on in its congregation, they don't
see the big picture of pastor performance statewide. So when it
comes to deciding who moves up to larger, more prestigious congregations (and the larger houses and higher pay scale that come
with them), the bishop makes that decision himself, together
with his Cabinet of District Superintendents at the Oklahoma
Methodists' Annual Conference. Promotion can be as effective a
lever as pay in directing performance.

Hartzell and Parsons find that the promotion decisions at the
conference go a long way toward realigning pastor incentives
with the Oklahoma church overall. Pastors are obliged to rotate
every few years to a new congregation, and in years when these
transfers take place, professions of faith—the pastor's work that
best lines up with the bishop's objectives—are what matter most
in advancing to larger, higher-paying churches. By comparing the
salary at a minister's old church to his earnings at the new one,

Hartzell and Parsons find that each new convert from outside Christianity translates into more than $200 in salary, not to mention the extra prestige and status from getting transferred to a bigger pulpit.

Likewise, attracting worshipers from other denominations generates over $250 in salary per convert at a new post. (Putting high-performing pastors in charge of larger congregations has the added benefit for the church of placing preachers in pulpits where their oratory and management talents can be spread over a larger membership base.) A sheep-stealing pastor doesn't see nearly the same promotion for his efforts; each new Methodist congregant adds less than $40 to his salary in rotation years.

The point of our account of how Methodists motivate their pastors isn't that money serves as their only or even their primary objective. These are men and women who, having completed four-plus years of postsecondary education, toil long hours for meager financial rewards. The upside for even the most successful pastors is still less than what a business school student earns a year or two after graduation. So while pay committees may use compensation as one additional instrument to get pastors to focus on what's good for the local community, to a large extent they can simply rely on pastors' intrinsic motivation to do the right thing.

By the same token, since most pastors are devoted to the Methodist Church's basic purpose of saving souls, any mismatch between the org's design and their pastoral incentives won't matter quite so much. They'll do the right thing not because they're angling for promotion or extra pay, but because it's the right thing to do. Yet even for these spiritually motivated men and women, the Oklahoma bishop *still* has to use promotion to prestigious congregations to undo some of the misaligned incentives put in place by local PPRCs, to ensure that the church overall serves its higher calling. The need to get everything to fit together just so is even greater for an organization where the motives of the employees and the goals of the org aren't quite so tightly aligned.

Adapt or Die: Reorganizing Procter & Gamble

The bishop's organizational challenges are decidedly modest compared to those of a *Fortune* 50 CEO setting the course for a globe-spanning empire and directing resources across dozens of divisions and hundreds or thousands of product lines. It's not just that a billion-dollar corporation may have a thousand times more employees and offices than Oklahoma's bishop—although that's true as well—but the CEO also can't appeal to a higher calling in motivating his minions. It has taken time, patience, and trial and error for the Methodists' efforts to create a well-functioning org, *even though* the church's mission, to serve God, helps inspire most of its members. A corporation has the much less inspiring objective of making money for shareholders.

With no calling higher than the lure of the almighty dollar, a corporate leader has to think that much harder about how to organize her enterprise to make sure that every employee, unit, product line, and division is aligned such that the org all comes together to be more than the sum of its many parts. The trials and errors of one company—among the most long-lived and successful corporations in history—illustrate just how hard it is to get it right.

Procter & Gamble's sprawling consumer products empire has its roots in the R&D labs that concocted Ivory Soap. The company was founded in the 1830s by soap maker James Gamble and candle-making apprentice William Procter at the prodding of their mutual father-in-law. It was a good match. Procter and Gamble thrived as a partnership, selling over $1 million worth of soap and candles—nearly $30 million in today's dollars—by 1859. Like most companies of the time, though, P&G remained very much a family business. It employed eighty workers at a single factory on Central Avenue in Cincinnati, where they could be policed and motivated through direct observation, in the same way Bill Hewlett and Dave Packard watched over HP in its early days.

By the mid-1880s, P&G had moved into a larger production complex, named Ivorydale, to accommodate its ever-expanding product line. Still a family affair, the company was managed by sundry Procter and Gamble sons and grandsons, who experimented with new soap formulations and watched over operations, which by that time were on a scale that could no longer be overseen with a walk across the factory floor. With labor unrest on the rise—as it was in the rest of the country at the time—Procter grandson William Cooper had the idea of giving workers a share of the profits, aligning employer and employee economic self-interests. Cooper's management innovation made for a happier, more productive workforce, according to official company history.

In the decades that followed, P&G built out from its chemistry-based expertise to produce innovations in everything from cooking oil to paper to pharmaceuticals. New products combined with marketing savvy to lead to even further diversification, including TV production in the 1930s: P&G's market research arm invented the "soap opera" in 1933, and the longest-running daytime drama in television history, *Guiding Light*, was produced by a P&G subsidiary until 2009.

From M-Form to Matrix

To cope with its growing size and complexity, P&G sought a new way of managing the org. In a process that was taking place in business empires across America, P&G evolved into a multidivisional org (known as the M-Form), in which largely autonomous operating divisions for soap, toiletries, and foods were given authority to develop, manufacture, and market their own products relatively unimpeded by a central P&G bureaucracy. The company pushed decisions even farther down the org chart with the invention of brand management in the 1930s, which empowered managers of individual products to chase after customer segments as they saw fit.

This led to inevitable but often productive conflicts. Sometimes, Camay and Ivory would go after the same customers, much as sheep-stealing pastors might try to poach one another's congregants. But the upside of local control was such that, on balance, it served the larger interests of P&G—higher profits for Camay and Ivory meant higher profits for P&G overall, just as local pastor oversight has been good for Oklahoma's Methodists. Despite their autonomy, product and brand managers ultimately answered to P&G's senior management, who had the final word and exercised this authority as needed to ensure the org's greater good. Top executives, for example, pushed perennial bestseller Tide through the R&D process against the wishes of detergent brand managers, who correctly saw it as a threat to their own market share.

This arrangement worked well for P&G, much as it did for other emerging industrial giants. But as business leaders looked to find ever more ways of wringing greater profits out of the org, they latched on to the idea of eliminating the redundancies that appeared in product divisions. Sales managers for Ivory, Tide, and other product lines covered the same regions, accountants kept separate books, manufacturing facilities acted independently. Think of the waste! So by the mid-1980s, P&G's execs decided it was time for an organizational reset. The solution was the matrix.

The matrix had its roots at NASA in the 1950s, where it was used to bring engineers together with scientists and administrative staffers to design rocket boosters, satellite panels, and other project-based tasks. It quickly caught on in business, but with product lines taking the place of the R&D projects that defined the matrix at NASA. Functional groups—sales, finance, manufacturing, R&D—were overlaid on the product groupings that had previously defined reporting structures.

Under the matrix, work was no longer "siloed" in individual brands or product lines. All scientists were integrated as an R&D group, just as manufacturing engineers, marketers, and sales associates were united by their respective functions. Sales could be coordinated across brands and categories, while scientists working on, say, dish detergent could share their discoveries and best practices with those who worked on laundry detergent or paper towels.

The matrix seemingly avoided the trade-off that companies had to face during their multidivisional days, between functions and products. As Columbia University professor Leonard Sayles put it, without irony, in a 1976 article advocating this new form of organizing, "Matrix management represents the effort, organizationally speaking, to 'have your cake and eat it too.'"[11]

P&G's version of the matrix came with an additional layer of complexity because of the company's global operations. By the early 1980s, P&G was operating in twenty-seven countries.

While Texans and New Yorkers have similar tastes in toothpaste and potato chips, their palates differ markedly from those in the United Kingdom, where P&G sells curry-flavored Pringles along with kebab and prawn cocktail, flavors that might not make it elsewhere. The gulf between British and American tastes as compared with those in Asia is even wider. (Salmon teriyaki chips, anyone? In Indonesia, apparently so.) Across P&G's dozens of product lines, customization proved critical to respond to varying regulations, levels of prosperity, customer idiosyncrasies—even differences in the size and shape of a baby's bottom. (Pampers is a P&G brand.)

The result was effectively a three-dimensional matrix, with separate reporting lines and hierarchies for products, functions, *and* geographies. An org with many bosses has its benefits. Where appropriate, accountants and sales reps could be shared across product lines to create "cross-product synergies" (business-speak for the whole being greater than the sum of its parts). Global product managers were able to coordinate the rollout of new products across all P&G's markets, getting innovations to market more rapidly. The consolidation of manufacturing under a single global supply chain helped to streamline and rationalize (another buzzword of the era) production. All the while, country managers could provide feedback and guidance on the needs of their local markets.

But you rarely get something for nothing, organizationally speaking, whatever a Columbia Business School professor might tell you. Handing control to competing bosses with disparate objectives led to tension and conflict. Coordinating the three groups created additional layers of meetings, bureaucracies, and confusion. Those living and working in the matrix bore the brunt of this collective confusion and tension. This may account for the mixed results experienced by the many companies that had adopted the matrix in the 1970s: it seemed to work for some but was abandoned by others.

Bosses from product lines, geographies, and functions pulled P&G and its employees in three separate directions. In the ranks of management, quality-obsessed R&D managers seeking to maximize performance at all costs butted heads with manufacturing managers evaluated on cost control. Country managers reveled in their newfound autonomy, paying little heed to the global costs of local customization.

Perhaps inevitably, in 1998 P&G began a billion-dollar restructuring to replace the matrix, called Organization 2005 (named for the date that the multi-year process would finally be completed). Under newly minted CEO Durk Jager's mantra of Stretch, Innovation, and Speed (SIS), the idea was for P&G to become an agile, nimble force of innovation—more strike team than Catholic hierarchy. Jager's initiative was meant to combat the P&G culture that had evolved under its then-legendary bureaucracy, a bureaucracy that had produced employees— Proctoids, they were called—known for total obedience and equally complete lack of inspiration. Reinforcing this new culture of initiative were streamlined decision-making rules that emphasized individual responsibility over decision making by committee, which had come to dominate P&G under the interwoven design of the matrix.

No one would call Organization 2005 a matrix, which had been blamed for the years of stagnant sales growth and a burgeoning bureaucracy. Yet it had the same conflicts and tensions between product managers and manufacturing bosses, some focused on quality, others on cost cutting, and the same clash of incentives: innovators were paid for innovating, cost cutters for cost cutting, salesmen for selling. The great irony, and the initial failure of the matrix, was that with all these high-powered, clearly directed incentives, there was too much bickering and backstabbing for anything to get done at all.

When Organization 2005 failed to turn the company around—granted, Durk Jager was given only seventeen months to prove himself—P&G promoted A. G. Lafley to the position of CEO. At the risk of diluting employees' clarity of purpose, Lafley baked a bit of intergroup empathy into the matrix. For example, cost cutters in manufacturing who elicited complaints from their counterparts in the rest of the company were docked points in their evaluations. And everyone in the company was given a broader set of performance criteria—market share, profit margins, sales, and the like—which made it feel more like they were playing on the same team.

Lafley's culture, seen largely as a return to the P&G of old, emphasized that all Proctoids were in this together. But his version of togetherness was built around an understanding that each P&G employee relied on the efforts and goodwill of others to get his job done. Likewise, each worker's good-faith efforts were needed by others to accomplish their own objectives. To some degree, it was a culture of "you scratch my back and someday I'll scratch yours." Lafley wrote his approach to employee relations into P&G's credo, adding the phrase, "mutual interdependence as a way of life." It was a culture fit for a matrix.

Fitting It All Together

It would be too easy to proclaim Durk Jager the loser, A. G. Lafley the winner, and say, "Follow Lafley's lead and all will be well." Despite all the ink spilled about his success (not least by Lafley himself), that might be the worst thing you could take away from this chapter. If there's a lesson from the P&G story, it isn't the failure of the matrix or the triumph of A. G. Lafley. It's a much more subtle storyline of the trial-and-error grasping for a better way of organizing. If P&G has got back on the right track in the past decade, it's in part because of the realization that multiple bosses create fewer conflicts if they have fewer reasons to butt heads.

Getting the org right is hard. Think of the Protestants' efforts and the fit between goals, beliefs, the market, and members' motivations. It involves lots of trial, lots of error, and the occasional epic failure, even with the best-intentioned efforts by the smartest of managers. A. G. Lafley benefited from all that was learned through the trials and tribulations of his predecessors, and more than likely from at least a little bit of luck. But understanding the basic economics of the org surely helped as well.

CHAPTER 4

In Praise of Squelching Innovation

THE CAMPUS AT THE U.S. MILITARY ACADEMY at West Point is all about winning. It's announced on the billboard at a security checkpoint where visitors enter the Academy ("2009 National Champs in Judo, Boxing, Orienteering, and Pistol"). It's plastered on the side of the chancellor's white clapboard residence ("Go Army, Beat Navy"). It's the primary objective espoused by the Office of the Directorate of Intercollegiate Athletics (Goal Number 1: "Compete to win"; Goal Number 2: "Beat Air Force, Beat Navy").

Athletics are just a means to the end of getting young, driven men and women to line up behind the much larger mission and purpose of the U.S. Army: "to fight and win our Nation's wars." Football and boxing are mere metaphors for the contests that cadets will face in the valleys of Afghanistan, the streets of Baghdad, and wherever future geopolitical interests may take them.

The emphasis on winning is partly about discipline. Recruits follow orders, from boot shining as extreme sport to doing push-ups at the command of classroom instructors. It's also about conformity, from the strict campus dress code (including well-shined boots) to the time each cadet sits down to lunch (12:05 p.m. precisely) in the cavernous dining hall along with her five thousand fellow cadets. While the cadets may find many of the routines pointlessly frustrating, coming as they do with an avalanche of demerits and punishments (after all, you can buy brass buttons that never need polishing), the leadership at West Point knows that the conformity and attention to detail that come with proper marching can save lives.

But the Academy is also the training ground for the officer corps, future leaders of the U.S. Army. (Army athletics Goal Number 3: "Develop scholar-athletes who lead the Corps.") Upon graduation, cadets take the rank of second lieutenant, entering their compulsory five years of military service with a platoon of, on average, thirty soldiers already under their command. In recent years, many were shipped straight to Iraq or Afghanistan, where they were forced to cope with the trials and challenges of keeping the peace, developing the local economy, and fighting in active combat.

In battle, the freshly minted second lieutenants (with a far more experienced noncommissioned officer riding herd) must internalize complicated rules of engagement and make sure their soldiers pay attention to a plethora of confusing and contradictory on-the-ground conditions. They also have to translate into action the vague strategic directives from generals sitting in the Pentagon: boost economic activity, fight insurgents, kill as few civilians as possible. Should the black market for benzene be shut down, or would it be better to leave it alone? Can local religious leaders be trusted? What's the right balance between community building and policing? Blind conformists who haven't had an original thought in their lives won't be able to figure out the answers for themselves. And the few West Point grads who eventually go on to wear a general's stars will need to give marching orders to tens or hundreds of thousands of soldiers.

So the army needs a cadre of officers who follow blindly, yet provide inspired leadership; who think outside the box, but stay inside it when they're told. These competing objectives require that the army strike a delicate balance between producing an org filled with sheep (as one reform-minded major called his fellow officers) and the chaos that they'd find if West Point churned out free-thinking innovators.

This challenge isn't limited to the U.S. Army, or the military more generally. Red-taped, over-sized orgs the world over recognize the tension inherent between centralization and innovation, and have searched for ways of seeding creativity and imagination amid the crushing burden of rules and cultures of following orders. How do you make sure everyone marches in lockstep, even as you figure out your org's next great innovation?

Orgs that fight for survival in the marketplace can't afford to get stupid or lazy, for fear of being supplanted by nimble start-ups, falling victim to what economist Joseph Schumpeter called "creative destruction," the "central fact" of capitalism. But if any organization had an incentive to get this balancing act right, you'd think it would be the U.S. Army. After all, West Point is all about winning, not just because it's really fun to beat Navy, but because losing in this context means people are going to die. In its struggle to find the right balance, though, the army begins with the premise, learned through decades of experience, that adherence to rules and following orders is an undeniable necessity.

The Ineluctable Necessity of Coordination

The Allied forces' crowning achievement in the Second World War was the D-Day invasion of June 6, 1944, code-named Operation Overlord. Winning wars is part heroism, but to get the heroes onto the beach alive requires cold, rational planning. Stephen Ambrose, a military historian, described Operation Overlord as "a planning operation that seemed infinite in scope." In Winston Churchill's words, the invasion was "the most complicated operation ever to take place," a claim that may still hold to this day.

General Dwight Eisenhower was the supreme commander of this infinitely complex set of interconnected assaults, which held as their objective a toehold in Normandy from which Allied forces could launch their Western European campaign against Hitler and bring the war to an end. In planning their defenses, German military strategists were all too aware of the importance of holding the coast of France. Eisenhower's German counterpart, Field Marshal Erwin Rommel, had directed the fortification of an Atlantic Wall involving a diabolical combination of millions of sea and land mines, reinforced concrete bunkers housing antitank and machine guns, and several divisions of Panzer tanks. Rivers were flooded to confound troops parachuting inland.

To overcome this strong defensive position, Eisenhower coordinated the landing of 175,000 men and their equipment, including 50,000 vehicles ranging from motorcycles to bulldozers. They were to storm ashore on the heels of a pre-assault naval and air bombardment to soften up German defenses with coordinated landings and attacks planned down to the second. On Omaha Beach, for example, at precisely 0625—just as the hammering from Allied ships and planes lifted—two companies of amphibious tanks were to come ashore to provide support to the coming waves of infantry landings. Five minutes later—H-Hour—a further company of tanks would land, with the first infantry touching down at various points along the beach one minute after that, and subsequent landings at H + 3, 30, 40, 50, 57, and 60 minutes. That was just the first hour.

Back in England many thousands more remained to manage the shipments of oil, food, and munitions to fuel the invasion. Even before this, an epic effort on the home front had redirected industrial production toward meeting the needs of Eisenhower and his fellow planners, and a transportation infrastructure to deliver the goods as needed. Months before the assault began, in early 1944, the Allies had begun to confound German logistical and resupply efforts through a sustained air attack against German factories and refineries.

Viewed from the grand sweep of history, this elaborately premeditated and choreographed attack was a relatively new way for a commanding general to think about war. Eisenhower once told an interviewer that before the battle is joined, plans are *everything*. According to historian John Keegan, this realization started with the Prussian army's defeat of Austria and France in 1866, largely on account of its extensive railway network (partly owned by the government), which was able to hurry troops to the front lines. This lesson was not lost on commanders of the rest of Europe's armies. The German army defending Normandy's beaches in 1944 had owned its own railway department since 1876, an acknowledgment of the role of coordinated logistics to ensure military access when needed.[1]

Careful planning (coupled with some remarkable heroism) paid off. After taking the beaches of Normandy, Allied forces

marched through France and into Belgium, taking the Nether-
lands and arriving on German soil before year's end. The force
that defeated Hitler went on to build and manage an arsenal
armed with tens of thousands of warheads and to keep the peace
throughout the Cold War.

Those who fought in the war went home to work in orgs
where life looked a lot like the army. Many of America's largest
companies had taken the same lessons as the military on the
value of logistics and planning in building the gargantuan businesses that fueled the Industrial Revolution. The modern org
chart itself—grouping the organization into divisions and con-
necting subordinates to managers and managers to bosses via a
set of unidirectional arrows—was invented in 1855 by Daniel
McCallum of the Erie Railway to keep track of men and resources in what was the largest railroad in the world at the
time. As with Eisenhower's army, McCallum sought to create in
Erie an organization with clear division of responsibilities, power
conferred on bosses in the chain of command, channels of communication to report on whether duties had been carried out,
and the means to allow the superintendent (McCallum himself)
to have a clear view on what was going on throughout the org
and the power to act on it.[2]

Bureaucratic, centrally planned orgs dominated the economic
landscape that Ronald Coase observed during his year in America. At that point there was no reason to doubt the model. The
pyramidal org had proved equally effective at building the country's railroads, rolling its steel, and refining its oil. It had defeated
the German war machine in Europe and the Japanese in the Pacific, coordinating divisions to achieve strategic and tactical goals,
and moved millions of men and millions of tons of materiel
around the world. *V* for Victory! The org chart, complete with

the president at the top of the pyramid, was rational and good—
Platonically so.

Yet the shortcomings of the military model were already in
full view to the soldiers of the 101st Airborne, dropped inland
the night before D-Day—who took a markedly different view
on the merits of army planning.[3] While the Eisenhower script
for the Normandy invasion had largely assumed away complications from bad weather, as the full moon on June 6 approached,
thick clouds hung over the French coast, frustrating Allied pilots' attempts to drop their men and machines in neat fighting
formation. Platoons were scattered, and ad hoc groups of fighting men formed organically on the ground. The paratroopers'
situation was complicated by two untested innovations presented by army brass in this, the biggest invasion the world had
ever seen.

The men had spent their evenings trying to figure out how
to use the new "leg bags" they'd been issued. British airborne
soldiers had already effectively deployed leg bags, which allowed
each soldier to have a place to stash machine gun tripods, medical
equipment, and the like—stuff that was unwieldy to carry on a
jump. A twenty-foot rope tethered the bag to the soldier's leg,
with a quick release to be pulled just before landing so that he
could drop onto his equipment and be prepared for combat.
The soldiers of the 101st loaded their bags with everything they
could think of: extra ammunition, mortar plates, Tommy guns.
As they joked about their "$10,000 jump" (the army offered a
$10,000 life insurance policy), each so-called stick of eighteen
men boarded their C-47s to partake of the second innovation:
airsickness pills. To this day, no one is quite sure what was in the
pills, but they put a good number of soldiers to sleep. Many of
them never woke up: they were killed when the planes they slept

in were shot down. And the pills left many more in a lightheaded daze when it came time for them to jump.

Those who did make the jump with their leg bags found that their pilots had been flying faster (150 miles per hour instead of 90 miles per hour) and lower than planned. This is entirely sensible for a pilot intent on evading enemy fire, but not so good if you're making a parachute jump. Because of the extra weight of the leg bags, the soldiers hit the ground only seconds after opening their chutes. And in those few seconds of descent, the ropes tying man to leg bag broke—the combined effect of the shock of emerging from a 150-mile-an-hour plane and bags overstuffed with more than three times their intended weight. So try asking a groggy, weaponless paratrooper on D-Day morning how Eisenhower and Co.'s planning worked for him.

The supreme planner himself might have agreed with the men of the 101st. After stating that plans are everything before the battle, Eisenhower added that plans were useless once the fighting began.[4] For the skeptical troops on the ground, he may have done well to point out that they were focused only on the negatives. Pre-attack planning conferred many advantages on Allied efforts. Imagine the sheer impossibility of landing hundreds of thousands of men and coordinating their attacks without it. It was an intricate jigsaw puzzle of interconnected offensive actions, the success of each depending critically on the effective execution of all others. While the leg bags didn't work as planned, many innovations succeeded, from amphibious tanks able to fire from the sea to provide cover to landing troops, to a massive rubber fuel hose laid under the Channel to resupply the invading force.

Going to War without Planning

To see the merits of Eisenhower's point of view, it's useful to take a look at what happens when you invade a country with insufficient care to planning, coordination, and centralization. Allied casualties for D-Day have been estimated at 10,000, including 2,500 dead. But things could have been far worse if they'd been managed by the admiral overseeing the invasion of a small Caribbean nation nearly three decades later.

In 1983, U.S. president Ronald Reagan used a bloody coup in Grenada, along with a perceived threat to American medical students, as a pretext to eliminate a Marxist regime allied to Fidel Castro's Cuba. During the invasion, code-named Operation Urgent Fury, the U.S. military faced a total defending force of around two thousand, most of them poorly equipped Grenadians and Cubans, with a smattering of Soviets, East Germans, and others.

Goliath prevailed, but not without loss of life of American troops. The Army Rangers who led the invasion, for example, were trapped with inadequate armor in part because of failures to coordinate radio frequencies among the different U.S. service branches participating in the invasion. As a consequence, Marine commanders who could have provided support never came to the rescue—the two forces were talking past one another. During the assault on the governor-general's mansion, a team of Navy SEALs was pinned down by Marine helicopters, whom they couldn't call off because of the same radio frequency snafu (a term first used during World War II: "situation normal, all fouled up"). They were eventually able to do so only by calling Fort Bragg on the telephone, collect. As one commenter noted, "Operation Urgent Fury became the military equivalent of a Japanese Kabuki dance created by three or four choreographers speaking different languages, all working independently of each other."[5]

Following the military's misadventures in Grenada, Ronald Reagan signed into law the Goldwater-Nichols Act in 1986, whose stated purpose was improving coordination and communication across the branches of service. Yet military traditions die hard, and just over a decade following the miscommunications at the Grenada landing, a pair of air force F-15 fighter jets shot down a pair of army Black Hawk helicopters over the no-fly zone in northern Iraq, killing all twenty-six passengers and crew aboard, a higher body count than in the entire Grenada operation. The culprit? A breakdown in communication across branches of the service, despite a raft of safeguards put in place to prevent exactly such a catastrophe.

The no-fly zone patrolled by the F-15s was part of a larger United Nations effort to set up a security zone in northern Iraq following atrocities by Saddam Hussein's Republican Guard against Kurds in the region. Humanitarian efforts on the ground were to be supported by air cover provided by aircraft from a coalition of nations, directed by the Combined Task Force under U.S. command. Several branches of the U.S. military (army and air force included) were part of the American contribution of troops to the task force.

On April 14, 1994, two F-15s crossed the border from Turkey into Iraq to "sanitize" the area of possible enemy aircraft. The pilot of the lead plane, Captain Eric Wickson, picked up a pair of unidentified helicopters flying at low altitude. A few days after UN sanctions were imposed in 1991, the Iraqis had sent a Soviet-built MiG fighter up from Baghdad to test the coalition's resolve. On passing into the no-fly zone, the MiG was immediately shot down, and things had been quiet since then. Nonetheless, the

helicopters weren't on the flow sheet, which listed coalition aircraft going into northern Iraq, and when the F-15s "squawked"
the universal IFF ("identification, friend or foe") signal at the
helicopters, nothing came back in response. After misidentifying
the Black Hawks in a visual flyby as Soviet-made Hinds used by
the Iraqis, Wickson and his wingman notified a nearby AWACS
(Airborne Warning and Control System) command plane of
their intent, and downed the two helicopters with a pair of heat-
seeking missiles. Only after returning to the coalition base in
Turkey did the flight crew learn of their terrible mistake.

The causes of the Black Hawk shoot-down involved a tragic
confluence of bad luck and poor coordination that collectively
led, once again, to a broken telephone between fighters equipped
for combat and unarmed helicopters.[6] Despite the newly integrated command of the armed forces, the army and air force had
developed very different ways of operating even within the unified task force. The helicopters never appeared on the F-15s' flow
sheet listing what was going into Iraqi airspace that day; the flow
sheet listed only "aircraft" which, according to air force definition, included only fixed-wing craft, not helicopters. The Black
Hawk pilots couldn't respond to the F-15s' friend-or-foe query
because a couple of years before the accident the air force had developed its own friend-or-foe signals—without telling the army.
And despite a protocol mandating that all aircraft switch to the
no-fly zone frequency on entering Iraqi territory, the Black Hawk
pilots followed the army convention of continuing to use their
"en route" frequency—even within the no-fly zone—so they were
never in communication with the same air traffic controller in the
AWACS as the fighter jets. In this case, the crossed signals proved
deadly.

The way we've related the story, it seems a shocking breach

of regulation that army pilots never switched radio frequency on leaving Turkey. Yet this was a convention that had evolved over three years of peace and tranquility in Iraqi airspace. Harvard Business School professor Scott Snook (who is a retired colonel in the U.S. Army, and was shot by friendly fire during the invasion of Grenada) calls this slow evolution "practical drift"— the idea that we keep adapting and changing practices within our own group at the expense of coordination with others.

From the perspective of any one group, their individual practices made sense. Army aircraft never flew very far inside Iraq— that was left to air force patrols—and it's dangerous to switch air traffic frequencies mid-flight. So at some point army pilots just agreed among themselves to stick to the "en route" frequency. Their failure was to take into account how their "local" decisions might interact with the larger unified force. And the missing Black Hawks on the flight plan flow sheet? Ask the air force clerk who filled in the sheet the morning of April 14, and she'll tell you. She recorded the Black Hawk flight plan in her logs, but for the airspace flow sheet, her job was to fill in the flight paths of all *aircraft*. Since helicopters travel close to the ground, while F-15s fly at high altitude, the two rarely met. So the air force adopted a convention of listing only the fixed-wing craft relevant to the F-15s' missions. Why clutter the flow sheet with irrelevant information? Besides, from her perspective she was following her orders to the letter.

Squelching Innovation with a Club

Seemingly oppressive bureaucracy does more than just aim to avoid disasters that can spring out of ineffective coordination.

It's also a way for bosses to keep the troops in line with the over-all mission of the org. It's a blunt instrument, but often it's the best that the hierarchy has to offer. The CEO or brigadier gen-eral can't reach down through the levels of the org to correct mis-takes at ground level—although sometimes he's tempted to—so the org has to adhere to a strict rule-following policy to effect the same end.

For McDonald's, keeping a lid on independent innovation reared its head very early in the company's history as Ray Kroc, who bought the small company from its founders in 1955, strug-gled to build a fast-food empire that provided cheap, consistent food. Kroc followed a franchise model, where local managers own their stores while still benefiting from the McDonald's brand and products. To Kroc, it was self-evident from the very start that centralized control was needed to maintain the com-pany's all-important brand and identity.

Kroc found many of the early owner-operators from the mem-bership rolls of the Rolling Green Country Club, near his home in central Illinois, including Bob Dondanville, an ad representa-tive for the *Ladies' Home Journal*. For Dondanville, ad sales was "a straightlaced occupation that belied his free-spirited character," according to John Love's book *McDonald's: Behind the Arches*, a comprehensive retelling of the McDonald's story. Unable to express himself in his day job of selling ads for a women's mag-azine, Dondanville found expression for his flamboyance in his McDonald's franchise. He wasn't going to sell just hamburgers.[7]

This was going to be a classy joint, selling hand-carved roast beef. And Dondanville, a publicity hound, was going to let every-one know it. According to Love, he "placed a huge roast in the front window...donned a chef's hat, and carved the roast himself in view of his customers." Separately, and apparently even more rankling to Kroc, was Dondanville's beard. Kroc was a stickler for careful grooming and had strict rules governing facial hair for McDonald's staff—rules that Dondanville ignored. Kroc reportedly tried to dupe Dondanville into shaving through a publicity stunt where he would serve the company's millionth hamburger, to great fanfare, and then sit in a barber chair at the front of his store (where the carving station sat) for a ceremonial shave. Dondanville served the millionth burger but kept his beard.

A roast beef innovation may have been good for Dondanville, but it wasn't something that would easily scale in Ray Kroc's vision of McDonald's nationwide. And if it was good for Dondanville's ego—he carved the roast with great relish—it may have been less so for profits. Dondanville reported struggling financially in those early days.

Despite their friendship, Kroc would never award another McDonald's franchise to Dondanville. He determined that the McDonald's brand needed careful, rule-following stewards. Contemporary company executives won't let beef-carving innovations endanger their profits, built on decades of reputation building. By 2010 the McDonald's brand was worth over $35 billion, according to one estimate.[8] While a garage start-up has almost nothing to lose, McDonald's risks losing billions of dollars if it lets its franchisees start drifting.

The potential loss of millions or billions (or even thousands, for that matter) can help put into context some of the apparent control freaks running global businesses. At Disney (2011 brand value, $29 billion) CEO Michael Eisner couldn't even let the rules do their job. Eisner was known to intervene in some of the details of movie making one might imagine would be best left to junior studio execs. In *The Big Picture*, a recent history of the movie business, Edward Jay Epstein describes Eisner's taking "a red pen to the script of the 2002 film *The Hot Chick*, circling twenty jokes he deemed inconsistent with Disney's image. He then e-mailed his request for changes to the studio executive in charge of the film, who passed the memo on to the producer. Of course, the changes were made."[9]

A glimpse at what might have been without Eisner's red-lined scripts and Ray Kroc's facial hair fixation can be seen in some of the small-scale innovation misfires that McDonald's has had over the years. The company has managed such blunders as made-to-order McPizza, delivered to your table (you go to the Golden Arches for something in a hurry, not table service, and to eat burgers, not one-stop fast-food shopping); the McLean Burger (the burger has to be quick and tasty, not healthy); and worst of all, a McAfrica sandwich, test marketed in Norway amid a massive famine in Ethiopia and elsewhere on the continent in 2002. The irony was too much for Norwegian customers.

Even if the vetting of new ideas at McDonald's HQ produces some mistakes, they're the inevitable consequence of the gambles that businesses make when they bring new products to market. While, in hindsight, it's easy to see McLean and McAfrica as massive McBlunders, they seemed like good bets at the time. They were calculated risks that didn't pay off. One can only imagine what would be left of the $35 billion brand if McDonald's employees and franchisees weren't kept on such a short leash.

The Cost of Nonconformity

In the army, conformity can save lives. In sprawling multinationals, it saves costs. Standardization is cheap; customization is expensive. Why are bulk burgers and fries so much cheaper than the handmade variety? It's partly technological. McDonald's frying innovations can easily be adopted by its franchisees if they're all making the same product. Coordinated, large-scale production also allows McDonald's to take care of all but the final frying in centralized potato processing facilities that cure, wash, peel, slice, blanch, and freeze the fries by the billion before shipping them across the country and around the world with the peace of mind that each precut potato will be compatible with the fryer it encounters at its destination. Each part of the production chain dovetails neatly with the next.

McDonald's still relies on the market, but only when it can accommodate the exacting standards of Kroc's legacy. When McDonald's opened operations in the former Soviet Union, it had to bring in house everything it needed to make its operations work—from cattle farms to provide beef, to wheat farms to supply basic ingredients for the buns, to potato farms to grow the right russet for its fries. McDonald's couldn't trust the local network and could not tolerate nonconformity, so the company just built the whole thing itself.[10]

For the customer, this obsession with consistency ensures that every McDonald's dining experience will be much the same wherever it takes place. A tourist from Peoria can thus find the comforts of home while gazing at the Eiffel Tower, sightseeing in Latin America, or grabbing a burger around the corner. With each fry like the next, McDonald's probably isn't where you've had the best fries in your life, but you've almost certainly had worse.

The main source of variability between Paris and Peoria involves the intrusion of human error and judgment, and McDonald's has worked hard to take even this out of the equation. Since early in the company's history, the legendary Potato Computer has taken the guesswork out of making the standard fry. These days the fry guy does little more than reload the fry machine and unload the fry dispenser. Even so, the McDonald's operations manual runs into the hundreds of pages.

Orgs that are mechanized have it easy, in a way. Less automated operations have the additional burden of promoting and enforcing conformity through training, rule books, and so on—much like the rule-and-demerit system at West Point. At the Cheesecake Factory, a chain with more than 150 restaurant locations across 35 states, each location has an identical menu of hundreds of items. Cooks are trained to follow exact instructions for every one of them, and the wait staff is given a script to ensure that you, the customer, encounter an eerily cheery and familiar server regardless of which Factory you visit.

Life at "casual dining" establishments such as the Cheesecake Factory—and Applebee's and T.G.I. Friday's—were singled out by the writers of the movie *Office Space* for particular mockery of standard practice. This took the form of a thinly fictionalized restaurant chain Chotchkie's, an establishment just slightly more regimented than its real-life inspirations. Part of Chotchkie's charm was the tchotchkes (Yiddish for "little knickknacks") worn by its employees. Company policy thus required that staff adorn themselves with "flair"—buttons that allowed them to "express themselves." This leads to an argument between Chotchkie waitress Joanna (played by Jennifer Aniston) and her manager, an exchange every low-level employee on earth has fantasized about having at some point in her standardized existence.

Joanna: You know what, Stan, if you want me to wear thirty-seven pieces of flair, like your pretty boy over there, Brian, why don't you just make the minimum thirty-seven pieces of flair? [Joanna wears the minimum pieces of flair, fifteen.]

Stan, Chotchkie's Manager: Well, I thought I remembered you saying that you wanted to express yourself.

Joanna: Yeah. You know what, yeah, I do. I do want to express myself, okay. And I don't need thirty-seven pieces of flair to do it. [Gives Stan the finger—her form of self-expression—and quits.]

The Cheesecake Factory's chief marketing officer, Mark Mears, calls its version of flair "Wow," as he told National Public Radio's Kelly Alexander. "It's all about getting to 'Wow,'" Mears explained. "That's a very important word to us. When I say we're over-the-top and multi-sensory, I mean 'Wow.' When the food comes out, it's a 'Wow,' when I taste it, it's a 'Wow.' The dessert presentation is a 'Wow.'"

What can you say except "Wow."

As much as it might grate on workers such as Joanna to hear it, Mark and Stan have a point. As *Time* magazine writer (and self-described food snob) John Cloud points out, we take a nostalgic view of local places offering "crunchy fried chicken and flaky blueberry pie" lovingly prepared by the fry cook who has manned his station for decades and by a lady whose baking wins big at the state fair. Yet in one outing to a recommended local establishment during a visit to Jamestown, North Dakota, Cloud found a reality that was much, much worse than what Applebee's or the Cheesecake Factory have on offer. A bison steak so tough and flavorless as to be inedible, accompanied by fries that tasted of old grease. It led Cloud to write "In Defense of Applebee's," which he also visited in Jamestown, and left satisfied, if not inspired. He plans to go back, knowing that "it will taste the same every time, and it will feel like it's supposed to, a neighborhood that's nowhere and everywhere." That is exactly the point.[11]

The upside of standardization is such that variability has come to be seen as the enemy of the good (and profits) in corporate America. This has spawned an array of operations gurus offering international quality standards certifications (ISO 9000 and 9001 being two prime examples) and Six Sigma solutions. This latter term, for those who have not been subjected to its practice, refers to manufacturing defect rates. A one sigma production line has a defect rate of 31 percent, while a six sigma process produces 3.4 defects for each 1,000,000 products produced. It has also given rise to legions of consultants offering help achieving ISO 9000 status, and "black belt" Six Sigma experts, the ninjas of standardization. Standardization boosts shareholder profits. Of course, Googling the phrase "six sigma sucks" returned 1.44 million hits.

Innovative Bureaucracies

McDonald's franchisees, who sit on the front lines of the fast-food wars, have immediate and pressing insights into what their customers need and want, insights that would never enter the minds of the execs back at Oak Brook headquarters. McDonald's management does take their suggestions seriously, and some of them have probably added billions to the McDonald's brand.[12] Franchise owners, in fact, supplied Kroc with some of his greatest hits. Menu mainstays such as the Egg McMuffin and Filet-O-Fish were local innovations that were invented in the 1960s and '70s and quickly spread to the rest of the company.

Yet head office approval was needed before a single fish filet or McMuffin could be served, and these local successes were only scaled up after careful screening, test marketing, and further tweaking. That is, there were many layers of approval and modification before a franchise idea became a McDonald's product, and as a result, there were surely some great ideas wallowing in obscurity along with the suggestion boxes full of terrible ones.

The Filet-O-Fish is a case in point. The fish sandwich was proposed in the early 1960s by Lou Groen, a franchisee in a heavily Catholic community who didn't do much burger business on meatless Fridays. He looked down the street at a nearby Bob's Big Boy that was doing a steady trade selling halibut sandwiches and proposed that McDonald's do the same. Groen was met with fish skeptics in Oak Brook, but after he flew to Illinois to make his case in person, he got his fish sandwich—halibut dipped in pancake batter and deep fried—approved. Friday sales increased as much as fivefold, and even on other days of the week, hamburger sales were higher, as burger lovers could now bring their meat-averse spouses and kids for a meal.

But Groen's fish sandwich proved no more scalable than Dondanville's hand-carved beef stunts. Groen similarly cut his halibut by hand, then set to work battering and blanching the fish to prepare it on-site for Friday sales. Halibut was in relatively short supply, and if the fish sandwich took off, McDonald's needs would test the limits of global fisheries. This is a real concern: as HBS professor Clayton Christensen has pointed out, if McDonald's were to move into shrimp, it could quickly deplete the world's supply.[13]

Eventually, product developers at McDonald's and its fish suppliers came up with a product that was cut, frozen, and breaded at a central plant, and shipped to franchises to be cooked in a specially developed fish fryer. It was made from cod, and topped with tartar sauce and a slice of cheese.[14] It was cheap to make, mass-producible, and transformed from a one-store niche product into a staple of McDonald's cuisine.

But as McDonald's grew, so, too, did the difficulties with innovation. Supply-chain concerns—figuring out what products wouldn't destroy entire species, and the types of food prep that could be done on an industrial scale—were much more complicated for a thirty-thousand-outlet operation than for the two hundred franchises that were in business when the Filet-O-Fish was introduced. The brand grew more valuable, and perhaps managers became more averse to risking product fiascos.

The *Wall Street Journal* reported in 2007 that it had been years since franchises had offered a marketable item. Suggestions still flow in from customers and franchisees, but product development has moved from franchise kitchens to the Culinary Innovation Center in Oak Brook, which, according to McDonald's, tests up to 1,800 new recipes a year. Out of this fast-food R&D lab have come products the company has used to enter the "snack" space for between-meal times, to produce higher-quality coffee to compete with newcomers such as Starbucks, and of course to design a better burger. McDonald's has bureaucratized, industrialized, and centralized the innovation process itself, and carefully feeds its findings back out to the larger organization.

The Skunkworks Model

McDonald's relies on market-research-driven R&D to come up with new products, and takes into account its need to balance resources, standardization, and distribution. What if a corporate bureaucracy wants to promote unfettered creativity in its purest form? That model of innovation—innovation as done by a small cadre outside the usual strictures of the org—dates back to 1943, the year when a team of elite, handpicked engineers at Lockheed came together through its Advanced Development Program to design and build an airframe around the Goblin jet engine supplied by the British. Under the direction of Clarence "Kelly" Johnson, the development team went to work in a rented circus tent separated from the rest of the company's employees with access strictly limited to those directly involved. The tent happened to be located next to a plastics factory, and the stench was such that this top-secret Lockheed program acquired the nickname Skunk Works—or, more commonly, skunkworks, a term now often used to describe any autonomous group within a larger org. (It's also trademarked by Lockheed Martin, which hawks everything from Skunk Works™ shot glasses to Skunk Works™ pen knives on its corporate website.)

At that point, the need to wall off the fighter development project from the rest of the company was surely driven primarily by secrecy. The air force couldn't count on thousands of Lockheed staff to keep the project under wraps. But it also insulated the group of independent-minded tinkerers from the checks and balances of Lockheed bureaucracy. (Although even innovators have bureaucracy, as embodied in "Kelly's 14 rules" posted on Lockheed's website. Rule Number 5: "There must be a minimum number of reports required, but important work must be recorded thoroughly." That is, a rule to minimize rules.)

Johnson's Skunk Works now sits in the pantheon of legendary innovation workshops. Lockheed Martin trumpets the fact that Skunk Works' first project, the XP-80, was undertaken with little more than a handshake and loose specifications for what air force generals were looking for, and was completed well ahead of schedule. That was merely Skunk Works' first success. It went on to develop a number of famous aircraft designs, including the U-2 spy plane, and kept up its reputation as an autonomous org-within-an-org where great scientists could do brilliant things, unhampered by bureaucracy.

Organizations every bit the equal of McDonald's in scale and complexity continue to embrace the skunkworks model. But the idea of skunkworks fell into disrepute when it came to be seen as just another cost center, albeit one full of inventive scientists thinking lofty thoughts. The problem was that these deep thoughts often were disconnected from the real world. In its more contemporary incarnation, the skunkworks model meets the McDonald's R&D lab at least halfway. Managers make sure that scientists and engineers maintain regular contact with marketing and sales to ensure that lofty scientific thinking ultimately finds application in a product that consumers want to pay for. The results have often been blockbuster commercial innovations, if not great scientific advances: The Apple Mac and IBM PC were the result of modern skunkworks-like projects. Motorola's wildly successful Razr cell phone was, too, produced in an independent lab fifty miles from Motorola's main R&D facility.[15]

Within the army, the elite Special Forces serves as an incubator for innovative military technologies and tactics. Special Forces personnel are deeply involved in army tactical operations, and have used their on-the-ground knowledge to pioneer such innovations as the use of night-vision goggles for piloting low-level nighttime flights and "fast-roping" to deploy quickly out of a helicopter.

But why not just have an army of Special Forces? It's elitist by design. Only the best and brightest even choose to apply, and only the best and brightest of those applicants make it through Special Forces Assessment and Selection. Put an infantryman into a Special Forces unit and you'll need your thicker rule book again. That's the give-and-take of it.

To bring these and other innovations "to market," the army has developed a team of outreach soldiers called the Asymmetric Warfare Group (AWG), so named because its mission is to aid the army in the "asymmetric" wars it now fights against Al Qaeda and other small but deadly enemies. The idea is to take battle-tested innovations developed on the front lines (by Special Forces and also regular infantry) and help them spread throughout the army. Yet, in doing so, the AWG faces many of the same challenges as McDonald's menu planners—sorting the wheat from the infinite chaff of tactics being practiced in platoons spread across the world (sorting the McMuffins from the McAfricas of military innovations); selling the product to change-averse local management (the seventy thousand carefully chosen conformists who make up the U.S. Army officer corps); and developing scalable products from local innovations (whether McMuffins or fast-roping techniques).

Both fast food and military life demand standardization, yet both McDonald's and the army recognize their limits. As Kroc's successors have expanded the McDonald's empire to 119 countries worldwide—it was 125, but the Arab Spring took its toll—they've had to accept that, globally, one size doesn't fit all. Food is a culturally sensitive product, American cultural imperialism notwithstanding.

Even McDonald's has had to bow to local preferences. The company opened its first restaurant in India in 1996, and now has a couple hundred locations. Just about the only menu item common to both Indian and American menus is the Filet-O-Fish. Most Indians don't eat beef or pork, so hamburgers are out. That's not to say there isn't a close facsimile of a McDonald's burger available. The R&D team has come up with a spicy burger made from potatoes and peas (McAloo Tikka), a lighter all-vegetable version (McVeggie), and a chicken Big Mac (Chicken Maharaja Mac). McDonald's India still focuses on scaling their successes, albeit on a more local level. There are almost as many McDonald's in India today as there were in the United States when the Filet-O-Fish was born—plenty of scale to work with but not too much to risk emptying the sea of shrimp. Even if every location in the world can't be the same, McDonald's can at least standardize its operations within each country, and aim to standardize the experience: all McDonald's global offerings look uncannily similar, regardless of the ingredients.

The U.S. Army also has to accommodate some local customization. While America's enemies all seem to share a fondness for improvised explosive devices (IEDs), recent wars have been fought in sparsely populated valleys in Afghanistan and crowded warrens of Baghdad's slums. AWG members are embedded with units in combat zones for two or three months at a time, to observe what they're doing well, and also to make suggestions for implementing tactics they've seen work effectively before in comparable circumstances. (In fact, odds are that the same AWG team was embedded with the force that the current unit came in to relieve, so they're able to compare the efficacy of tactics deployed against the same enemy in exactly the same locale.) Through the AWG, the army hopes to come up with general counterinsurgency policies but apply them with careful consideration to local circumstances. It is trying to avoid the counterinsurgency equivalent of offering a 100 percent all-beef patty to customers in Mumbai.

Experimenting with Innovation

In the end, most orgs find a middle ground. They cordon off some part of the organization, call it skunkworks, and put some checks and balances into unbridled innovation, stifling some creativity and initiative but ensuring that things don't get out of hand. If choosing between freedom and bureaucracy is a matter of degrees rather than extremes, then how much innovation is enough? Sure, Scott Urban and his one-man spectacle workshop will have less bureaucracy and oversight than McDonald's, but that doesn't give much direction to McDonald's bosses who have to figure out if their checks and balances have gone overboard.

There are some guidelines. Orgs that have a lot to lose from mistakes anywhere in the production line should have triple checks and stern oversight even at the expense of building a more inspired space craft—the failure of a single O-ring was enough to doom the *Challenger* space shuttle. Orgs that need coordination—to keep costs down in a global supply chain or to storm the beaches at Normandy—will naturally have more central planners and bureaucrats.

But the "right" level of control remains ambiguous. Coupled with the fact that there are obvious downsides to any choice— you can always point to the blunders of out-of-control employees or the stultifying effects of bureaucracy to make the case in either direction—it's perhaps not surprising that conventional wisdom on how to design the perfectly innovative yet fully accountable org lurches back and forth between the two.

As companies grow, they do find that the little inefficiencies they've elided in the name of creativity pile up. All of a sudden, they realize that they've ceded too much control to the front lines, or that they've centralized too much in the name of efficiency, and ended up stifling creativity. Naturally they want to fix the problem, aided and abetted by change consultants and management gurus peddling the latest panacea for corporate ills. In response to what he saw as crushing bureaucracy endangering America's innovative edge, Tom Peters sang the praises of free-thinking innovation in *Thriving on Chaos*. As orgs simplified and shortened their manuals and protocols, the inevitable response arrived. Management scholar Chris Bart argued that orgs were *gagging on chaos*—the idea that oversimplified orgs lacked the bureaucracy to steer the innovation process or otherwise set their directions.

Of course, they were both right—but more in a sense of tinkering and fine-tuning to find the right balance, responding to changed circumstance, and reacting to growth and change in the org itself.

The apparent yo-yoing can be senseless, for sure, but it can also reflect the earnest search for the steadily moving target of the optimal org.

A 2010 *Wall Street Journal* article described this process at work in the pharmaceutical industry, where already gigantic drug companies went through a wave of mega-mergers at the turn of the twentieth century. Sanofi and Synthélabo became Sanofi-Synthélabo, then merged with Aventis (itself the product of an earlier union of Hoechst and Rhône-Poulenc) to produce Sanofi-Aventis, the fourth-largest pharmaceutical company by prescription drug sales (they dropped the "Aventis," and 25 percent of their U.S. workforce, in 2011). Glaxo partnered with Wellcome in 1995, and combined with SmithKline Beecham (which itself was the result of a 1988 merger between SmithKline Beckman and Beecham) five years later, resulting in GlaxoSmithKline, the fourth-largest pharmaceutical company in the world, period.

These corporate agglomerations produced—in addition to a profusion of compounded, hyphenated names—immensely powerful sales and marketing teams. It was hoped that they would also produce even more powerful R&D departments, sprouting new drugs for marketers to sell. Drug companies need innovation to survive. Their inventions are protected from competition for twenty years by patents. And when those patents expire, the companies face challenges from cheap, generic competitors, who drive down prices and profits.

The assumption that bigger R&D departments would lead to bigger profits had seemed reasonable. Before the mid-1970s, in fact, drug development took place almost exclusively inside large pharmaceutical companies, the only ones with the financial resources to take billion-dollar bets on new product development.

Drug development, the reasoning went, was an industrial process like any other. Armies of chemists developed massive "libraries" of chemical compounds that served as the basic input into research. These molecules were then handed off for "high throughput screening," and the most promising compounds were passed on for the scale-intensive activities of testing and production. Somewhere in a distant office several layers of bureaucracy removed from bench scientists, R&D chiefs passed judgment on what future research directions might be, seeing the big picture of what held greatest promise. Scale, it was thought, could be as effective in mass-producing new drugs as it was at churning out burgers.[16]

But when he was asked to reflect on the mergers, the CEO of Sanofi-Aventis described the post-merger era as the "lost decade." The newly merged research staffs failed to produce the next wave of billion-dollar inventions. Why? The combined R&D labs were saddled with innovation-stifling bureaucracy.

That "lost decade" saw the center of gravity of R&D innovation continue its shift away from Big Pharma to biotech start-ups, where basic knowledge developed in university labs was nurtured and cultivated into promising drugs by small teams of highly motivated scientists. It turned out that much of the drug development process involved art as well as science; holistic thinking, not the rational division of labor; individual motivation at the expense of checks and balances; creativity, not the straitjacketing oversight of profit-minded executives.

This realization led to a subsequent explosion in alliances between pharmaceutical giants and biotech companies—partnerships that more than tripled during the 1990s. And it's the reason that drug companies are doing an about-face on the industrial model of R&D. Glaxo first deconstructed its thousands of R&D employees into semiautonomous groups of four hundred, each with its own budget and greater discretion to manage its own fortunes. They've subsequently broken these up into even smaller groups of twenty to sixty "discovery performance units," or DPUs. (Not even Glaxo's freethinkers are spared bureaucratic-ese.) Biotech companies acquired by Glaxo can maintain some distance from corporate bureaucracies, as they are given independent DPU status rather than fully digested by the company.

Unless you completely take the start-up out of the corporation, though, you can't take corporate influence out of the start-up. DPU managers know they're on a three-year clock. Unless they have something to show for their independent efforts at the end of that time, their funding will disappear. In the meantime, DPUs still need to get sign-off on some funding requests from the larger Glaxo bureaucracy, and also must contend with meddling visitors from non-research company execs. Skunkworks it is not.

But it may be the best that an enormous bureaucracy can do in its effort to achieve a new way of innovating amid the ever-present need for oversight.

The Army's Workaround

West Point claims to be the oldest continually occupied military post in America, dating back to the Revolutionary War. Formally commissioned as the U.S. Military Academy in 1802, the school initially focused on practical sciences, a reflection of the Founders' disdain for their reliance on foreign-born artillerists and engineers during the revolution. Military discipline and a focus on civil engineering came in the early nineteenth century, and West Point sent professionally trained engineers to help build the young nation's infrastructure. A West Point graduate was the chief engineer for the Panama Canal. Graduates fought on both sides during the Civil War, after which the curriculum took a turn toward leadership and continuing military education. After World War I, West Point began to focus on physical fitness as part of military preparedness. After World War II, the curriculum shifted again, taking account of "dramatic developments in science and technology, the increasing need to understand other cultures and the rising level of general education in the Army."[17]

That short history is a long way of saying that it's not as if the U.S. Army were unaware of the challenge of centralization versus innovation, or the need for innovators. The officers who rotate through the West Point teaching staff and the recruits they train are part of USMA's recognition of this need, and a workaround that's worth exploring. Today, the academy includes not just engineers but all the departments you'd find at top-ranked U.S. colleges, aimed toward producing the army's future leaders.

West Point's Department of Social Sciences is known on campus as SOSH. The faculty is part civilian (staffed with PhDs in economics and political science like any other social science department in the U.S.), and part mid-career officers (many with PhDs). The military members of the SOSH faculty wear the same officer's uniform, attend the same Army-Navy games, and follow many of the same rules of others in the academy. They're mostly West Point products themselves. Many are on the fast track to top posts, and use their time at SOSH to develop unconventional ideas on the direction in which the army should be led.[18]

Others are longhaired (by army standards) "dissidents" who chafe at the army's culture of conformity and are likely to serve out their careers as academically focused scholars. Regardless, the department provides some of these soldier-scholars with a safe space to think differently, share new ideas with other entrepreneurially minded officers, and test out their thinking on solving the problems that beset the army.

Lieutenant Colonel Reid Sawyer had at least one foot in the egghead dissident camp.[19] He's a West Point grad and a member of the army's elite Special Forces. Although he entered the Special Forces as a logistics expert—he lists debating as his main extracurricular activity at West Point—he can nonetheless rappel out of a helicopter and snipe a target from a thousand yards. From 2008 to 2011 he ran the Combating Terrorism Center at West Point, an antiterrorism think tank and training center within the army.

So far, twenty-first-century warfare has been waged against

loose global networks of terrorist cells rather than fought against standing armies. Colonel Sawyer's work centered on this future of U.S. military challenges: how to protect U.S. cities from attack, and develop capabilities for tracking down insurgents amid hostile populations in places such as Somalia and Afghanistan. He believes, like many others, that these conflicts will require a very different military org from the one that stormed the Normandy beaches in 1944 (and the oil fields of Kuwait in 1991), one that recognizes that "one valley is different from the next" and that the army is "fighting different enemies in different places." Sawyer is in his mid-forties, exactly the age for him to have seen a generation of officers, both his peers and those much younger, complete tours in Iraq and Afghanistan, where they were required to keep the peace in the valley under their command or track down urban insurgencies. They may have been told to "take the hill" by central command but never handed a rule book explaining how. On returning to the United States, they were confronted with the absurdities of spit-shining boots and marching to nowhere.

The Combating Terrorism Center serves as an internal consulting firm to the armed forces and other orgs such as the FBI and local police departments involved in the fight against terrorism. Sawyer can reel off the many roadblocks and frustrations he experienced trying to help the army and others actually do their jobs in combating terrorism: one agency's refusal to share its "terrorism primer" with others, not for reasons of national security, but because they didn't want to share something they'd paid Sawyer to produce; the slow proliferation of innovations across the military; and the oversight and scrutiny that the Center faces. Sawyer was, in his own words, "fighting an insurgency against army bureaucracy."

Lieutenant Colonel David Lyle may not be an insurgent, but he views the way the army is organized with at least a bit of respectful questioning. His goal isn't to dismantle the bureaucracy, but to make it function based on logical analysis rather than doing things the way they've always been done. He is straightforward, literal, and earnest. Lyle, too, is a West Point grad, an engineer by training—near the top of his class. After his initial stint as an officer, he went on to earn a PhD in economics at MIT, a department considered by many to be the best in the world. One of Lyle's thesis advisers describes him as "precocious," and there's good evidence to back up that view. While most of MIT's econ students take five years to complete their coursework and write a dissertation, Lyle finished in three.

Broadly, Lyle's graduate work focused on the impact of different ways of organizing soldiers at West Point: Do cadets get higher grades if exposed to West Point superstars in classes? (They do.) Should cadets with different skill sets be thrown together to form classes with a varied mix, or should cadets be tracked by ability? (A mix is better.) Now back at the army, Lyle would like to apply his theories of human resource allocation to make the army bureaucracy work more efficiently. True to his engineering roots, he views the army as essentially a problem in resource optimization, one that's currently operating well below its potential.

Currently, junior officers are assigned to tasks in much the same way loaves of bread and pairs of shoes were allocated in the Soviet Union—by administrative fiat. In the army's case, assignments are essentially random, going to whichever engineer is at the top of the queue when a job comes up. The luck of the draw determines who will manage a bridge project in Alaska, regardless of whether the chosen soldier wants to live in Alaska, or whether he or she knows all that much about bridges. The machine needs a cog, and as far as the machine is concerned, any generically qualified soldier will do. That's what the army's training aims to do: produce reasonably well-prepared generalists for an array of well-defined tasks.

Lyle's solution is to bring the market inside the org, developing systems to collect and distribute the kind of granular information that will allow senior officers looking for bridge engineers to compete for the best candidates, and giving junior officers the chance to express preferences for where they're stationed and what they're told to do—a market for engineers within the org, regulated by army bureaucracy.

The job of managing this market-within-a-bureaucracy will fall to the military's top generals, who already oversee the army's budget, manage its relations with Congress, strategize on marketing to potential recruits, and sell new initiatives to current soldiers. This makes the job description of four-star general sound more like that of a corporate executive than a soldier, which Lyle believes is an accurate reflection of the army's needs. He points out that Eisenhower was promoted to lead the D-Day invasion because he was a better planner than General George Patton, not necessarily a better warrior.

Lyle works alongside Colonel Jeff Peterson, head of SOSH's economics department. Whereas Lyle is a tinkerer and social engineer, Colonel Peterson sees the human side of army economics. Peterson is soft-spoken in conversation, yet a commanding physical presence. He came to run the economics group after leading the Stryker Cavalry Task Force in policing what had been one of the most violent corridors in post-conflict Baghdad. Peterson's job was to keep the peace in Haifa Street, which had been one of the bloodiest battlegrounds in the city. The street is lined with densely packed apartment high-rises, which made house-by-house clearing of the area an impossible task.

Peterson attributes a large part of his success in curtailing insurgent attacks to luck,[20] and is quick to point out that the battle that broke the back of insurgent elements on Haifa Street was fought before he arrived, by the 1-23 Infantry unit under the command of Lieutenant Colonel Van Smiley. But maintaining control of the area surely owed something to the other pillars of counterinsurgency—a recent army innovation—as practiced by Peterson and his men: control, partnership, civil works, and governance. While securing and controlling Haifa Street was a crucial precondition to ending attacks, it was just as important to maintain relative calm through improved economic development, coming through small-scale development projects structured to ensure that funds weren't lost or stolen.

Not all the soldiers in Peterson's unit were happy with his approach. According to Peterson, after weeks of experimentation, discussion, and taking stock of their situation, some soldiers still believed they should be fighting a traditional war. One journalist who spent time with the unit summed up these sentiments with the following quote from an infantryman: "We joined up to fight the bad guys and kill the bad guys, and we trained for that, and that's what we should be doing." Peterson's response? "They can think whatever they think, but they have to be soldiers and do their job—and no matter what they think, that's exactly what they do."

When Colonel Peterson left Iraq in 2007, many pointed to Haifa Street as a model for how the military could "win" in Iraq. From among the posts offered to him on his return home, Peterson chose SOSH, seeing it as a place where he could turn his experiences in Iraq into some guiding principles for how the army could manage its combat operations. He has come to believe that army bureaucracy isn't going to find a way of coming up with better orders, so everyone, from the top of the chain of command to the lowliest infantryman, will need to learn to think for himself. He would like to train cadets, the officer corps of the future, to experiment and approach the army way with Lieutenant Colonel Lyle's respectful questioning. He'd like to create an army of innovators.

These men of West Point bring three very different perspectives and approaches to reforming the military. For the most part, they're not trying to change the military model in which commands (and everything else) flow downhill. But they want to change a system that's very, and appropriately, resistant to change. If the past is any indication, there's a reasonable chance that the well-meaning and well-conceived innovations of Sawyer, Lyle, and Peterson will be squashed by the same army culture of blind adherence to rules. And there's an even better chance that any change will come at a glacial pace. And yet the army allows West Point and SOSH to foster such relatively radical innovation in recognition that it can't afford to lose all such thinkers. The army knows it has to have some innovation in its back pocket.

CHAPTER 5

What Management Is Good For

T HE BRITISH EMPIRE WAS BUILT, at least in part, on finding ways to extract value from its territories. And one of the best ways to wring value out of Mumbai (known as Bombay until 1995) was through cheap cloth production. The first textile mill opened in the mid-nineteenth century in what came to be known as the neighborhood of Girangaon, which translates from the Marathi as "mill village." The industry as a whole took off with Mumbai's increasing importance as a deepwater port after the Suez Canal opened in 1869.

These days, Girangaon no longer houses Mumbai's mills, most of which shut down after the eighteen-month-long Great Bombay Textile Strike of 1982–83. Thousands upon thousands of square feet of factory space are becoming outposts at the other end of the consumer economy (malls and luxury apartments) and the remaining textile industry has migrated north.

If we head out on the NH 8 (that's the national highway between Mumbai and New Delhi), we'll arrive in Tarapur and Umbergaon, the two largest remaining textile towns in the state of

Maharashtra, in an hour and two, respectively, north of the city by car. For the most part, the textile communities of Tarapur and Umbergaon operate in a state of stunning inefficiency and outright peril, with inventory rotting in storerooms and heavy machinery blocking passageways. Some of these same factories were also the site of an experiment aimed at answering the timeless question that dogs the modern org: Are managers good for anything? And if so, what? And if they are good for something: really?

The answer will surprise and maybe upset those who routinely seethe with rage over the latest boneheaded move from their own manager or who can recall with barely checked anger some managerial transgression from the past. Because what our Indian textile manufacturers really needed, the ultimate solution to their problems, was a bunch of MBAs: men and women trained to create systems to keep tabs on and direct workers and processes, to make sure shipments ran on time and supplies didn't walk off the storeroom shelves, to let the owner know that everything was moving along properly and efficiently.

Most people who have done time in a cubicle imagine a world without managers as a kind of paradise where workers are unshackled by pointless bureaucracy, meaningless paperwork, and incompetent bosses. A place where stuff actually gets done. The textile factories of Tarapur and Umbergaon provide a very different view, and the management experiment offers a stark demonstration of what managers are good for. Really.

An Experiment in Good Management

The experiment in the Indian textile factories, a joint venture of economists at the World Bank and Stanford University, aimed to assess whether good management practices were in fact good for business. You might think this is an easy question to answer, one way or the other. But most people can't even agree on what management is, exactly.

The researchers leading the textile management study didn't aspire to define management, merely to find a workable description that they could put into practice in Indian factories. They built off the previous efforts of one member of the team, Nick Bloom, a Stanford economics professor, who had already developed a definition of good management as part of a long-running effort to measure and compare management practices around the world.

The World Management Survey (WMS) is as close to science as you can get in the fuzzy field of management. It's a set of questions designed to evaluate managerial practices in three areas: monitoring, setting and meeting targets, and establishing incentives. The survey was developed in collaboration with McKinsey, a top-tier consulting firm, and administered by teams of MBA students—Bloom describes them as a "loud, brash and self-confident bunch"—who had the requisite skills to interview managers in manufacturing firms around the world about how they spent their days. It was a massive operation involving extended interviews with thousands of managers in ten thousand companies spread across more than twenty countries. The end product was a standardized measure that the WMS used to compare management quality around the world.

The results, which can be found at worldmanagementsurvey .org, wouldn't surprise the laborers of Tarapur. India ranked third from the bottom, just ahead of China and Brazil. Companies from the United States, Japan, and Germany—three of the world's richest countries—took the top three spots.

You might see a problem here. The survey naturally reflects the gospel of good management according to McKinsey, which many perceive to be a Western-centric view of what constitutes effective management. If we define good management as the way organizations are run in America, of course American companies will come out looking good, and the less "Western" a country, the farther it'll be from "good" American practices.

Bloom was also troubled by the lack of any clear sense of cause and effect. Is American management what made U.S. companies profitable and efficient? American companies differ from Indian ones in lots of ways apart from management practices. Making this sort of cross-country productivity comparison is like comparing Harvard MBAs to high school dropouts. And even if McKinsey-style systems worked for American companies, who knows if they would be effective in streamlining textile production in Indian factories? Which is why Bloom started looking for ways to determine if Western-style good management would benefit non-Western organizations. The cotton weavers of Tarapur and Umbergaon were to serve as his testing ground for introducing a set of management best practices into a set of organizations that previously had none.

Bloom and Co. titled the product of their efforts "Does Management Matter?" The original academic paper enumerated thirty-eight practices similar to those in the WMS, including routines to record and analyze quality defects, production and inventory tracking systems, and clear assignment of job roles and responsibilities.

The World Bank covered the cost of bringing in experts from the consulting firm Accenture to provide their usual advice— essentially implementing the thirty-eight elements of management for a group of midsize textile companies that spin cotton

yarn into cloth that's then sent on to dyers for sale on the whole-
sale market.[1] The cotton weavers would get Accenture's services
free.

The researchers initially approached sixty-six Indian firms.
Only seventeen (with twenty factories among them) agreed to
participate; the other forty-nine weren't interested in $250,000
worth of free consulting services—a resounding statement on the
perceived value of management practice. Fourteen factories were
ultimately provided with the full consulting experience, while six
others served as a control group, much as a medical study has a
group of patients who are left alone to benchmark the effect of a
new treatment.[2]

Before/After

Before the consultants arrived, chaos reigned in the factories.
Bloom recounts seeing storerooms strewn with rotting yarn, un-
sorted by color, quality, or any other attribute—employees had
to rummage about to find the requisite product, if it was there to
be found at all. Many spindles were crushed, so yarn had to be
rewound each time a worker needed a new spindle. Factory floors
were a mess, and hallways were blocked by heavy machinery and
littered with broken machine parts and discarded tools. Equipment was in a state of disrepair, dirty, and often well past expiry
dates. One owner wore the key to the stockroom on a piece of
string around his neck, so he had to be called every time someone
wanted more material. At one factory, the workers had to move a
heavy piece of equipment whenever they needed to open a loading bay. The org wasn't in much better shape than the physical
plant. On average, the factories were using only about ten of the

thirty-eight management best practices that Accenture and the investigators were planning to promote.

Before the consultants began dispensing their advice, each of the twenty factories received a one-month diagnosis of its management and performance—a kind of management health check. The fourteen factories selected to work with Accenture then received four months of management practice upgrades. The other six, the control group, were left to their own devices after the diagnostic phase. For the most part, the same managers were kept in place, but the ad hoc ways of getting things done were replaced by the standard protocols of modern management, the kinds of things the Accenture consultants had gone to business school to learn. Finally, Accenture did a follow-up evaluation in all twenty factories to assess whether performance had improved after the consultants' intervention.

The before/after photographs of stockrooms and production lines tell pretty much the whole story.[3] Out of disarray and confusion arose order: In storerooms, bags of yarn were now carefully stacked and arranged, and elevated to protect against dampness. Offices previously cluttered with random stacks of paper were now equipped with charts to prioritize and track the flow of inputs and outputs working their way through newly organized assembly lines. Defects were cut in half, and inventories fell by nearly 20 percent, even as output increased by 5 percent. Overall, the authors calculate that profits at each factory—assuming the new practices remained in effect—would improve by over $200,000 per year. Even if the firms had paid full cost for Accenture's services, extra profits in the first year alone would have covered the expense, with higher earnings in future years being all gravy.[4]

Better management also led to a further round of changes in

the factories, separate from those instituted by Accenture's consultants. All the new monitoring and control mechanisms created a flood of information that had the potential to overwhelm the factory boss. To cope with the deluge of data, the Accenture factories began using computers more intensively, a change that was probably good for the job prospects of computer-literate workers, less so for unskilled laborers now at risk of being "made redundant" by the factories' improved efficiency.

Equipped with new details on the operations of each individual factory, the company boss might feel more comfortable yielding greater discretion to each factory manager. Any drop in production—or mysterious disappearance of yarn from the supply room—would raise computerized red flags. Indeed, the researchers found that there was more delegation of responsibility to factory managers after the new management practices were put in place.

Managing in a World without Managers

Let's be clear: the Indian factories didn't *not* have management. Quite the contrary, they were probably doing the best they could with what they had, which had enabled each company to grow into a relatively large and complex operation. The firms had been around for an average of twenty years, and some were diversified into other activities besides textile manufacturing, such as real estate and retail operations. On average, they had 270 employees, assets of $13 million, and yearly sales of $7.5 million. One appeared on the Mumbai Stock Exchange. If these plants had been located in the United States, they'd have been in the top 2 percent of American firms by employment and the top 5 percent by sales.

To understand how they got by—and why they performed better after Accenture's makeover—it's instructive to look at what was going on inside the most efficient firm the researchers encountered in Tarapur before the intervention took place.

Basic economic theory, not to mention common sense, would predict that the most efficient producer would grow to be the largest. The factory that produces at lowest cost can afford to undercut its competitors, grabbing a larger share of the market. This feeds a virtuous circle of efficiency: the more you do something, the better you do it (the so-called "experience curve"), further enabling the cheapest producer to undercut his competitors even more.[5] At some point these efficiencies are overwhelmed by the challenges of coordinating an ever-larger cotton weaving empire (that was Ronald Coase's insight on the limits to a firm's expansion), providing an opening for competitors to survive. But when the dust has settled on the market for woven cotton or anything else, the most efficiently run firm will be the biggest.

Yet the best-run cotton weaver in Tarapur had only a single factory. Many of his competitors had expanded to multiple sites, employing more laborers and selling more cloth than the man who should have been the Cotton King of Tarapur. Bloom met with this would-be cotton king—Mr. Samata, we'll call him (translated from the Hindi as "Mr. Efficiency," more or less)— as part of his fieldwork leading up to the management experiment, and asked why his operation had remained so modest. Mr. Samata explained, sadly but matter-of-factly, with a shake of his head, "No sons, no brothers."

Mr. Samata wasn't alone. As Bloom and his coauthors put it in one of their reports, "In every firm in our sample all senior managerial positions are held by members of the owning family. The number of adult males available to fill senior positions thus becomes a binding constraint on growth." Why are sons and brothers critical for expansion, swappable for well-trained MBA grads in managing the firm?

Mr. Samata can personally keep tabs on the goings-on in a single plant. He was by necessity a practitioner of "management by walking around," just as Bill Hewlett and Dave Packard were during the early history of HP. While Bill and Dave wanted everyone to feel part of the HP family, Mr. Samata maintained his foot patrol to ensure that yarn and other supplies weren't disappearing into employees' pockets. He wore the key to the supply closet on a string around his neck because he couldn't trust that one of his employees, given an unlocked door, wouldn't walk away with a bunch of yarn.

If he opened another factory, he'd need to find someone to manage that site by walking around as well, and that would mean trusting someone else with a key of his own, on a string around his neck. That involved a leap of faith that Mr. Samata apparently wasn't willing to make. How could he ensure that his proxy wasn't pilfering inventory of yarn or finished cloth, or actual funds, taking extra-long breaks, or allowing employees to do all the above? If profits were lower or costs higher at the new factory than at the one supervised by Mr. Samata himself, who's to know whether it was because the factory manager had his hand in the till, or simply because he wasn't as efficient as Mr. Samata?[6]

This is where brothers and sons come in. While not incapable of treachery or deceit, they're the only ones whom Mr. Samata felt he could have relied on to act as his surrogate in a growing textile empire. Sons know they'll inherit at least part of the family fortune, so they'll want to grow it to serve their own selfish ends. Brothers sometimes share ownership of a company—if it's a family business, it was likely passed down from their father before them—so their interests are also well aligned. And if brothers start squabbling over who is stealing from whom, there's always a higher authority to appeal to: Mom. Bloom asked about brothers- and sons-in-law, but apparently they're not to be trusted. Whom are you going to appeal to, your mother-in-law? Not likely. And sisters and daughters were simply not part of the equation. (In the event of a family wedding, one of the brothers or sons has to stay behind to keep watch over the factory, lest it be stripped bare during the weekend's festivities.)

The alternative to dependable relatives would be to put in place systems for tracking inventory, monitoring performance, and generally keeping tabs on the goings-on in each factory: management. It's what empowered business to move beyond the "no brothers, no sons" world of Mr. Samata in the first place.

The Origins of Management

The condition of these Indian factories isn't so far removed from the general state of the org before the twentieth century. This history of how we got from that pre-corporation past to our cubicle-filled bonanza was first tackled by business historian Alfred D. Chandler Jr.

By the time Chandler published his masterwork, *The Visible Hand*, in 1977, professional managers dominated the workings of industrial capitalism and the work life of white-collar employees everywhere. In six hundred–plus pages, Chandler was able to tell them why. His title was a play on Adam Smith's idea of the invisible hand, that powerful and ubiquitous metaphor for the intricacies of market capitalism. Chandler's visible hand was the very tangible force that directed resources inside individual businesses—the decisions of the professional manager.

Chandler divided the history of business into two periods, with the great separation coming around 1850 just as the Industrial Revolution was picking up steam. Economic activity in the earlier era was dominated by family-owned businesses— businesses run by the Mr. Samatas of the preindustrial world. These family firms, which had existed in much the same form for centuries, were run by a single person, in one location, and focused on a particular type of product.

In a stripped-down description of an eighteenth-century economy, plantations farmed the land, and miners extracted ore and refined it into a usable product. Both sold their output to resident merchants—the middlemen who enabled Smith's invisible hand to work its magic. These traders in turn passed on the wheat, iron, and other inputs to artisans and craftsmen to make final goods (bread and tools and clothing), which were then sold back to the farmers and miners through the very same merchants who'd purchased their output.

The plantations, artisans, and resident merchants alike were comprised of partnerships that employed business practices that were pretty similar to what the merchants of Venice used during the Renaissance, such as double-entry accounting and trade credit relationships.

Then, in the mid-nineteenth century, came the transcontinental railroads, the first enterprise, in Chandler's view, run on modern management principles. It was a case of necessity's being the mother of invention. With the arrival of the steam locomotive, railroads could move both people and freight much faster than the horse-drawn trains that preceded them. There was only a single line of track in those days, so if a train was running south, there had better not be one headed north. It was thus a business that required careful control and coordination if there weren't to be head-on collisions, but also to ensure that enough trains were running to turn a profit. At the same time, the cost of building and maintaining a railroad network swamped that of earlier enterprises such as cotton plantations and textile mills, so such networks couldn't be managed as family businesses. It was far too expensive an undertaking even for the country's wealthiest dynasties. Those wishing to build railroads raised capital in New York, spurring the development of the city's investment industry, and the railroads were directed by professional managers who could keep the trains running on time.

These imperatives forced the railroad into the age of modern management. Job functions were well defined. Each existed within geographically dispersed units with coordinated operations. Org charts were created showing lines of authority and communication. Multiple layers of management were introduced to organize individual business units and subunits. Cost accounting was developed to monitor performance across operations. With data only hours old, managers could accurately track trains, estimate the cost of moving one ton of freight one mile, and determine whether they should adjust the rates. These managers coordinated activity, applying the same techniques (accounting, finance, statistics) to the same data (costs, timing, routes) to produce optimal results. Good, better, best—this was the drumbeat of efficiency.[7]

Mass production and mass retail, both of which were enabled by the fast, reliable transportation of the railroads, adopted these techniques themselves to great effect. Chandler found that these modern large-scale firms prospered because they had higher productivity, lower costs, and higher profits. The managerial class became a necessity to coordinate the increasingly complex and interdependent system of commerce. The managerial revolution had come to America.

Although Chandler's book saw the light of day only in the late 1970s, he had started writing it in the 1950s, when he was also helping Alfred P. Sloan, the longtime president and CEO of GM, with his memoir, *My Years with General Motors*. Sloan himself was a leading practitioner of the new science of management, showing up in *The Visible Hand* in the capstone chapter on the "Maturing of Modern Business Enterprise," and their discussions started Chandler thinking about the origins of managerial capitalism. *The Visible Hand* is very much a reflection of the time in which it was conceived and written—smack in the middle of the period that gave rise to the idea of the American Century. The first *Fortune* 500 list, published in 1955, included such corporate behemoths as General Motors, Exxon, U.S. Steel, General Electric, Chrysler, Armour, and DuPont.[8] What drove this American Century, in Chandler's view, was an army of professional managers.

While Chandler's subtitle, *The Managerial Revolution in American Business*, evokes the majesty of twentieth-century enterprise, this was, after all, the period of *The Man in the Gray Flannel Suit*, *The Organization Man*, and *The Lonely Crowd*—where men had given up the rugged individualistic spirit of the Protestant work ethic to conform and fit in. Financial journalist Michael Lewis called it "the deplorable, metronomic life of the American businessman," who dressed in the aforementioned gray flannel suit, kissed the wife, patted Junior on the head, commuted to work ("packed like lemmings into shiny metal boxes," in Gordon Sumner's memorable phrase), and droned on with his peers, who behaved exactly as he did, down to the length of their hair and grass and their choice of television shows and scotch and gin.[9]

By the time *The Visible Hand* hit the shelves in 1977, the country had lived through the countercultural revolution of the prior decade, and moved on from the mid-century fashion of conformity. The industrial giants that gave birth to the managerial revolution no longer seemed quite so invincible. The United States was facing the deepest recession since the Great Depression, and, perhaps most tellingly, the railroads had largely collapsed economically. (Amtrak, which is government owned, took over intercity rail service in 1971.)

Still, the need remained for managers and management to run the next generation of *Fortune* 500 corporations, and smaller orgs, too. Chandler's point—that middle management as a technology enabled the org as we know it—was undeniable, even as the fashions of the day had changed from gray flannel to three-piece suits with wide lapels to Steve Jobs's jeans and black turtleneck and Mark Zuckerberg's signature hoodie. The IT revolution may have flattened hierarchies and replaced typing pools with laptops, but management and managers persist. Management reduced costs and made the org, of many shapes and sizes, more efficient.

In fact, we now have a whole infrastructure around training the "general manager," the master of business administration, or MBA, which emerged along with Chandler's managerial revolution over a century ago. Before the MBA, America's new modern enterprises had a notable lack of middle managers to organize and run America's rapidly growing businesses. As Edmund James, an early proponent of management education, noted in 1903, American banks "existed in a chronic state of fear bordering on panic," while the railways that Chandler pointed to as a sign of modern management's successes had "grown clear beyond [managers'] ability to control," with the companies that oversaw over three quarters of the country's railway miles passing into bankruptcy.

No wonder. The curricula of business schools at the time provided woefully inadequate preparation for the new class of professional manager, dominated as they were by the subjects of bookkeeping, arithmetic, and penmanship (one school even had a department of Normal Penmanship and a separate department for Plain Penmanship). This demand for better-trained managers spurred universities, often reluctantly, to take on the mission of educating businessmen. And so the MBA was born; managers and management proliferated. By one estimate, the fraction of American workers devoted to managing grew nearly fourfold between 1900 and 1980.[10]

The Harvard Business School opened its MBA program for business in 1910, and its marketing materials still reflect its original mission to churn out professional managers to lead American business, with propositions and promises such as "Change is the one thing you can expect with certainty. That's why we have carefully crafted the MBA Curriculum to help you develop a capacity for analysis, assessment, judgment, and action that you can exercise throughout the course of any career you choose to pursue."[11]

While many HBS graduates take jobs in management, around a quarter of each class goes into consulting, becoming just the kind of worker bees with rolled-up sleeves that Accenture let loose on the Indian factories, teaching the world how to quantify, organize, and manage.

The Science of Shoveling

In the 1890s, just as the United States entered the second industrial revolution and the transcontinental railroad finished erasing the American frontier, one of the world's first business consultants, Frederick Winslow Taylor, gave birth to the idea of "scientific management" (also known as Taylorism) by applying the scientific method to manufacturing processes. Taylor's business card read "Systematizing Shop Management and Manufacturing Costs a Specialty," an expertise he'd developed working as an industrial apprentice patternmaker, a machine shop laborer, a gang boss, foreman, research director, and finally chief engineer. He'd also earned his correspondence degree in mechanical engineering.

Based on these experiences, Taylor tried to understand why differences existed among workers' productivity and how best to get everyone up to top speed. His answer? Standardization. He thought his main tools, time and motion studies, would help him discover the "one best way" to do any given task. In Taylor's view, managing workers involved figuring out, say, the most efficient way to shovel (the "best" weight to lift with a shovel was, according to Taylor's study, 21 pounds) and making sure each worker used it.

Scientific management was the "worker as interchangeable cog" approach—one that many modern office workers might relate to. If Taylor's original ideas have been tempered by at least a bit of humanity in their modern application, the principles of Taylorism are still at the core of what is considered good management, whether reflected in the HBS curriculum, Six Sigma certifications for reducing defects, or the best-practice checklist at Accenture. Decisions on how to deploy organizational resources have to be based on information: which types of cloth are selling fastest, which ones generate the highest profits, which employees deserve promotion, and which ones need to be let go. It was this avalanche of data that led the railroads to develop nineteenth-century information systems. To rise above the disarray that reigns on Tarapur's factory floors requires modern information systems to manage their records.

Not everyone needs to know the last detail of what's happening in the factory. The foreman who manages inventory, for instance, does need to keep tabs on pretty much every scrap of yarn. But higher up the org pyramid—where Mr. Samata and other factory owners sit, or to Alfred P. Sloan's corner office at GM—executives need to see only summary information on the flow of goods through the production process. Too much detail would be overwhelming.

So not only does effective management require efficient information gathering, but also the facts and figures need to be distributed to those who need them. Mr. Samata shouldn't be micromanaging the storage closet, though in the absence of effective management systems, he does. And Alfred P. Sloan shouldn't be agonizing over how to distribute tasks on the assembly line, or manage the formation of a hubcap design team. Top managers should occupy themselves with the larger strategic questions facing their companies: Should we expand to a second plant? Bring parts production in house? Raise prices on next year's model? Call the union's bluff in wage negotiations? Once these decisions are made, instructions make their way back down the hierarchy—yet more flow of information—on what needs to get done; then the process repeats itself. If management systems are working properly, it's possible to keep tabs on whether everything is getting done, and also figure out what to do next.

Mr. Samata didn't command such a hierarchy, and his lack of modern management left him with the supply closet key around his neck. By contrast, Alfred P. Sloan wrote in a 1924 essay on GM's management, "[senior executives] do not do much routine work with details. They never get up to us. I work fairly hard, but on exceptions."[12]

The costs to this system are obvious: you have a critical piece of information to deliver to your boss's boss's boss, but company rules prevent you from doing so. And you feel divorced from the decisions that are driving the direction of the company.

(There's another reason why you can't go around the chain of command to snitch on your boss, and it has to do with getting the most out of our middle managers.[13] Think about a book editor whose job it is to find and sign new talent. She enjoys hobnobbing with authors, and has interests that run a bit more literary than commercial. The publisher's CEO may nonetheless choose to give the editor full authority over signing new authors, to ensure that she goes all out to find promising proposals. If the editor constantly worries that she's going to be overruled, her efforts will be halfhearted. If the editor's assistant finds that his boss is taking too many lunches with high-brow literati, he can threaten to take this information to his boss's boss. The only way the CEO can truly commit to giving his editors autonomy in signing authors—and ensure they'll put in the long hours to develop the necessary relationships—is to adhere to a rule of communicating to lower-level subordinates only through their supervisors.)

The fundamental role of managers, at least in the economic logic of the org, is in large part the gathering and processing of information to be passed up and down the org chart, to extend the control of the owners and to filter and sort employee intelligence. Without this flow of information, we're back to the world of Mr. Samata, or even the single-person org of Scott Urban and his spectacles.

The Dark Side of Management, Part I: Rising to One's Level of Managerial Incompetence

If you're under fifty, you've almost surely never heard of Dr. Laurence Peter. There's even a good chance you don't even know his principle by name. But unless you've lived a hermit's life, you'll recognize it when you see it: "In a hierarchy, each employee tends to rise to his level of incompetence." This is the Peter Principle. Once an employee reaches his level of incompetence, his superiors will recommend no further promotion, leading to "Peter's Corollary": "Every post tends to be occupied by an employee incompetent to execute its duties," a pithy expression of the gripes and discontent of managers and the managed masses alike.

Dr. Peter introduced his principle in the January 1967 issue of *Esquire* magazine, and spun its ideas out into a slim book a couple of years later, subtitled *Why Things Always Go Wrong*. It introduced what Peter claimed, tongue firmly in cheek, as the "salutary science of hierarchiology."

The book *The Peter Principle* is a playful take on organizational dysfunction, what one reviewer labeled "deadpan satire in the jocular-jugular vein." It's filled with taxonomies of hierarchical ills, and includes a comprehensive glossary, from *Alger complex* to *utter irrelevance*. Choice entries: *tabular gigantism* ("an obsession with bigger desk than his colleagues") and *papyromania* (an obsessive cluttering of one's desk with piles of paper in an attempt to mask incompetence by creating the illusion of having too much work to do). The final chapter, "The Darwinian Exception," argues that dinosaurs were victims of the ill effects of the Peter Principle: They rose to dominate the earth and thus reached beyond their abilities and went extinct. Dr. Peter suggests that humanity may suffer the same fate—an argument that's perhaps a mischievous case of overreach by Dr. Peter himself.

Playfulness aside, Dr. Peter struck a deeper chord among the managed of the world. *The Peter Principle* spent a year and a half near the top of the *New York Times* bestseller list. Dr. Peter became a fixture on the talk show circuit, and business groups around the country enlisted him for speaking engagements. Some of America's largest corporations even offered him consulting gigs. (He declined—to accept the offers would have been to reach beyond his own level of competence.)

The principle and its success are yet another backlash against Chandler's managerial revolution, which had empowered American business while emasculating its armies of employees, wearing them down through protocol and bureaucracy. The principle provided an appealing logic: the skills of lower-level tasks aren't necessarily informative of what's needed to lead and manage others. (Michael Scott of TV's *The Office* was an award-winning salesman, which led to promotion to regional manager—where he proved hopelessly inept.) And it subverts the organizational hierarchy in the peon's favor: one of the principle's consequences is that "work is accomplished by those employees who have not yet reached their level of incompetence"—that is, the lowly cubicle dweller, not the manager in the corner office. In Peter's scheme, "managing upward" becomes a subtle dance in which workers manage their superiors to limit the damage they can do.

Serious scholars have taken an interest in Dr. Peter's work—in part because it's true, at least to some degree: if you promote people to management based on the fact that they've demonstrated skills at lower-level work, there's no evidence that they'll be good managers.[14] Even if companies follow the best feasible promotion rules, it's still possible to end up with substandard managers. In his article "The Peter Principle: A Theory of Decline," Edward Lazear, a Stanford labor economist and former chair of George W. Bush's Council of Economic Advisers, points out that an employee may work hard only until he gets a big promotion, at which point he'll take some time to relax. In this variation on the Peter Principle, managers aren't stupid, just lazy. Yet Lazear doesn't suggest that companies should do things any differently. The prize of a bigger paycheck, higher status, and a corner office spurs lower-level employees to compete for the coveted promotion. The value of their increased effort can easily outweigh the cost of slacking managers.

(At the odder end of the spectrum, three complexity scholars from the University of Catania, Italy, won the 2010 "IgNobel" Prize, an American parody of the Swedish Nobel, for providing an alternative to Peter's incompetence trap. They demonstrated mathematically that organizations would become more efficient if they promoted people at random.)[15]

Peter does have advice for those employees who know their limits and want to avoid promotion: self-sabotage, or "Peter's Parry." Such "creative incompetence" will help the employee who is happy in his current position take steps to appear less desirable for a place in the ranks above. Subtly painting your personal life as morally questionable, wearing too much perfume or cologne, and parking in the company president's reserved space from time to time are among Peter's favored examples. This strategy comes with a caveat, though: don't be so incompetent that you get fired.

Hiring managers randomly or intentionally sabotaging one's own promotion seems a bit ridiculous. If we all know effective managers when we see them, why not just promote people who are good managers, regardless of whether they were good at what they did before? The problem is that managerial talent is hard to glean from performance as a salesman or engineer.

This certainly hasn't stopped companies from trying. Google, always the data-driven org, has done its best to encode what makes a good manager. Its efforts were born of the realization that, while promotions at the company had been made based largely on technical expertise, really good engineers didn't make really good managers. The Peter Principle was alive and well at one of the leading tech giants of the twenty-first century.

Through an initiative called Project Oxygen, Google tried to capture the common attributes of managers of its most productive teams, and distilled its findings into a list of eight qualities of great managers.[16] Most items on the list—"Have a clear vision and strategy," for example—aren't necessarily that easy to spot in up-and-coming engineers, however. So Google's list may be useful for training new managers but still not very helpful in spotting raw talent. Except maybe item eight, "Technical Skills," which are easy to spot and quantify. It could be that adhering to the Peter Principle isn't so absurd after all.

The Dark Side of Management, Part II: Managers versus the Managed

Without managers, orgs would likely come to a grinding halt. Or at least, like the Indian textile factories, they might end up with heavy equipment blocking passageways and owners wearing inventory keys around their necks. Or as one popular manager of computer programmers who moonlights as an online management guru puts it: WHILE YOU WERE USELESSLY STARING AT THAT ONE BUG THIS MORNING I WAS KEEPING THIS ORGANIZATION MOVING PAL.[17]

When you examine how managers spend their days, however, it doesn't feel as if they're the engines that make orgs run. Take, for instance, one of the natural habitats of the manager: meetings. Meetings can feel like a grand waste of time, ill conceived, at best—and some of them certainly are. Paul Graham, a computer programmer and venture capitalist, points out that meetings, while part and parcel of the manager's toolkit, cost the "maker"—that is, the worker who's actually trying to produce something—valuable time. Graham writes, "There are two types of schedule, which I'll call the manager's schedule and the maker's schedule. The manager's schedule is for bosses. It's embodied in the traditional appointment book, with each day cut into one-hour intervals. You can block off several hours for a single task if you need to, but by default you change what you're doing every hour." He goes on: "When you're operating on the maker's schedule, meetings are a disaster. A single meeting can blow a whole afternoon, by breaking it into two pieces, each too small to do anything hard in."[18]

Like the Peter Principle, this message feels like a dose of blessed common sense in the world of organizational nonsense, focusing as it does on the fact that it is the average worker who actually gets stuff done. Without makers, this line of reasoning goes, there'd be no org at all. Fair enough—and what average worker wouldn't want to hear that? But at least some of the apparent pointlessness of meetings reflects the inherent inefficiency in ferreting out "soft" information, the state of affairs that can't be coded into a spreadsheet. Meetings' written counterparts (memos and reports) similarly serve to collect information to feed the org, while distracting the maker from the "real" work that needs to get done.

Large organizations need to impose some degree of uniformity (part of the manager's role) for the same reason that McDonald's doesn't allow franchisees to offer hand-carved roast beef sandwiches—quality control over the inputs of production, including information. Meetings and memos and reports, the essential tools of management, serve this function, even though they may resemble nothing but disruption to the work lives of those who feel they are the ones actually producing something.

From this confluence (organizational necessity and maker hostility) managers are at least twice damned. They're watching over and coordinating the hard work the market couldn't handle—hence all the soft information and meetings, which are critical but disagreeable aspects of organizational life. In pinning this unpleasantness on managers, we're falling prey to what psychologists call the fundamental attribution error: we blame the person, not their dysfunctional situation. If a waitress is curt, we assume it's because she's a rude and ornery person, instead of observing that she's overwhelmed with the lunchtime rush. Similarly, we blame managers for oppressing us, when in fact that's the only way they can do their jobs.

It's also a sad fact that most of us, given the choice, often don't really want to be at work. The beach or work? Spend time with your family or work? Travel or work? In his script for the movie *Heist*, David Mamet wrote, "Everyone wants *money*. That's why they call it *money*." You could shift that ever so slightly: "No one wants to *work*. That's why it's called *work*."

Company founders such as Scott Urban are driven by an intrinsic motivation, passionate about changing the world, inventing revolutionary technologies, and generally making the world a better place. You can see it in how their eyes light up when they talk about their companies. Early employees tend to share the same fervor. But once you get to the nth hire, intrinsic motivation is often overtaken by that magic paycheck that shows up in your bank account every couple of weeks. It's the manager's job to make sure that someone whose eyes don't light up when she discusses the business still does her job efficiently. And no matter how much you love your job, there are always things you'd rather not do.

To someone who'd rather be playing solitaire or just taking a little time to plan his next vacation online, or even a dedicated worker who's doing one part of a job that's more fun instead of another that's less fun but equally necessary, a manager's oversight is often going to seem unwelcome.

But your manager's job isn't to be your best friend; it's to make you work hard. A good boss from an employee's perspective is one with empathy and understanding. From the org's perspective, empathy is fine as long as it doesn't get in the way of productivity. And there's ample evidence that it's possible to have too much of a good thing. In a study of Cambodian textile manufacturers, giving direct supervisors empathy training made for happier employees who liked their bosses more but were no more productive.[19]

Meanwhile, there are ways that managers can boost productivity, despite the resulting destructive effects on morale. Remember CompStat, the data-driven approach to policing that Peter Moskos encountered in his time as a Baltimore cop? With block-by-block details on crimes committed each week, CompStat enabled police leadership to flag hotspots before they got out of hand, and to hold precinct commanders' feet to the fire if they failed to make their numbers. According to a 2012 *New York* magazine profile of the NYPD, the department had "two striking characteristics: its effectiveness and its unhappiness." Crime had fallen by over a third in the post-CompStat era, accompanied by a comparable decline in police officer morale.

And what about the good employees, you ask? Which is to say, why can't *your* manager leave *you* alone? (You surely are one of the good ones.) Well, remember what every serial killer's neighbors says: "He was nice and quiet. A good neighbor." Yeah, until they started digging up bodies in his backyard. Or until Mr. Samata takes an inventory of the supply closet.[20]

Better Management Can Save Lives

In case the Indian experiment in management isn't sufficiently convincing, a stark comparison of the relative value of managers versus makers comes from the Wharton School's Ethan Mollick, who examined the manufacturers of 854 computer games, together accounting for over $4 billion in revenue, to figure out which parts of the org contributed most to the products' success. Computer games are developed on a project-by-project basis, with a core team of several dozen programmers and engineers working intensively together on a single game for months at a time. They're overseen by a producer who is ultimately responsible for making sure everything gets done on time and on budget. The game's development is driven by the project designer, who guides the team in going from drawing board concept to software reality. The designer is the quintessential innovator and maker, the creative engine that drives software development. The producer is a much-maligned project manager, keeping tabs on costs and deadlines.

The project-based nature of game production means that designers, producers, and programming teams are constantly coming together in different permutations, sometimes within the same company and sometimes in different ones. This enabled Mollick to decompose the relative contributions of designer, producer, and firm in making a game succeed or fail. For example, if a designer *always* generates blockbusters, irrespective of his pairing with producer or company, then we can likely assign his success to his own creative brilliance rather than to lucky partnerships. Similarly, producers responsible for multiple flops can probably be blamed for their failures. The extent to which success or failure follows producers or designers from project to project gives a sense of the importance of each job in determining a game's fate.

Mollick's findings upend the assumption that makers matter more than managers. He finds that 30 percent of the differences in revenue among games could be attributed to the producer and the designer alone, but most came from the producer.

As Mollick drily puts it, "Variation among middle managers has a particularly large impact on firm performance, much larger than that of those individuals who are assigned innovative roles. Middle managers are necessary to facilitate firm performance in creative, innovative, and knowledge-intensive industries." The boring manager, in other words, meant more to the success of the project than did the designer, no matter how fancy his glasses.

These findings are echoed by some additional work that Stanford's Nick Bloom and his coauthors did in extending their World Management Survey. In a wide range of sectors, including health care, education, retail, and manufacturing, they've documented management practices in companies, nonprofits, and government agencies across the globe. There's wide variation in the management competencies across institutions, which gave the researchers a chance to see whether high scores on the management checklist were associated with more profits and productivity.

The results are startling. Based on a survey of 1,500 schools across North America and Europe, the researchers conclude that students at better-managed schools get higher test scores. In their study of Canadian, American, and British retail firms, they found that relatively low-performing family-run companies have weak management practices when compared with highly productive multinational chains. And in their hospital study, they found that management turns out to be literally a matter of life and death. Countries with better-managed hospitals had higher survival rates for heart attacks, shorter wait times, and better surgery outcomes. While the studies are not without their shortcomings—there are many other differences between hospitals in Sweden and Italy apart from management practice—their findings should at least make the managed of the world think a little harder about what their bosses do.

CHAPTER 6

The View from the Corner Office

A $90,000 AREA RUG, a pair of guest chairs that cost almost as much, a $35,000 toilet, and a $1,400 trash can—these are just a few of the miscellaneous expenses from a remodeling of John Thain's office when he took over as Merrill Lynch CEO in December 2007. The total bill came to an astonishing $1.2 million—nearly enough to buy five average single-family homes.

Those same remodeling expenses contributed to Thain's resignation just over a year later and helped to define the popular image of the CEO living a life of extreme privilege—gold-plated faucets, oak-paneled offices, country club memberships, and chauffeur-driven limousines, all paid for through corporate largess. (Thain's limo tab included $230,000 for his driver—$85,000 in salary, the rest in overtime and a bonus.)

In the days of the "organization man," corporate leaders got their hands dirty running companies, Harvard Business School professor Rakesh Khurana explains. They worked their way up through the org, no more visible or famous to the outside world than anyone else in the company. But all that changed in the

1980s, with larger-than-life figures such as Lee Iacocca, Steve Jobs, and Jack Welch. Men, mostly, with outsize charisma and overgrown egos who were worshiped with quasi-religious fervor by the markets and the public alike for their ability to swoop down from the heavens as corporate saviors, producing results and driving up the stock price.[1]

While the stock market and business press continue to see CEOs as playing an important role in their companies' performance, since 2008 the larger public has seen them more as responsible for an epic wave of business failures. Detroit's leaders couldn't see beyond gas-guzzling SUVs, even with an oil price of $120 per barrel. (Pilloried for chartering private jets to get to D.C. to testify before Congress, they ended up driving from Detroit in a kind of cross-country perp walk.) And supposedly infallible banking execs were left holding trillions in subprime mortgages worth pennies on the dollar.

Depending on whom you ask and the day of the week, then, CEOs are either brilliant or hopelessly incompetent. Regardless of what CEOs are actually worth, they earn millions—and increasingly billions. But what do they actually *do*? And do they deserve it?

A Day in the Life of a CEO

Henry Mintzberg is one of a small group of researchers who have worked to give us a glimpse of what goes on in the rarefied world of the CEO. Since he appeared on the scene nearly four decades ago, Mintzberg has been called a management guru—a balding, opinionated, and combative one. His background isn't in management but in mechanical engineering. He learned about organizations as a peon at the Canadian National Railway. In his memoir, he suggests that watching collisions between two fast-moving boxcars is an excellent way to understand the basic mechanics of corporate mergers.

After a few years, Mintzberg left CN to go to graduate school, more out of inertia than any directed intention of acquiring credentials to climb his way up the railroad hierarchy. He enrolled in a master's program at what was then called the Sloan School of Industrial Management at MIT.[2] A year later, with his doctoral coursework out of the way, all that lay between Mintzberg and a PhD was his thesis. He spent six months twiddling his thumbs and waiting for deep thoughts and big questions to descend from the skies. That was when the director of NASA, James Webb, who'd gotten the Apollo spacecraft into orbit, approached one of Mintzberg's thesis advisers and asked to be studied as a manager. Since no one else at Sloan was interested in management or managers, at least according to Mintzberg, shadowing Webb and figuring out what managers do landed in his lap.

Mintzberg never got to follow Webb, but he did run with his idea, tracking five other leaders for his dissertation on what managers—in particular, chief executives—actually do. The bosses he followed ran organizations of vastly different types and purposes: John Knowles of Mass General, a nonprofit hospital; Charlie Brown, head of the Newton, Massachusetts, school system; James Gavin, CEO of the consulting firm Arthur D. Little; watch magnate Harry B. (for Bulova) Henshel; and Bernard O'Keefe, CEO of high-tech defense contractor EG&G.

Mintzberg's five CEOs were a long way from constituting a scientific sample, and his collection of anecdotes was insufficient for what academics would now regard as serious data analysis. But Mintzberg's results have since been confirmed by the more recent work of HBS professor Raffaella Sadun, who, along with colleagues Oriana Bandiera and Andrea Prat of the London School of Economics, replicated Mintzberg's time diary exercise nearly fifty years later with a far more scientific sampling of over a hundred CEOs. Sadun and her colleagues came to much the same conclusion regarding how CEOs spend their days, even though their CEOs were Italian captains of industry—leaders of Italy's equivalent of *Fortune* 500 orgs—and lived in a markedly different era from that of the leaders in Mintzberg's study. (Mintzberg's CEOs had no e-mail. They didn't even have conference calling or fax machines.)

Despite enormous differences in customers, products, and size of organizations, Mintzberg's five CEOs and Sadun's one hundred Italians all spent their days in much the same way: going to meetings.

The CEO Diaries

Mintzberg combined the insights from his observations of five CEOs with the findings of a number of other time-use studies of managers around the world, distilled them down to a terse ten-page article titled "The Manager's Job," and got it published in *Harvard Business Review*. His description of CEO "folklore and fact" launched his career.

Mintzberg's time diaries showed lives filled with interruption. In a total of five weeks of observation, he recorded few instances of a CEO alone and without disruption for more than fifteen minutes straight. Half their activities lasted fewer than nine minutes—and this was in the pre-BlackBerry age—while only 10 percent went on for more than an hour.[3] Those hour-long stretches were taken up with hour-long meetings, mostly to catch up on the latest fire to be extinguished or dispute to be mediated. More than 90 percent of Mintzberg's managers' face time was impromptu rather than planned.

Mintzberg's conclusions flew in the face of what was then the accepted wisdom of his colleagues at the Sloan School, who viewed management as a science, akin to physics or chemistry. The org's constituent parts, whether men or machinery, were meant to behave in predictable ways, dictated by immutable laws of social science, discoverable by astute observers, and manageable by competent CEOs. Managing an organization was essentially an engineering problem, with all the information the CEO needed to guide the org provided by management information systems (MIS) developed by management scientists at Sloan and elsewhere. The CEO, in this view, should be fine-tuning the gears of the org, and at the same time figuring out just what purpose the machine should be put to next.

Yet, as Mintzberg wrote in "The Manager's Job," a CEO's day-to-day activities were scarcely unchanged from those of his predecessors a century before. Most of his information came through conversation rather than MIS printouts, and the brief periods of alone time were spent catching up on correspondence or flipping through the day's newspaper rather than in solitary reflection.

To analyze the job of a CEO with greater scientific rigor, Sadun and her colleagues farmed out the task of collecting time diaries to the CEOs' personal assistants, who spend their lives mapping out the moment-to-moment activities of their bosses 365 days of the year. In the words of famed GE CEO Jack Welch's longtime PA, Rosanne Badowski, "For more than fourteen years, I've been a human answering machine, auto dialer, word processor, filtering system, and fact checker; been a sounding board, schlepper, buddy, and bearer of good and bad tidings; served as a scold, diplomat, repairperson, cheerleader and naysayer; and performed dozens of other roles under the title of 'assistant.'"[4]

The Italian PAs didn't record details of activities that lasted fewer than fifteen minutes. They were too busy schlepping, buddying, repairing, and naysaying—and so missed out on some of the stop-start details of modern CEOs' lives. These short spurts of activity took up around a fifth of the average CEO's time—nearly ten hours a week, almost exactly the same as back in Mintzberg's graduate school days. Of the thirty-seven hours of work time remaining, only about five were used in solitary tasks. The rest (thirty-two hours a week) were spent mostly with in-person meetings, with a smattering of conference calls and ribbon cuttings to fill out the CEOs' calendars.

The computer revolution seems to have changed mostly the ways CEOs spend their time alone, rather than causing them to seek more solitary moments at the expense of personal contact. Instead of reading newspapers and magazines, they keep tabs on various blogs and Twitter feeds to stay informed on what's going on in the world. Much of their correspondence is now sent through smartphones rather than dictated to secretaries. But personal interaction has survived the imposition of e-mail and information systems, and the virtual office revolution never arrived. Video conferencing and telecommuting have not replaced flesh-and-blood interaction.

Yet suggesting that Steve Jobs's duties at Apple consisted of going to meetings is a bit like saying that Shakespeare wrote words. True, yes, but pretty thin for explaining what made Steve Jobs Steve Jobs.

So what goes on at those meetings? Despite its imperfections, the meeting (rather than spreadsheets, reports, or MIS printouts) remains the most effective way of gathering details on what's really going on around the org, and for spreading the CEO's vision, unadulterated by garbled retelling, to his many minions. Hence the CEO's calendar remains as meeting filled today as it was in 1968—or even 1868, for that matter. And there's no reason to expect that things will change anytime soon.

What Only Meetings Can Do

CEOs may snatch a glance at budgets, printouts, and other hard data in the nine-minute stretches of uninterrupted time they can call their own. And the management engineers are present in spirit at the CEO's many meetings, which often involve the discussion of balance sheets and reports. But top managers spend so much time with meetings because spreadsheets and reports simply can't equip them with the knowledge required to run their organizations.[5]

The management engineers at the Sloan School, who hoped to replace meetings with their data reports, had in mind a theory of decision making that was heavily influenced by computer science research on information processing. From a computing perspective, the flow of information in a bureaucracy follows the reporting lines of an org chart up through the ranks, until it reaches the root of the "upside-down tree" that is a corporate hierarchy. The ultimate recipient of all information is the CEO. The many facts and figures flowing up the tree would utterly overwhelm any individual brain, so at each step, managers vet data for their relevance, then organize them, simplify them, and kick them up one more level in the chain of command for further processing. And this is so, to an extent. As we saw in chapter 5, those at the top of the org don't get status updates on every machine or employee, just the repackaged and aggregated information they need to make high-level strategic decisions.[6]

But a lot of this information can't be packaged into a written document. In explaining why reports will never replace meetings for the boss, Mintzberg quotes the historian and presidential biographer Richard Neustadt, who studied the information-gathering practices of presidents Truman, Roosevelt, and Eisenhower. The decisions that come under the president's powers— managing geopolitics, the Congress, the economy—are arguably much more complex than deciding whether to order more toasters or T-shirts to stock Walmart's shelves. For instance, in 2010 the U.S. federal government had more than two million employees on the payroll, comparable to the largest corporate employer in the world, Walmart. In the same year, President Obama oversaw a budget of well over $3 trillion, as compared to Walmart's $400 billion in revenues.

Yet even the leaders of the free world get informed in ways that would seem hopelessly inefficient to the computer engineers of MIT. Neustadt found, "It is not information of a general sort that helps a President see personal stakes; not summaries, not surveys, not the bland amalgams. Rather . . . it is the odds and ends of 'tangible detail' that pieced together in his mind illuminate the issues put before him. To help himself, he must reach out as widely as he can for every scrap of fact, opinion, and gossip bearing on his interests and relationships as President. He must become his own director of central intelligence." President Obama didn't decide to launch the mission that killed Osama bin Laden based on intelligence reports and satellite images alone.

In their description of what leaders do, Harvard Business School professors Michael Porter and Nitin Nohria also quote Neustadt to account for the meeting-filled days of CEOs.[7] Porter and Nohria go on to point out that a boss might need some talent to wheedle out of his underlings the odds and ends of tangible detail, even in person. This ability is, in part, what makes the CEO different. For example, it's easy to imagine the Ivory brand manager at Procter & Gamble trying to avoid presenting inauspicious soap-related anecdotes and details when meeting with the boss, lest the CEO shut down or sell off the P&G soap division and "decide" Ivory's brand manager out of a job.

This is one reason for the many pre-meetings among lower-level employees: to carefully orchestrate any interaction with the CEO to ensure he gets a favorable perspective on how things are going at Ivory, with the desired net result of more P&G resources getting allocated to its soap business. Even the impromptu meetings and interactions that present constant interruptions to the CEO's workday have at least a bit of spin in their presentation, with snippets presented with the intention of pleasing the boss or influencing his decisions in favor of the presenter.

We have a permanent record of the heights (or depths) of flattery to which some underlings will go, in the form of wiretaps by Italian prosecutors of phone calls to that country's then prime minister, Silvio Berlusconi, in 2007, while he was under investigation for charges of corruption.

Underling: "Presidente! Good Evening, Presidente. How are you?"

Presidente: "Getting by..."

Underling: "No…Getting by in grand form, I must say, even with so many difficulties…You remain the most beloved figure in the country…"

Presidente: "Politically, I'm nowhere…but socially they mistake me for the Pope."

Underling: "That's just my point, you are the most beloved in the country, I say this without any intent to flatter…"

It only goes downhill from there. Clearly, Berlusconi is going to have a tough time getting the information he needs to run Italy (and fight his prosecution) from exchanges like this one.

The pre-meeting meetings and yes-men of the org make meetings all the more important, as they provide an opportunity for the CEO to question, gauge a human response, and formulate his or her own judgment.

Just as CEOs can gather the soft information they need only through face-to-face meetings, relatively little of what they decide can be properly delivered to the corporate masses via mass e-mailings, the annual report, or other written documents. Ambiguity and divergent readings of the CEO's message are just as much of a problem on the way down the hierarchy as on the way up. The precise meaning of each word out of the CEO's mouth brings to mind Bill Clinton's storied response to allegations that he had lied to the American people, which, in Clinton's telling, "depends on what the meaning of the word 'is' is." And you thought you knew.

In Nohria and Porter's words, the CEO can't communicate any of his message in "high fidelity." The message gets garbled and misinterpreted (sometimes deliberately) as it works its way through the org, across shareholders, and among customers. So in the 80-plus percent of his time that's spent information-gathering through face-to-face interaction, the CEO is also broadcasting his message constantly through example, stories, and many other odds and ends of tangible detail to clarify what exactly is meant by "relentless focus on innovation" or "building our core business" and other vague statements made in annual reports or press releases.[8] The CEO helps to clarify what these platitudes mean in practice, and direct the company by example.

What Only the CEO Can Do

CEOs use meetings to glean intelligence and to convey their particular vision of what the org ought to be doing—to gather and send soft information that can't be contained in MIS reports and their contemporary equivalents. But what is it that they accomplish with these meetings and information that only they can do?

A. G. Lafley—who himself attained guru status with his turnaround of P&G—published his musings on the subject in the aptly titled "What Only the CEO Can Do" in the *Harvard Business Review* in 2009. Lafley observed that most of the actual *doing* within a company is delegated. So what's left?

Lafley answers his own question with the words of yet another management guru, Peter Drucker, who died as he was composing his theory of corporate leadership, leaving behind only a sketch of his thoughts on the matter. Drucker wrote (and Lafley transcribed), "The CEO is the link between the Inside that is 'the organization' and the Outside of society, economy, technology, markets, and customers. Inside there are only costs. Results are only on the outside."

Consider the job titles of the various so-called C-Suite execs who sit just one level below the CEO. The chief operating officer manages daily operations, ensuring that products keep running off the assembly line, with a view limited by his primary objective of optimizing internal resource use. The chief financial officer is essentially the head bean counter, seeing little beyond the balance sheet or profit-and-loss statements. For chief marketing officers, the customer is king—their job is to make sure people keep buying the product at least as fast as the company can make it, without undue consideration of the cost.

Together, these chief officers' perspectives on the company bring to mind a terribly overused yet still helpful Indian parable of a group of blind men asked to describe an elephant, but each given the chance to feel only one part of the animal's body. The blind man who touches a leg says the elephant looks like a pillar; the tail toucher claims an elephant is like a rope; the one who feels the trunk compares the elephant to a tree branch; the belly toucher asserts that it's like a wall; and the tusk feeler insists the elephant feels like a solid pipe.

To understand the sum total of what it means to be an elephant requires a view of how the many pieces fit together; the CEO is the great integrator of the many views of the elephant. However imperfect and imprecise his or her overall perspective may be, it's the only one we've got. In the land of the blind, the one-eyed man is CEO.

Every attempt at describing the CEO's job starts with his or her responsibility in setting strategy for the org (although recent years have also seen a proliferation of chief strategy officers), or, in Lafley's words, "deciding what business you are in."[9] In some sense, all decisions in an org are the ultimate responsibility of the CEO, but most of them get handed off to others so the boss doesn't have to sweat the small stuff. A. G. Lafley couldn't possibly have had the time to watch over the development of each new generation of Tide formula or pass judgment on whether detergent should be lemon-scented or lime. So he delegates the right to make these decisions to those below him, who in turn pass them on down the chain of command.

But questions such as "Should Apple get into the phone business?" can't be farmed out to one department or another within the company. They depend on whether customers want iPhones, whether Apple can make a better iPhone than other orgs, and also what it costs to deliver the iPhone to market. Figuring out whether iPhones should be manufactured in China or Korea can be delegated to the COO, and marketing can at least partly be left to the CMO. But the ultimate decision as to whether to make the iPhone in the first place falls to the one person in the company with the wider perspective needed to make such grand strategic decisions, the CEO. In the case of Apple, Steve Jobs mostly seemed to get it right, with the iPhone and iPad as Exhibits A and B of his epic successes (and the Lisa as an unfortunate detour into failure during his first tenure leading the company).

Doing It in Style

Jobs had a reputation as a particularly controlling boss, described in *Fortune* as "a corporate dictator who makes every critical decision—and oodles of seemingly noncritical calls too, from the design of the shuttle buses that ferry employees to and from San Francisco to what food will be served in the cafeteria."[10] While perhaps not as extreme as Jobs's domination of Apple, most CEOs do exercise considerable control over the direction their companies take, and reach very different conclusions. It matters who sits at the top. "Chainsaw" Al Dunlap (also known as "Rambo in Pinstripes") was a notorious downsizer and cost cutter, laying off thousands in the name of "streamlining" as leader of Scott Paper and then at Sunbeam.

Sandy Weill, on the other hand, was an "acquirer" who used his companies to Hoover up smaller ones to build massive corporate conglomerates. In two decades as CEO of financial services behemoth Shearson, Weill brought fifteen other firms under his control. By the time he sold the company to American Express, it had become Shearson Loeb Rhoades, the added names the result of just a few of these many acquisitions. He then moved on to run a tiny consumer finance company, Commercial Credit, which he parlayed into ownership of the banking giant Citigroup, again through a strategy of serial acquisition (including the reacquisition of his former firm, Shearson, which by that time had morphed through merger into Shearson Lehman).

Researchers Antoinette Schoar and Marianne Bertrand, who followed the careers of thousands of CEOs from company to company, found that there is indeed an individual style to the way bosses manage, one that moves with them. Some are acquirers like Weill; others Dunlapesque cost cutters; some load up with debt, while others hold cash; some invest in their companies' futures, while others focus only on next quarter's earnings. All these seemingly inconsequential differences in style can add up to big differences in how the overall org behaves, and perhaps even how much it makes in profits. This in turn can help to explain why CEOs make millions.[11]

CEOs, never known for their modesty, seem perfectly content with their extraordinary levels of pay. When Dow Jones reporter Kaveri Niththyananthan questioned the CEO of United Kingdom–based EasyJet, Andy Harrison, about his 2009 compensation of nearly $4.5 million, Harrison smiled and replied, "I'm worth it."[12]

Harrison's sense of self-worth echoed the response of Ford CEO Alan Mulally to a congressman who suggested that he should take a salary of one dollar, given the near-bankrupt state of the U.S. auto industry. No, replied Mulally. "I think I am okay where I am"—this in a year when he took home nearly $17 million in compensation.

Responses such as Harrison's and Mulally's might seem an affront to the working stiff toiling away for a paycheck a thousand times smaller. But what Mulally and Harrison no doubt had in mind were the profit numbers at EasyJet and Ford—Mulally's $17 million payday came on the heels of a billion-dollar turnaround that transformed a $970 million loss into profits of nearly $700 million just a year later, even as its peers GM and Chrysler begged for emergency funds to stay afloat.[13] Profits had fallen by 64 percent the year Harrison claimed to be worth his millions, but he could point to five straight years of profits as EasyJet CEO—a rare achievement in the airline business. Perhaps CEOs can be forgiven their hubris if they really are the only ones capable of seeing the big picture.

Are CEOs really so much smarter (and better at running meetings) than the rest of us? Possibly. But that's not the right question to ask. To claim they're worth it, Mulally and Harrison don't even have to be all that much better than the runner-up for the job.

Think about what you'd be willing to pay a professional card counter to play blackjack on your behalf.[14] The best card counters on the planet can skew the odds in their favor only by a few percentage points. While that sliver of an advantage in a penny ante game means only a few more pennies, at a high-rollers table, a few percentage points matter a lot. A player who wins just 51 percent of the time when making $10,000 bets will make $20,000 for himself and his investors for every hundred hands he plays. This is why casinos have banned counting and actively work to kick card counters out when they're discovered at the tables.[15]

The novice who loses more often than he wins will soon be out of cash and would do well to hire an expert as his proxy, paying tens of thousands a day for what amounts to a slight tilting of the odds on each hand. When the stakes get to the billions, you'd be willing to pay someone *millions*, even if their edge were only a few fractions of a percent.[16] And so we get to Harrison's and Mulally's claims that they're "worth it." No one else in the org has quite the same reach with regard to the impact of his or her decisions—the productivity of the chief marketing officer and chief operating officer depends on whether the CEO has taken the firm in the right direction, and so on down the line—and the value of a CEO who makes the right choices is commensurately a lot higher than even that of his or her immediate underlings.[17]

In "superstar economies," as in the market for CEOs, even a slight edge in ability can translate into enormous payoffs when the stakes get big. That's why Major League pitchers earn so much more than triple-A players, despite throwing fastballs only a couple of miles an hour faster. The theory also explains why, say, superstar baseball players sign contracts that run into the hundreds of millions when the lowest earners in baseball make the league minimum ("only" $480,000 at the beginning of the 2012 season). Given the benefits of being able to charge higher prices or sell more merchandise in baseball's largest markets, not to mention potential earnings from television broadcast rights, they're worth it. Top brain surgeons similarly earn a hefty premium if their success rates are a couple of percentage points higher than the next best set of hands, although the logic here is a little different. In this case, it's not that the impact of their skills ripples across an entire org or that they're watched closely by millions of viewers. Rather, when your brain is on the line, many customers are willing to pay a lot more than a few percentage points extra for a slightly higher chance of a good outcome.[18]

The Market Value of a CEO

The superstar theory runs up against some unfortunate realities in the case of many CEOs. Most obviously, some CEOs made immense sums of money while bankrupting their companies. Superstars? Hardly. However, in parsing CEOs' collective track record, it's important to keep in mind that sometimes good decisions result nonetheless in bad outcomes. Apple's Newton, a rudimentary personal digital assistant, or PDA, flopped in the 1990s, but may have simply been slightly ahead of its time. Later generations of palmtop computers, including Apple's iPhone, have sold millions. And good CEOs on occasion make bad decisions. Coke's disastrous launch of New Coke and the company's quick withdrawal of the too-sweet product from the market were orchestrated by Roberto Goizueta, the CEO also credited with successes such as Diet Coke and the "Coke is it!" campaign.

Excuses aside, sometimes bad people do end up running billion-dollar companies. Exhibit A, for the incompetents: Tony Hayward, the "most incompetent CEO in living memory" after BP's Gulf spill.[19] Exhibit B, for the felons: Jeff Skilling, former

Enron CEO, serving a twenty-four-year prison sentence. Exhibit C, representing the full spectrum from incompetence to felony: financial services in 2008.

Where does the weight of the evidence lie? Are CEOs more right than not? More competent than inept? Do CEOs earn their keep? While we can't answer that question definitively, there is a way of figuring out what investors think the answer is.

If one day a CEO is running a company and the next day, suddenly, through no fault of his own, he's gone, the difference between how investors value the company with and without him tells us something about what they think the boss is contributing to the bottom line. Usually, a CEO disappears because he's fired for doing a bad job, so the company is clearly better off without him. But sometimes his plane crashes, he dies unexpectedly in the middle of the night, or otherwise departs from the corner office for reasons unrelated to his performance in running the company. These sorts of "shocks" to company leadership are what researchers use to measure the value of a CEO.

In the years before Jobs's departure from Apple, before his death in 2011, Apple investors came perilously close to confronting this kind of "might have been" scenario as a result of Jobs's health problems, starting with a diagnosis of pancreatic cancer in 2004. As some measure of perceptions of Jobs's fragile health, the *Bloomberg* newswire mistakenly posted Jobs's obituary in 2008, with blanks for age and reason of death waiting to be filled in for quick publication. That was before his liver transplant the following year, which Apple's legendarily tight-lipped PR department kept under wraps until well after his operation. The secrecy around his health alone says a great deal about how consumers and investors felt about an Apple without Jobs.

These surprise health scares gave a preview of what investors thought a Jobs-less Apple was worth. Its stock price fell by 10 percent on a quickly debunked rumor on a CNN website that Jobs had suffered a heart attack. Apple's share price once rose just because Jobs showed up, looking well rested, at his favorite frozen yogurt joint. (By the time Jobs actually announced his resignation, in August 2011, the market had already been expecting the news for some time, so investors hardly blinked.)

Steve Jobs was an exceptional case. A lesser CEO's departure wouldn't necessarily spell disaster for company profits or stock price. After a few months of searching, the position would be filled with the "runner-up" for the job, perhaps one of his senior executives, or an outsider parachuting in to fill the leadership vacuum. In the case of Jobs, runner-up and current Apple CEO Tim Cook may have been a distant second, but that's probably not the case most of the time.

To get a sense of the value of leaders more broadly, in the early 1980s a team of accountants collected data on stock prices surrounding the sudden deaths of fifty-three CEOs and other senior executives.[20] They found enormous variability in how the stock price moved in response. One company's price fell by about 10 percent in the days surrounding the CEO's death. At the other extreme, another's price shot up by more than 20 percent.

What kind of leader elicits that sort of market euphoria when he moves on to the Great Hierarchy in the Sky? To uncover the situations where investors celebrate a CEO's passing, the accountants focused their attention on the deaths of CEOs who had also founded the companies they ran. Having an idea with billion-dollar potential isn't the same as having the skills to manage a billion-dollar company. Google founders Sergey Brin and Larry Page handed off the top management job to Eric Schmidt within a few years of the company's founding. Under Schmidt's leadership, Google came to be worth hundreds of billions. (He's recently passed the mantle back to Page, who, Google investors hope, has learned over the past decade what's needed to run the company.) Bill Hewlett and Dave Packard took turns as Hewlett-Packard CEO, leading the company through to 1978. Both also knew when to call it quits—leadership was passed on to John Young decades before either founder died.

But many successful entrepreneurs hang on to the bitter end. Occidental Petroleum founder Armand Hammer was still CEO when he died on December 11, 1990, at the age of ninety-two. Even if the sounds of champagne corks popping weren't to be heard on Wall Street that day, at least there were sighs of relief. Occidental's stock price jumped close to 10 percent on the news of Hammer's death.

Many founders seem to follow Hammer's lead, clinging too long to the title of CEO. The death of a founder CEO, according to the accountants' calculations, resulted in share price increases of about 3.5 percent. Nonfounders' deaths were mostly regarded as bad news, leading to share price declines averaging 1 percent.

It turns out that founder-led companies can extend their losing streaks if they so choose. In his work on leadership succession at founder-run and other family-controlled firms, Francisco Pérez-González, a Stanford University economist, quotes both Thomas Paine ("One of the strongest natural proofs of the folly of hereditary right in kings, is, that nature disapproves it, otherwise she would not so frequently turn it into ridicule by giving mankind an ass for a lion") and John Tyson, who inherited his job as Tyson Foods CEO ("The only reason I was on the payroll is because I was the son of the boss"). Leaders who see their children as heirs to the corporate throne aren't considering the full set of potential CEO candidates in search of the best person for the job.

It's no wonder a founder's departure, or the exit of a CEO from any family-run company, has a salutary effect on stock price and profits only in cases where leadership wasn't handed off to yet another family member.[21]

The Boss's Boss

Despite his exalted station, the CEO is, in most cases, merely a hired hand. Owners employ corporate leaders to manage things on their behalf. And it is these owners who ultimately have the right to hire and fire the boss, and to decide if he deserves a salary of $1 (as a number of CEOs of slumping companies have taken in recent years) or a $100 million bonus.

For most big companies, ownership is spread thinly across many thousands of shareholders whose savings of a few hundred or a few thousand shares of stock represent tiny stakes in the company. Very few shareholders have enough of an interest in the company's fortunes to put in the time that's needed to figure out if the CEO should keep his job, and if not, who should take his place. Given their tiny sliver of ownership, their votes would hardly count for much anyway.

Even if shareholders took seriously the job of selecting a leader, evaluating a CEO is tricky, at best. The direction of the stock price might be one useful measure, but one that can be misleading. Why pay John Watson more because Chevron's stock is gaining when the market is booming overall? You could look at whether Chevron's stock price outperformed the market. But that could reward Watson even if Chevron's shares increased in value just because the price of oil went up, increasing oil company profits through no effort of Watson's. Making an apples-to-apples comparison of Chevron's performance relative to Exxon-Mobil and ConocoPhillips gets us closer to an assessment of Watson's effectiveness. But given the minutes-long time horizon of some hedge fund managers and day traders, this may give Watson the unfortunate incentive to juke the numbers to inflate performance in the short run to the detriment of the long-term health of the company.

Even if investors could effectively evaluate the boss's performance, how should they translate it into rewards? Can our small shareholders make informed choices on cash versus stock versus stock options—never mind the infinite flavors of options now in existence—if they don't even know what an option is?

Most of the time, stockholders don't need to trouble themselves with any of this. Instead, they hire a group of wise men and women to watch over the boss on their behalf: the board of directors. With a board in place, shareholders don't need to vote on whether the CEO is doing his job or confer with him on major strategic decisions. They deputize the board to do it for them.

But this only pushes back the layers of conflicting incentives one step further. How do shareholders find individuals with the expertise and dispassionate objectivity to represent their interests in monitoring and evaluating the CEO? Evaluating a dozen or so potential board members is no easier than assessing the performance of the CEO. Some very wealthy investors with outsize shareholdings will make sure they themselves are given a seat at the boardroom table. Of Walmart's fifteen-person board, two are members of the Walton clan that founded the company and who still collectively own 40 percent of the company's shares. Jim and S. Robson Walton have considerable skin in the game of keeping a careful watch over CEO Michael Duke and the rest of Walmart's management.[22]

The composition of other boards can be somewhat more suspect. *BusinessWeek* magazine voted Disney's board the worst in America in 1999 and 2000, in part because it was shamelessly stacked with cronies of CEO Michael Eisner. It included, among others, Eisner's attorney, his architect, the principal of an elementary school once attended by his children, and the president of a university that received a $1 million Eisner donation. The same board approved more than $1 billion in pay for Eisner during his years running Disney.[23]

If it's unfair to malign all corporate boards on the basis of an incestuously rotten one at Disney, conflicts of a different sort are much more prevalent in the boardroom: back-scratching CEOs sitting on one another's boards. Most boards include at least one top executive from another company. There's an obvious logic to this: Who better to provide the critical knowledge of how to run a major corporation than someone who runs (or used to run) a major corporation? Unfortunately, this also means that CEOs can form a tight-knit club of gentlemanly back scratchers: If I sit on your board and you sit on mine, we can come to an understanding (unspoken or otherwise) to take care of each other.[24]

Cornell economist Kevin Hallock has estimated that during the 1990s, executive-exchange programs of this kind—they're known as *board interlocks*—were entirely commonplace. Eight percent of boards had at least one interlock, with the percentage rising to 20 if you threw in retired execs. A study by the watchdog group The Corporate Library even dug up an unseemly corporate ménage à trois in 2002 among Anheuser-Busch, phone company SBC Communications, and Emerson Electric, which shared a three-way interlock of CEOs.

The consequences of having two bosses responsible for monitoring and rewarding each other are all too predictable. Some of the most flagrant effects were documented by *New York Times* reporter Alison Leigh Cowan in the early 1990s. At that time, CEOs could even set each other's pay by sitting on compensation committees, the group within the board that sets the pay packages of the CEO and other top executives. And so it came to pass that, in 1992, B. F. Goodrich CEO John D. Ong was among the four board members setting the pay of grocery chain Kroger CEO Joseph A. Pichler, who was in turn one of four Goodrich board members deciding how much pay Ong's performance warranted. Apparently, it isn't even necessary for CEOs to sit on the comp committee for them to help their friends. Hallock's study found that CEOs at interlocked companies earned as much as 17 percent more than leaders of companies without interlocks.

The board member sharing that produces such incestuous relationships might also have an upside. Academics who study networks have spilled much ink analyzing whether the web of board connections among companies serves any useful purpose. Perhaps it allows best practices to spread to other companies through their board members, or it may be the result of many companies chasing after scarce executive talent to help guide their companies, leading to the same faces appearing again and again in America's boardrooms.[25] Regardless of whether interlocks make boards more effective, executives themselves clearly profit handsomely from them.

A Rising Tide Lifts All Salaries

While the bottom 99 percent have seen their wages stagnate, CEO pay continues its relentless rise. In 1960, CEO pay was 30 times an average worker's salary. By 2005 the ratio was nearly

110 times. Indeed, in Alison Leigh Cowan's *Times* piece on board interlocks in the 1990s, it's almost quaint to read about anxieties over Ong's pay reaching *nearly $2 million*! How times have changed.

Economists Carola Frydman and Raven Saks went back to 1936, collecting pay information on *Fortune* 50 executives from old 10-k forms, the reports companies file annually with government regulators. What they found was that CEO pay really didn't change all that much from 1936 through to 1976, even though the pay of average Americans tripled over the same time period. (In fact, things got so bad for CEOs in the 1940s that the *Wall Street Journal* ran an article describing banking executives as "The New Poor," the result of wartime earnings limits.)

But sometime in the mid-1970s, CEO pay began to rise, slowly at first, then accelerating rapidly over the subsequent decades. Over the whole 1936–2005 period, CEO pay follows a pattern that looks like what scholars call a *J-curve*. Alison Cowan's alarm over pay in 1992 came near the bottom of the J-curve's period of great acceleration: the current era of envy, hand-wringing, and collective anger over the bigger slices of the American economic pie extracted by CEOs was just beginning.

Those who rail against the rise in CEO pay—the hand-wringers and lynch mobs pointing to weak boards and inter-locked CEOs—don't really have a satisfactory explanation for the J-curve. Even if CEOs manage to pocket ill-gotten gains at shareholders' expense, it's hard to argue that companies are *less* carefully monitored than they were in 1975. We have more watchdogs such as The Corporate Library; new rules such as the Sarbanes-Oxley law passed in 2002, which puts more pressure on boards to pay attention to whether managers are doing their jobs; more disclosure requirements and more stringent rules about interlocks and other connections (companies can't get away with the boardroom back scratching that Cowan reported on in 1992); and of course we have the Internet, which allows dirty laundry to be broadcast freely to the masses. Yet CEO pay keeps rising.

The defenders of rising pay, including many CEOs themselves, also have some explaining to do. Are CEOs really so much smarter now than they were in 1950? Are their skills so much more valuable now than they were back then? Maybe. Between 1980 and 2005 the value of America's largest companies grew six times, so perhaps it's not unreasonable that bosses' pay grew sixfold as well—except that corporations experienced a similar growth spurt in the 1950s and '60s, when CEO pay remained flat.

Both groups are probably at least partly right, as unsatisfying as that answer may be. Nineteen seventy-five wasn't simply the year when executive pay began to rise. It's also when CEO compensation started becoming more and more sensitive to company (and hence CEO) performance. And as with the *level* of compensation, pay-for-performance really took off a decade later. It was in 1990 that HBS professors Michael Jensen and Kevin Murphy published a highly influential *Harvard Business Review* article that blasted boards for paying their CEOs "like bureaucrats." Jensen and Murphy argued that it was counterproductive to pay CEOs flat salaries largely unaffected by the ups and downs of the organizations they ran. What they needed was incentive pay that rewarded a job well done with a massive bonus, and that punished weak performers with a lump of coal or a pink slip. CEOs today don't just get paid a lot more than executives just below them in the org chart; their pay is also much more sensitive to overall company performance, reflecting their disproportionate impact on the bottom line.[26]

It's hard to say how much credit, or blame, Jensen and Murphy can take for the J-curve and the commensurate rise in pay-for-performance. They were either ahead of the curve, or they were echoing a shift in attitudes that was taking place in American boardrooms at the time. To get incentives strong enough—to the point where executives felt as if they personally had millions of dollars on the line—they naturally had to start heading up the J-curve.

Amid the gold rush to the top end of the corporate pay scale, it's easy to see how all sorts of outrageous payouts could have been rationalized to shareholders. While boards could sell the idea that CEO pay had to be linked to the performance of the company, in many cases the impeccable logic of pay-for-performance ended up serving the CEO's interests alone. In fact, Michael Jensen, the original high priest of performance pay himself, has been born again as a performance pay critic, penning essays with titles ranging from modestly revisionist, such as "CEO Incentives: It's Not How Much You Pay, but How," to more philosophical treatises on the failure of integrity in corporate America and beyond, such as "Integrity: A Positive Model That Incorporates the Normative Phenomena of Morality, Ethics, and Legality." Now even Jensen would admit that the people who think CEO pay has gotten out of hand probably have a point.

The Logic of Unintended Consequences

The often angry interchanges between the advocates and critics of high pay obscure the fact that there are reasons CEO pay may have risen that are neither sinister in origin nor optimal in design. For example, some recent scholars have pinned the blame on the seemingly innocuous and altogether common practice of bench-marking pay against what CEOs earn at other companies. It's a natural consideration for the board's compensation committee, which needs to provide an inducement to keep the CEO from leaving for greener pastures at other companies competing for his services.

How much is enough? It makes sense to see what competing firms—the ones that might try to lure your CEO away from his current job—are spending to reward and retain their leaders. That's where the CEO peer group comparison comes in. Who is the "right" peer? You probably want to pick someone running a company in the same industry, of similar size, of comparable profitability, and with similar experience (similar tenure at the firm, and so on). Depending on your industry, however, there might still be dozens of CEOs who meet these criteria. How do you decide who makes your list of comparables?

To make sure that compensation committees were staying honest in picking peers, regulators mandated in 2006 that peer groups be filed with the Securities and Exchange Commission. This allowed shareholders and watchdog groups to ensure that, say, Chevron's board didn't pick Disney's Eisner as a benchmark to inflate Watson's salary. It also provided financial economists Michael Faulkender and Jun Yang with an opportunity to compare the chosen peers with the peer might-have-beens, to see whether boards cherry-picked the comparison group in subtler ways. The researchers combed through the SEC filings of more than six hundred companies, recording the set of peer CEOs that informed executive compensation decisions. For each CEO, they also assembled their own group of peers based on their calculations of which other executives were most similar. A thoroughly compromised compensation committee would pick peer firms that were larger, more profitable, and otherwise more likely to have high-earning CEOs than their own. Yet Faulkender and Yang found that, by and large, there was enormous overlap between their list of peers and the ones actually chosen, illustrating that compensation committees were for the most part being "kept honest" in choosing pay benchmarks.[27]

Nonetheless, discretion in peer selection did have its benefits, at least for the CEOs. The peer CEOs chosen by compensation committees had total earnings that averaged nearly $850,000 more than those of the ignored potential peers found by the researchers. The authors also calculate that each dollar of extra pay among peer CEOs was used to justify an extra $0.50 in pay, so that the favorable selection of peers resulted in more than $400,000 extra for the CEO's pay. That $400,000 may not sound like a lot to a public accustomed to reading of hundred-million-dollar bonuses to Wall Street superstars. But relative to the average CEO, with earnings of around $6.5 million—still an exorbitant sum in historical terms—it represents a more than 5 percent pay hike.

More important, one executive's raise feeds into the pay hikes of others, as yet other companies will use the now 5 percent higher paycheck as a peer comparison next year. Add to the mix the fact that, every year, a few corporate leaders are awarded outsize paychecks that allow them to leapfrog their competitors' pay (perhaps because of an exceptionally weak board, threats of retirement, or other unusual circumstances) and become the new standard for pay comparisons, and it's easy to see how a few decades of favorable peer lists could snowball into the enormous incomes we're seeing today. In fact, according to the calculations of sociologists Tom DiPrete, Greg Eirich, and Matthew Pittinsky, the positive feedback loop and interrelatedness among

CEOs' pay could account for much of the recent rise in executive pay.[28]

Why do compensation committees err on the side of generosity in spending shareholders' dollars on CEO pay? Well, don't you want your circle of friends to be a little better than average? For board members who like to think they have an above-average CEO, this may translate into the choice of a relatively favorable pay package and a set of peers to match. Also, while boards may not be the CEO's lapdogs, they still have to face him or her at future meetings (or at the country club), so when given discretion in matters of pay, it's not surprising that the board may be predisposed to being bighearted in setting the boss's pay.

This explanation for runaway salaries in the corner office isn't going to sell a lot of newspapers. It lacks any insidious backroom conspiracy to spin into a story of intrigue. Yet for the very same reasons, it comes across as a more likely account for the rise in CEO pay. Compensation committees, and corporate boards more generally, are mostly comprised not of conscienceless scoundrels but of normal people who are doing their best to attract and retain leaders. And peer comparison is actually one useful way, albeit an imperfect one, of figuring out "what the market will bear" in setting CEO compensation. The same might be said of the larger debate around CEOs and the boards that evaluate and reward them—they possess mostly well-meaning intent that more than occasionally falls prey to human fallibility.

Getting Paid to Get Fired

The public's collective sense of outrage toward high-paid executives is never greater than when those executives get fired and

walk away under the shelter of enormous golden parachutes. Stan
O'Neal stepped down as Merrill Lynch CEO in 2007, amid ac-
cusations of creating a culture of reckless risk taking and pushing
Merrill to build its business of repackaging and reselling subprime loans. He left with a package worth over $160 million.
Bob Nardelli's golden handshake is one for the record book—
a $210 million gift for leaving Home Depot in 2007 after six
bad years of leadership that left the company with its lowest profits in a decade. Why should the pink slips of O'Neal, Nardelli,
and other failed leaders be accompanied by tens or hundreds
of millions in severance pay? This seemingly absurd system of
compensating CEOs for getting fired goes back to a perfectly reasonable attempt to get CEOs to create even more value for their
companies. The golden parachute was written into the employment contract of, appropriately enough, the CEO of an airline
company, TWA, in 1961. But the practice never really took off
until the merger wave of the 1980s was in full swing, when execs
started pondering whether it was smarter to seek out merger opportunities to make money for shareholders, or hold on to their
jobs instead. Mostly they opted for the latter (keeping their jobs)
by discouraging the advances of corporate suitors, often to the
detriment of the stock price.[29]

Creating incentives to motivate CEOs to seek out merger opportunities turned out to matter a lot, since one of the best ways
for corporate leaders to create value is to make the company a target for merger or acquisition. When larger orgs gobble up smaller
ones, it's usually at a premium to what the smaller orgs are worth
on their own, so shareholders (the owners of the org) get to cash
out at a big profit. But the combined firm needs only one boss, so
odds are one of the two CEOs in the merger is out of a job. Ironically, one of the most value-enhancing ways a CEO can spend his

time (shopping his company around for acquisition) also results in his getting fired. No CEO is going to pursue those options unless there's a financial upside to doing so.

Shareholders responded by providing CEOs with the escape valve that, the reasoning went, would encourage them to work in the long-term best interests of their companies. Looking back on that decade in 1988, Harvard Business School economist Michael Jensen (the same HBS professor who railed against boards for paying their CEOs like bureaucrats) wrote that, while there had been abuses of executive escape chutes—he notes, in particular, one company that packed golden parachutes for more than two hundred managers, thereby making it impossibly expensive for any buyer to take the company over—in general they created a lot of value for investors, who welcomed the takeover-motivating effects. Jensen also argued that what was good for CEOs' retirement accounts was also good for society in general, since it encouraged CEOs to open the door to corporate raiders, who stripped their purchases of waste and other inefficiencies to produce more valuable companies.[30] By this line of reasoning, golden parachutes make the world a better place by making companies more efficient. That can be hard to swallow.

Why don't regular employees get paid to get fired? CEOs are doing their jobs right only if once in a while it gets them fired, which isn't the case for lower-level employees. This reminds us of another peculiarity of the trade-offs in getting incentives right. If the contract says you get a big bonus check if you lose your job when the company is taken over, that works to align CEO incentives with those of shareholders, but it also means that executives whose ineptitude *also* makes their companies ripe for takeover will be rewarded for their incompetence. And, of course, when we see pay-for-incompetence, we shake our heads at the corruption and injustice of corporate America, rather than thinking of it as an unfortunate side effect of generally well-designed incentives.

Once you start breaking down executive privilege into its various components to try to understand why it exists, it's possible to see the logic of why CEOs get all sorts of perks. The modern poster child of executive excess, the corporate jet, is surely an unnecessary luxury for many corporate leaders—that's why when companies are taken over by cost-cutting private equity investors, the jets are often the first thing to go. But they don't get rid of private fleets altogether. Given that the job of a CEO is all about face-to-face meetings, many spend their days on the road, traveling among the company's various locales, and making sales calls to customers and investors. If their time truly is so valuable, what's an extra million or so to ensure that they're not stuck in airport security lines or otherwise kept from focusing on company business?

This efficiency-minded view of the corporate jet is borne out in a study by Raghuram Rajan and Julie Wulf. Rajan and Wulf show that companies headquartered outside major metropolitan areas are more likely to have their own private planes. For executives at these companies, a jet saves them from the extra hassles and layovers involved in flying to and from the out-of-the-way places where the company is based. The headquarters location is itself the result of trade-offs—cheap land and low labor costs weighed against the extra costs (e.g., corporate jets) of isolation. And what of chauffeur-driven limos? A cheap way of maximizing work time while stuck in traffic. The same Rajan-Wulf study found that execs in densely packed urban areas, where you're likely to encounter traffic jams during a morning commute, were much more likely to get the chauffeur perk.[31]

"I Could Do That!"

With the financial system a mess in 2009, the Obama administration proposed limiting pay to $500,000 for banking CEOs. This triggered an entirely predictable uproar from the finance industry. Where would we find the talent needed to run America's largest banks for such a paltry sum? It probably wasn't even enough to cover the mortgage payments of most Wall Street bankers, who themselves would soon be part of the default and foreclosure problem, if we weren't careful. What would become of these pillars of commerce without the best and brightest running the show?

Of course, many would be happy to take a job that came with a salary that would put its recipient within the top 1 percent of U.S. household incomes. And as to the talent question, after the previous years' debacle, many thought to themselves, "I could do that!" If running a bank or any other corporation is just a matter of sitting through meetings and asking a few of the right questions ("You made loans to *whom*?" "*How* exactly would that work?"), then these naysayers might have a point. Some investors did ask such questions, and walked away from the financial crisis of 2008 with millions or billions more.[32]

Did CEOs know anything about the loans that were squirreled away inside the collateralized debt obligations (CDOs), credit-default swaps (CDS), and other arcane instruments their companies invested in on borrowed money? One assumes not, since these loans turned out to be valueless. They delegated that task, and didn't ask the right questions, or at least not enough of them. They bought into the money-for-nothing storyline of ever-increasing housing prices that represented either an endless economic boom or a bubble soon to burst.

But while business is booming, who has the courage to explain to seize-the-day investors why you're taking a pass on what seems like the most profitable financial innovation in history? Citigroup CEO Charles Prince articulated this unspeakable reality (also an expression of Wall Street's reckless disregard for risk) just before losing his job in 2007: "As long as the music is playing, you've got to get up and dance. We're still dancing." And you have to compare—CEOs who were more vigilant saved their shareholders from the worst of the crisis. Chuck Prince's Citigroup was worth a tenth of its precrisis highs in 2010. Morgan Stanley was worth little more than a third. JPMorgan Chase took a relatively modest haircut, falling around 20 percent from the insane heights it reached amid the housing boom. Many attribute Morgan's performance—outstanding, relatively speaking—to the vigilance and leadership of Jamie Dimon, who may have been the only top finance CEO to drill down into the dubious subprime content of his company's investments. You would have paid a lot in 2008 to have your bank run by someone who really understood his business, such as Jamie Dimon. (Even Dimon has had his occasional epic blunder—as when JPMorgan took a multibillion-dollar loss on bad trades in the spring of 2012, a mistake that nearly cost Dimon his job.)

Before joining the shareholder activists and lynch mobs calling for CEOs to be held accountable and stripped of their obvious excesses, it's worth pausing to think about why those perks existed in the first place. From the corporate jet to the golden handshake, they were all designed with the intention of making CEOs maximize shareholder profits. If it appears excessive and undeserved, also remember that it might not be the case that you really *could* do that.

CHAPTER 7

The Economics of Org Culture

O N SEPTEMBER 7, 2009, a storm cloud of crisis hung over the normally sunny island nation of Samoa. Sose Annandale, owner of the Sinalei Reef Resort and Spa, warned, "A major disaster looms." Paul Caffarelli, manager of the Siufaga Resort, worried about the safety of his guests. "I'm seriously considering closing the resort," said Caffarelli, "because I'd rather not have income than deal with the damage." Another islander, Toleafoa Toailoa, described the coming events as "a nightmare."[1]

What was this momentous event that would bring death and destruction raining down on 180,000 Samoans? Tsunami? Civil war?

At six in the morning on September 8, 2009, with sirens blaring, church bells ringing, and horns honking, Samoa would switch from driving on the right side of the road to driving on the left.

Why did Samoans drive on the right in the first place? It was nothing more than an accident of history, the result of German colonization at the beginning of the twentieth century. If the British Empire had extended to Samoa, as it had to the island's nearest neighbors, they would have driven on the left as well. But through historical happenstance, they didn't.

Samoa would have been better off with left-handed cars and roads that would have put them in sync with their South Pacific neighbors, making it easier and cheaper to import cars, for instance. Yet until September 8, 2009, the Samoans persisted in their right-handed ways. They'd developed a system of laws, habits, and customs to accommodate this one minor bit of local culture—what economists would call an *equilibrium*—and if you took many islanders at their word, the seemingly trivial task of changing that culture was going to prove to be very difficult indeed.

An Ill-Defined Culture

Culture is fiendishly difficult to define. It's the expectation that everyone will wear jeans and T-shirts to the office at Silicon Valley start-ups. Show up in a jacket and tie, and you'd better be prepared for both questions and ridicule. At a blue-chip law firm, it's the opposite. But culture goes beyond superficial matters such as office dress code or habit. It's a sense of loyalty that makes some people work long hours at low pay, a belief in the glories of capitalism that motivates others to work in the service of the almighty dollar, and the force that compels a marine to risk his life for God and country.

Many economists look down their noses at the very notion of culture, and many scholars from other disciplines would question whether economics is up to the task of examining the topic at all. Yet economists' knack for stripping every aspect of human existence, culture included, down to its bare, utilitarian essentials turns out to be helpful in figuring out what org culture is and how it works.

Economists define org culture, in part, as what tells us how to behave when we can't turn to a formal contract or set of rules for guidance.[2] It's part coordination and part conscience, ensuring that we do the right thing, organizationally speaking—directing people to conform to a set of norms and behaviors that benefit the group as a whole. Culture serves as another lever for making sure people do their jobs and work well with others, something that orgs can rely on when the blunt instrument of incentives doesn't work or the reach of rules or surveillance is limited. Twinges of guilt at stealing from the supply closet and a norm of working till ten each night, for example, are workplace cultures that make employees do the right thing without the promise of cash bonuses or the threat of dismissal. And while there was a law in Samoa that told islanders to drive on the right, it wasn't really needed. In its absence, Samoans would have adopted a convention of always driving on one side of the road or the other to avoid needless collisions. That's the nature of an equilibrium: everything in perfect balance.

But out of this simple economic definition come more questions than answers. And much of the time, it's hard to square the cultures we observe with some economic ideal of pure efficiency. As Leo Tolstoy wrote, "Every unhappy family is unhappy in its own way." As far as culture is concerned, each org risks finding its own, perfectly balanced way of being dysfunctional.

The Economic Science of Culture

The economic science of org culture plays out not in cubicles or office complexes but within the confines of computer labs, where researchers tweak and manipulate lab cultures in much the same way geneticists study the behavior and evolution of fruit flies. Instead of rows of microscopes and Bunsen burners, these labs are made up of small cubicles, each one fitted with a computer workstation. Medical scientists seed Petri dishes with rudimentary life forms and watch their rapid-fire evolution over a matter of months. Economists Roberto Weber and Colin Camerer similarly developed a way of fast-tracking cultural evolution, and doing it in the sterile, well-controlled environment of a computer lab at Carnegie Mellon University, in an experiment that aimed to understand what happens when cultures collide.[3]

Each participant in their experiment viewed a matrix of sixteen office scenes on a computer screen. The participants were randomly paired up and put in the roles of "manager" and "employee." Managers' screens highlighted and numbered eight of the pictures. Their job was to communicate to the employee, via instant messaging, the eight highlighted scenes in order. For each one, the employee had to identify the picture the manager was describing. Each pair repeated the task twenty times, and the partners were paid at the end of the experiment based on their completion times across all rounds.

What Camerer and Weber had in mind as "culture" was the written shorthand that sprang up in each pair that helped them identify pictures more quickly and accurately as their relationship progressed and their shared understanding of the pictures deepened and expanded. They give the example of one manager who, in the first round, describes a picture as "The one with three people: two men and one woman. The woman is sitting on the left. They're all looking at two computers that look like they have some PowerPoint graphs or charts. The two men are wearing ties and the woman has short, blond hair. One guy is pointing at one of the charts." A few rounds later, the description is abbreviated to "PowerPoint." The partners took just a few IM exchanges to develop a common understanding of the shorthand's meaning.

In the first round of play, it took an average pair a bit more than four minutes to identify the eight pictures. After ten rounds, the time was down to just over a minute; after twenty rounds an average group took less than fifty seconds.

The experimenters, in sorting through the communications, noticed that their two-person cultures also drew on a wider set of shared experiences, much as the Tokyo offices of Toyota and Honda share a common Japanese set of norms, despite some differences in corporate cultures between the two firms. One pair started describing a picture simply as "Uday Rao," because a person in the scene resembled a professor, Uday Rao, who taught a class both were taking. Without this shared background, they might have struggled more to find a common language.

Each group spent a little time working out a method that worked for them and then stuck to it, changing only when pressured to do so. That's a pretty fair description of the haphazard way cultures evolve, and how they get stuck in holding patterns.

Consider the accident of how three quarters of the world's population came to drive on the right. To understand how we got here, you have to start with an explanation of why traffic used to travel on the left, a norm that goes back to the right-handedness of most humans. According to one theory, back in the days when men rode horses and never left their castles without a weapon at arm's reach, they carried their swords in left-sided scabbards for easy drawing by right-handed knights. Wearing swords on the left helped ensure the development of a left-sided riding norm, since passing horsemen didn't want to bump scabbards. (It was also useful to have your fighting hand closer to passing traffic, in the event of a disagreement.) Right-handed riders also found it easier to mount and dismount on the left, and a left-riding rule allowed them to do so out of the stream of horse traffic. By the same reasoning, British coachmen sat on the right side of their coaches to best position themselves to draw their swords at oncoming bandits.

Why the switch to the right side of the road? According to a 1935 *Popular Science* article, it's because drivers in continental Europe didn't sit in their coaches but up front on one of their horses, the postilion system of driving. Sitting on the left horse allowed right-handed riders to wield their whips to spur on either of the two coach-pulling horses. American coachmen similarly rode on horseback, which accounts for the right-sided norm in the New World.[4]

The rest, as they say, is history. We don't get around in wagons anymore, but it's costly to switch sides, so we still drive on the right, and so does most of Europe. The few holdouts switched to driving on the right because it's too costly to be the odd country out when your citizens drive across borders. Portugal switched in 1928, while Sweden and Iceland held out till the late 1960s. Conquering armies took care of those who didn't change willingly. As Hitler's troops marched through Austria and Hungary, they left behind right-driving rules in their wake. German conquests are also responsible for Samoa's right-sided norm, leaving that country incompatible with its British-colonized neighbors, New Zealand and Australia.

Right-handed knights, riding in coaches versus wagons, Western imperial ambitions—now ancient history—together account for Samoans driving on the right in 2009, just as we can explain, in retrospect, how a pair of Carnegie Mellon students got settled into referring to one particular scene as "Uday Rao." Groups settle into different routines that become a matter of self-reinforcing habit over time. That's exactly what Camerer and Weber produced in their lab.

Getting Past the Origins of Culture

For Camerer and Weber, though, the formation of these micro-cultures was merely a means to an end. The two researchers had the ultimate objective of looking at what happens when cultures collide as in, say, a corporate merger. In the lab, cultural collision was engineered by adding a second employee under each manager, who was then required to describe the eight assigned scenes to his two underlings simultaneously. Managers were paid based on the average speed of their two charges, so most stuck to their "PowerPoint" and "Uday Rao" shorthands to communicate with their old partners.

Not surprisingly, reliance on the old culture proved to be confusing to the new hires, who weren't aware of the underlying meaning of the shorthand. In the case of Uday Rao, the misunderstanding was amplified by the fact that, unlike the members of the original team, the new employee wasn't in Professor Rao's class. The manager may as well have been communicating with his new employee in a foreign language; and to some extent, he was.

In one frustrated exchange, a manager tried to describe a scene that has coffee mugs on a table in the foreground and a cupboard at the back. He had come to use the shorthand "coffee mugs" during the first stage of the experiment to describe the picture. But there were coffee mugs in other pictures, too, thus confusing his new employee, who had referred to the picture as "cupboard in back" with his pre-merger partner. After a minute or so, they settled on what turned out to be the correct "coffee mug" scene, and to verify that they were focused on the same picture, the employee asked whether there was a cupboard in the back. Her manager shot back, "I don't know. Just look for the coffee mugs!" In another exchange, a new employee angrily interrupted a manager's description with "Stop telling me what they're wearing and just tell me how many people are in the picture!"

Inevitably, after a while, the three-person groups came up with picture descriptors they all understood. An additional half-dozen rounds was all most teams needed to get back under a minute to identify the eight scenes. Yet it was harder to adjust than participants expected. More than three quarters predicted a more modest effect of the merger on performance.

And despite the eventual adjustment to the new three-person "firms," simmering resentment remained. In a post-experiment questionnaire the original employees consistently rated the manager as better at his or her job than did the new employees. The feeling was mutual. Managers rated the new employee as less competent than his or her original partners. This was true *even though* everyone recognized that neither was to blame. In fact, the new employee's job was rated as harder by all members of the team.

Camerer and Weber's lab experiment provides a stark illustration of just how important it is that we have a shared culture in the first place. Take it away, and employees end up in standoffs defined by misperception and recrimination.

In this case, changed circumstances were thrust upon participants by experimenters who could effectively play god within
the confines of the Carnegie Mellon computer lab. But one can
easily imagine that without this external pressure, teams would
have kept to their insular and familiar communities. And when
the logic of uniting does bring two cultures together, the whole
may nonetheless fail to add up to the sum of its parts. Corporate
empire builders, dreaming of cost synergies, shared strengths and
capabilities, and other "technical" rationales for mergers, would
do well to think of the unanticipated challenges of Carnegie Mellon undergrads in adapting to the simplest of cultural collisions
imaginable.

Sustaining Good Cultures

One lesson from Camerer and Weber's experiment is how easy
it is to slip into a culture of distrust rooted in misperception,
even in a case where everyone in the group has exactly the same
objective. Where there's office intrigue—complete with competing interests, hidden agendas, and other sources of conflict—it's
a wonder things don't always degenerate into backstabbing and
suspicion. Yet companies do somehow maintain healthy cultures
of trust and reciprocity.

One example is the Boston Consulting Group, number two
on *Fortune*'s list of 100 Best Companies to Work For in 2012.
A new recruit to BCG worries relatively little about whether he'll
get stuck with an exploitative supervisor. BCG employees know
they'll work long hours and live out of hotel rooms while assigned to out-of-town projects for weeks at a time. But they also
know they'll receive fair attribution and reward for their accom-

plishments. Don't take *Fortune*'s word for it; you can check out employees' reviews on company rating websites such as glassdoor .com. These days, word travels much faster, and far beyond the water cooler.

Other companies have equally well-established cultures of exploitation. They got as far as mistrust and anger and decided to stay there. Anyone who has read *Liar's Poker*, Michael Lewis's classic account of his two-year stint as a Salomon Brothers bond trader, knows that you'd be crazy to trust bosses, coworkers, or anyone else if your new job were at Salomon. (Lewis on career development at Salomon: "to get the best job, you had to weather the most abuse"; on dealing with colleagues: "lift weights or learn karate.") Enlightened self-interest isn't going to help much when first-year analysts come in expecting to get screwed. They aren't going to put themselves out on a limb to help their bosses, so what's to be gained from *not* exploiting them? It's impossible for any individual to escape the bad equilibrium of a poisoned culture.

Clearly, prospective hires who valued a nurturing workplace—the ones who might be fair-minded bosses themselves when promoted—looked elsewhere for employment. Not only do reputations inform what employees do on the first day on the job, but they also help make sure that the right kinds of employees match themselves to the company that suits their sensibilities.

Yet BCG would be ill-advised to stand idly by expecting its kinder, gentler culture to be self-perpetuating. Sadly, the "good" BCG culture is much more fragile than the backstabbing free-for-all of 1980s-era Salomon Brothers, in much the same way that an individual's reputation is only as good as yesterday's behavior. Exploit a few employees, and glassdoor.com and its ilk will take care of the rest.

How, then, can organizations that prize good behavior ensure that employees sustain it?

Lessons from Nuclear War

Game theory, the field of economics that tries to model how people behave when put in positions of conflict or cooperation, provides a useful tool for thinking through how to maintain a good org culture.[5] The field came to public prominence with the success of the movie *A Beautiful Mind*, but as a mathematical discipline it goes back to the eighteenth century. Analyzing strategic interactions, after all, has a long history.

But it took the onset of the Cold War to really bring game theory into the modern age, when economists and mathematicians used it to analyze strategic military interactions such as long-distance bombing campaigns, jet fighter pursuit, and deterrence by mutually assured destruction (MAD). The mathematical tools developed to figure out how to deal with a nuclear USSR are now applied by economists to explain Walmart's price wars with Amazon, to develop auction bidding strategies (and to design better auctions), and even to help us to make sense of office politics.

Imagine you show up for your first day of work and your new boss asks you to develop a presentation for the CEO—for the next morning. Is it worth pulling an all-nighter for this person you've just met? Do you expect appropriate attribution and reward for your efforts? Having completed the job and handed off the fruits of your labor, what's to keep the boss from taking credit for your words and presentation?

It's a leap of faith, but one that might ultimately work in the best interests of both parties. If you expect the boss to be exploitative, you won't put your best work into the job. He'll be embarrassed in front of his boss; so will you. From his perspective, if he doesn't expect effort above and beyond what he can wheedle out of you by hovering near your desk, then he may as well at least take full credit, fairly or not, for whatever is produced. In this workplace culture, bosses don't expect high-quality work, employees expect to get screwed by their bosses and so slack off, and both sides validate each other's expectations with their actions.

To escape from this bad equilibrium, good bosses need to make a convincing case that they'll treat others fairly. Unfortunately you, the new recruit, have to put in your all-nighter before finding out whether the boss's promises are sincere or just cheap talk.

What might keep even the coldest and most calculating of bosses honest? In a "one-shot" interaction, absolutely nothing. But your relationship with your new manager is more akin to what game theorists call a *repeated game*, where boss and employee are destined to play out the give-and-take of working together for days, months, or even years to come. A good boss develops a reputation for "playing nice"—giving generous attribution when called for, letting the staff go home early on Friday afternoon if they've spent all night on Thursday prepping for a presentation, bringing in dinner Thursday evening to boost morale. In turn, he attracts loyal employees, who reciprocate by trusting him and working hard on his behalf. The fair boss doesn't have to be a fair-minded person, but he'll behave as if he were one, motivated by the long-term benefits of give-and-take relationships with his employees. (But only so long as the upside outweighs the one-time gain from exploiting those around him. The difference between fair bosses and those masquerading as fair will come out the day he starts thinking about looking for a new job.)

At the same time, this trust is fragile, potentially undermined by a single act of managerial bullying or opportunism. Those who feel the sting of injustice aren't going to keep quiet about it. Trust thus broken is hard to mend, making it very hard to rehabilitate a reputation that's flipped from good to bad.

This view of trust—quick to disintegrate and difficult to restore—is the result of people using what economists call *trigger strategies* to maintain cooperative relationships. For a boss and his subordinates, cooperation can be sustained because both sides know that even the hint of exploitation will trigger a lapse into suspicion and distrust, which is harmful to everyone. All parties refrain from deploying bad behavior that may end up leading to mutually assured destruction.

None of this does much to help the freshly minted MBA who hasn't yet had a chance to develop a reputation as a boss, good or bad. What allows him to start off on the right foot is that org cultures are much larger than any one individual, and they color what's expected from entire organizations. A company-wide culture of give-and-take is maintained by the same trigger strategy threat, where opportunism by anyone can lead to systemic cultural collapse. Everyone has an incentive to make sure this doesn't happen—because who wants to be stuck in a coldhearted, backstabbing culture?

Sweet Revenge

The problem with triggers (maintaining office détente using game theory) is that they easily lead to an org where everyone treads lightly, waiting for someone to pull the trigger, ironically building a culture where everyone behaves but no one invests deeply in relationships that make them vulnerable to exploitation. The United States and the Soviet Union never had what we might call warm relations, even though a "hot" war never broke out.

Bosses and coworkers, who collectively benefit from a kinder, gentler, more cooperative workplace, need to ensure that it's costly for any bad apples to show their true, self-serving colors. It's not sufficient merely to distrust those who are outed as Machiavellian. They weren't kept honest by the upside of a good culture to begin with. They need to be caught and punished, lest the entire company degenerate into a vicious circle of distrust and recrimination. The bigger the punishment, the better. This could help explain why some companies make such emphatic statements about their no-asshole policies—for example, firing otherwise highly productive workers who disrupt the norms of a place.[6]

Even better might be to leave retribution to coworkers and peers. Not many organizations would proudly advertise as a strength their collective vindictiveness against violators of the unwritten rules of the workplace. ("Come work for us! If you screw up, everyone will come down on you like a ton of bricks!") Yet revenge is useful for maintaining an environment of cooperation and sacrifice. It's helpful to recognize the long-term benefits from collaboration, sure, but it's even better if anyone contemplating a departure from the norm sees how rule breakers are mercilessly and swiftly punished.

The problem with revenge, though, is that it takes effort. And it's much easier to let someone else take care of it. Why waste your time for nothing in return when you can leave the dirty

work to others? Why risk retaliation, or damaging your own reputation, in the process of taking down a coworker who has done
wrong?

It's the kind of question that would occur only to an economist. You don't go about settling scores in hope of financial
reward or promotion. We humans are vindictive creatures who
seek revenge for the sheer pleasure of it. The Roman poet Juvenal
had it right: "Revenge is the weak pleasure of a little and narrow
mind"—but, perhaps fortunately for our purposes, this describes
most of us.

A classic economic experiment sheds some light on this venge-
ful side of humanity. Behavioral economists Ernst Fehr and
Simon Gächter ran a lab study that shows exactly how much we
value retribution.[7] Their experiment grouped students from the
University of Zurich at random into four-person teams to play a
"public goods game with punishment." Each team member was
given twenty tokens (to be converted into Swiss francs at the end
of the experiment), which he could either keep for himself or
contribute to the common pool of team funds. For every token
contributed to the fund, Fehr and Gächter returned 1.6 tokens
to be shared equally among the group. That's the "public goods"
aspect to the game: by sacrificing tokens, individuals made the
group better off. In fact, the way to maximize the tokens the
team earns is to have everyone contribute everything to the public
pool.

But there's a tension between what's good for the group and
what's best for the individual. For each token contributed, you
get only 0.4 tokens back (the other 1.2 go to the other team
members). Why not let the other three donate *their* tokens, and
keep your twenty for yourself?

When everyone thinks this way, we find ourselves back in the every-player-for-himself culture of Salomon Brothers. Indeed, Fehr and Gächter found that their students quickly converged on this Wall Street culture after a few rounds of play. Some participants initially tried to instill a norm of contributing to the common pool, but after three or four rounds they grew frustrated with their uncooperative teammates, and average contributions dropped to nearly zero.

That's where the punishment comes in. In a variant on the original game, the students were also given the option of subtracting tokens from their teammates, after observing how much they'd contributed to the team's fund. But punishment didn't come cheap. For each punishment "point" assigned to another team member, the punisher lost one or more tokens himself. Participants nonetheless chose to mete out punishment to anyone giving less than others in the group. This had the virtuous effect of quickly bullying selfish teammates into upping their contributions: after a few rounds of punishment, most participants, fearing retribution, contributed their full twenty tokens to the common pool. The teams didn't need to waste tokens on getting revenge. The mere threat of it was enough to keep everyone honest.[8] Remember this the next time you and your coworkers plan for your end-of-the-year performance review.

Getting More Than You Paid For

It's not just vengeance and retribution that compel humans to give up financial gain for emotional satisfaction. Sometimes people *do* act nice just because it's the right thing to do. Even economists recognize this.

But this isn't the case, it would seem, for Massey Energy, the now-defunct mining company behind the Upper Big Branch coal mine disaster of 2010. It's hard to view the leadership of Massey Energy through any lens beyond profit maximization at any cost. Twenty-nine miners were killed in an explosion at the mine, which had accumulated more than five hundred citations the preceding year from the Mine Safety and Health Administration, two hundred of them for "significant and substantial" violations considered "reasonably likely to result in a reasonably serious injury or illness."

Yet Massey's leadership seemed to want people to think it had a vision beyond the bottom line. In 2009 the company published an ill-timed inaugural corporate social responsibility report, which provided "an overview of our long-standing tradition of stewardship of our most important resources: Our people and our planet."[9]

There's something nearly beyond belief about a company such as Massey Energy presenting itself as a noble steward of Appalachian forests and streams, caring for its workers and community as if they were family, given the lawsuits against the company for poisoning West Virginia's drinking water, and its long and much-publicized history of poor safety practices. The mystery isn't why Massey had such a worker-hostile culture in the first place. Treating runoff from open-pit mines is expensive, as are practices that prevent workplace injuries, which also slow down the pace of coal extraction. Maximizing profit can easily and inexorably lead to safety violations. A management culture of profit-at-all-costs certainly keeps shareholders and profit-sharing executives happy with their investments and bonuses.[10] But why would Massey even bother to pretend to care?

Because it can be cheaper to get workers to put in long hours motivated by a desire to help their coworkers than by issuing overtime checks. Furthermore, if work requires collaboration, it makes life easier if employees value cooperation for its own sake. So if Massey CEO Don Blankenship thought he could get his workers to buy into an image of Massey as a kinder and gentler company, it could be yet another lever for increasing profits.

Odds are that Massey's workers never marched off into the coal mines singing merrily like the Seven Dwarfs. But a company such as Ben and Jerry's, with a long history of corporate charity and do-gooding, might get its servers to scoop a little bit faster believing they're serving a higher purpose.

If you're skeptical that concerns beyond self-interest matter to people, don't take our word for it. Try the following experiment: take a random person off the street, put him in a windowless lab, and give him ten dollars to split (or not) with a random, anonymous stranger. While there's admittedly a high probability he'll keep the whole thing for himself, there's also a very good chance he'll divide it evenly, handing off five dollars to someone he'll never, ever meet.

This so-called dictator game (the person tasked with dividing the pie is the dictator) has been repeated endlessly in experiments around the world, with subjects ranging from Cal Tech computer geeks to seminomadic Kenyan herdsmen. The findings from these cross-cultural dictator experiments seem to reveal a universal human sharing instinct: when made dictator, many people choose to divide the pie fifty-fifty.[11]

The extent to which people make sacrifices in lab experiments for the good of others turns out to be remarkably malleable. When subjects participate in a simple two-person public goods game like the one played by Zurich students, they're twice as likely to cooperate with one another if you tell them it's the "Community Game" as when they're told it's the "Wall Street

Game." Exactly the same game, but a different cue as to the culture they're meant to conform to.

It's clearly in the org's interest to cue up the kind of culture that's going to encourage people to work together to the org's benefit. This may be why supposedly profit-maximizing companies such as Massey attempt to evoke dewy-eyed emotions in what they put on their corporate websites and in their company mission statements. Are corporations truly nurturing entities that care mainly about saving the planet and making children smile? Maybe some of them are. By convincing its staff and customers that the company doesn't just serve the interests of shareholders but has some higher calling, a company may well be tapping into the same public-minded sentiments that make people give to charity, and may compel random strangers to be generous in dictator game experiments. The org challenge is to convert group identity into higher profits.

This raises the question of just how much unpaid work and loyalty a company gets by creating a sense of greater purpose. Some hint of it comes from comparing the earnings of employees at not-for-profit charities and those at for-profit corporations. People work for charities because they want to heal the sick, feed and clothe the poor, or save rainforests from clear-cutting. Often they'll take a cut in pay to do so.

By estimating just how much less compensation the same kind of professionals in the nonprofit sector are willing to take relative to their private-sector counterparts, you can get a sense of how much a "higher purpose" is actually worth. Both for-profits and nonprofits need accountants, IT experts, and clerical personnel—similar employees often with near-identical qualifications. If a chartered public accountant with a dozen years' experience earns half as much minding the books at Save the Children as a similarly experienced CPA working at P&G, perhaps P&G could get its accountants to work twice as hard (or cut their salaries in half), if only they could be convinced that the social value of P&G's mission was on par with that of Save the Children.

Labor economists have tried to calculate this "compensating wage differential" (the amount of money that compensates for taking a less satisfying job) between nonprofits and for-profits. The estimates range anywhere from 20 percent to more than 50 percent—in other words, a lot of free labor and motivation if you can just get the messaging right.

Ben and Jerry's, and maybe even Massey, may have been on to something after all.

No *I* in *Team*

The most powerful force that compels individuals to take one for the team isn't so much charity as a sense of loyalty to the group. What group? It may not matter that much: the color of your T-shirt, the make of the car you drive, even whether or not you estimate a similar number of dots on a page.

This was the finding of a series of pioneering experiments conducted in the 1970s by social psychologist Henri Tajfel, who demonstrated just how easy it is to get human beings to form group allegiances and loyalties. In one study, Tajfel had subjects estimate the number of dots on a screen, and told them they'd be divided into teams based on whether they overestimated or underestimated the actual number of dots. In reality, they were grouped randomly. Each subject was informed of his "team," then escorted to a separate cubicle and told to give other subjects "rewards" and "penalties" that would be translated into payments at the end of the experiment. As bizarre as it sounds, the low-dot subjects handed out rewards to other "low-dotters" and punished those who were different from themselves on the basis of nothing more than the number of dots they thought they'd seen on a computer screen. Tajfel coined the term "minimal group paradigm" to describe the tiny nudge that's required to form group identities.[12]

If it's possible to generate a sense of togetherness based on dot-counting—or even less: just assigning individuals to different colors will suffice to create blue-team loyalty and red-team loyalty—how hard can it be to persuade employees to identify with the place they spend at least half their waking hours? Not very.

But it's worth noting that "we're in this together" can mean working together for or against the org. For example, a study of farm workers in England found that when workers in a group were paid based on how much each employee picked relative to the others, everyone harvested at a slower rate. The slowdown was greatest when the team of pickers was made up of friends, who were best able to collude against their employer. (In the first part of the experiment, the workers were picking a fruit that grew low to the ground, such as strawberries. When the workers switched to harvesting a crop that grew on bushes that grew to a height such that they couldn't keep tabs on one another's efforts, the harvest rate immediately picked up. It seemed that friends could be trusted only if kept in sight.)

If that's where togetherness takes us, the org may be better off with the largely value-free workplace ethic that Lewis encountered at Salomon.

Of course, Tajfel required only the most modest of sacrifices for his subjects. Minimal group identity may be enough to shift a few dollars here or there to those of our own kind. In organizations where there may come a time when it's required, literally or metaphorically, to jump on a grenade for the sake of the group, identity formation may be cultivated through intensive indoctrination that borders on cultlike brainwashing.

The army is a curious case, if we think of rules and culture as substituting for one another as forms of motivation. Life in the military is bounded by rules too numerous to mention, rules that border on the nonsensical. The consequences of insubordination even during peacetime are severe: dishonorable discharge, loss of pay and/or rank, and confinement.[13] It's all necessary for an immense operation with lots of interconnected parts to stay synchronized, where the consequences of miscommunication are the downing of friendly helicopters or the stranding of fighting units amid enemy fire.

But coordination can take you only so far when part of the job requires putting your life on the line for the good of the platoon. In the heat of battle, when performance is valued most, jumping on a grenade can't be mandated by army regulation, nor is it done with the expectation of future rewards, financial or otherwise.[14] It's a matter of honor, born of the army culture of sacrifice.

It takes the indoctrination and complete immersion of boot camp and beyond to convert raw recruits into honor-bound soldiers who will identify so strongly with the army and its code that they'll die for them.

It's no wonder companies invest in team-building exercises, despite the eye rolling they induce among employees. Even if no one is literally going to take a bullet to boost next month's sales numbers, it may help to motivate everyone to work that little bit harder to close a deal for the sake of the team.

Leading Change

Culture is useful in precisely those situations where there's more than one way groups can "decide" to do things, such as driving on the left or right side of the road. Even if we're all made better off by switching all at once to the new custom or norm, each individual remains jointly bound to the old way of doing things. Stepping out of line means head-on collision with the dominant culture. We can't change our ways one person at a time. What's required is public statements from someone whose opinion we respect—and even more important, someone whose opinion we know *everyone else* respects—to point us in the same new direction. But culture tends to be squishy, which makes it harder for leaders even to define the change they're trying to get people to follow.

Consider this example from Robert Gibbons and Rebecca Henderson, two organizational economists, about Merck, a pharmaceutical company that wishes to become more research-focused and tries to attract freshly minted PhD scientists with the promise that their jobs will be "almost like at a university lab." The hope is that this will allow Merck, with an empty pipeline of new products, to attract the very best and brightest young scientists, ones who are motivated by curiosity rather than paychecks, and who are also more likely to lay the scientific foundations for developing the next wave of blockbuster drugs.

For aspiring scientists, the decision between academic jobs and joining a corporate bureaucracy hinges critically on the meaning of *almost*. The company never pretends to be *exactly* like a university. It's set up to make money for shareholders, so it can't always indulge itself in the kind of knowledge-for-knowledge's-sake exploration as an academic setting. Yet it is this freedom in pursuit of innovation that it needs in order to develop new ideas.[15]

No contract can clearly delineate the line that's drawn between these sometimes competing considerations. If you can't contractually define *almost*, what can organizations and those leading them do to reassure their research staff that they'll have the autonomy to pursue scientific discoveries? Current and future employees instead learn the definition of *almost* through stories and anecdotes that circulate within the org and beyond. Culture is learned through direct experience and stories, not rule books or style manuals.

Many of the stories that form the backbone of organizational culture sometimes feel manufactured—and they may very well be—to clarify the extremes to which an organization will go to back up its value and culture statements with tangible action. Cultures of customer orientation are explained through accounts of employees going to insane lengths to satisfy insane customer demands. Clothing retailer Nordstrom, for example, corroborates its stated policy of outstanding customer service with celebrated anecdotes about eager-to-please "Nordies," such as one who gift-wrapped clothes bought at Macy's, and another who cheerfully provided a refund on tire chains, though Nordstrom has never sold automotive accessories of any kind.[16] These customer-centric employees were presumably lavished with praise and possibly promotion, further reinforcing the sense of what's valued at the company.

In an org that wants to change, though, the challenge is for the leader to discuss what the new culture ought to be and then to put money where his or her mouth is—demonstrating to everyone just how serious the org is about the change. Does "almost" at a pharmaceutical company mean that scientists can set their own hours or go to conferences at will, just like an academic department? Then let's see the HR practices and budget to accommodate those practices.

Leaders may even want to engineer a crisis so they can show what's truly valued by the company. It's easy to turn down inappropriate customers when business is good. But only the truly committed will say, "Thanks, but we're not interested in your money," when teetering on the edge of bankruptcy. Bob Sutton, a Stanford University psychologist, gives the example of the Van Aartrijk Group, a small marketing strategy firm, which has an explicit "No Assholes Policy" for both employees and customers. Founder Peter van Aartrijk recounts a story from the company's early days, of a client CEO who chewed out a Van Aartrijk tech guy for a PowerPoint malfunction. Van Aartrijk swallowed hard and told the customer the company didn't want to take on more work. He lost a lucrative account, but also made it clear that he really meant it when he said he wanted to keep assholes away from his young firm.[17]

It's what Gibbons describes as "nearly going off the rails." You don't really know the depths of commitment to a principle until the organization confronts life-and-death circumstances.

So for changing culture, leadership matters—or, to turn it around, shaping culture may be the very definition of leadership. Once you get beyond tautological descriptions (from the Merriam-Webster dictionary: "leadership—the act of leading"), most attempts at capturing what leaders do center on setting the direction for an organization.

It's another reason why CEOs spend 80 percent of their workdays in face-to-face meetings. Most of what's required to set the organization's course are the ineffable directives and guidance that can't be expressed or enforced through a rule book, written

memo, or incentive contract—the very stuff that collectively constitutes organizational culture.

The Price of Change

Things *can* change. And once new ways of doing things develop,
it's hard to believe it was ever any other way. Consider Samoa's
shift to driving on the left.

Samoa's parliament passed the bill prescribing the change in
2008, over the protests of thousands of islanders, who organized
their interests through People Against Switching Sides (PASS).
Despite PASS's court challenges, the right-to-left switch took
place as planned on September 8, 2009. Despite a year of lead
time, the government still hadn't retrofitted enough buses with
left-sided doors to keep the country's public transportation system running, causing havoc and delays in the days that followed.
On September 12 came the first real casualty of the switch,
when a bus driving on the wrong side of the road plowed into a
twelve-year-old boy, putting him in critical condition. From the
opposition came a chorus of "I told you so."

But by the middle of September, there was nothing else to report. Life had returned to normal—albeit a new normal, with
left-sided driving that made it easier and cheaper for Samoans to
import cars from relatives and neighbors in nearby Australia and
New Zealand.

If there's a final lesson from Samoa's roadside switch, it's that
amid the pain and discomfort of change, it's worth remembering
that, as Bill Clinton told Americans in 1993, "The price of doing
the same old thing is far higher than the price of change."

CHAPTER 8

Disaster and Change

J OHN BROWNE BEGAN HIS CAREER at British Petroleum as an apprentice while working toward a physics degree at Cambridge University. In 1969, after graduation, he took a full-time position with the company and stayed with BP for nearly four decades. His résumé describes a rapid ascent of the petro-corporate hierarchy—petroleum engineer followed by regional petroleum engineer; then up through the rungs of management: Aberdeen office manager, treasurer of BP Financial, and a string of successively more senior executive positions that landed him in the CEO's office in 1995.

When Browne started at BP, the British government was still its largest shareholder, and the company was run like a government bureaucracy. BP's oil empire was ruled from a three-thousand-strong head office in London, which issued directives to its numerous operations across the globe. Local employees followed orders. Refineries were allocated a volume and mix of crude to process; gas stations were told how much gas was available to sell each week, regardless of the implications for profits.

In the 1960s, BP was a reflection of the Soviet economy, where Kremlin economists decided how many potato sacks should be sent to Minsk from the Russian heartland, whether the people of Minsk liked potatoes or preferred wheat. As with the bureaucrats in the Soviet Union, where there was little to be gained from producing more potatoes or wheat, locally disempowered BP managers didn't benefit from being more productive, so why bother trying? And so the shelves in Minsk grocery stores were often empty, and BP consistently lost millions of pounds each year.

Browne's predecessor as CEO, Richard Horton, had taken the helm in 1990 with a pledge to axe thousands of central office jobs. This was just about the time Margaret Thatcher was liquidating the British government's ownership stake in BP. Drilling for oil isn't as tricky an organizational undertaking as policing Baltimore's Eastern District or managing child welfare services. It's easy enough to measure how much oil is coming out of the ground and at what cost, and also to track demand. So, the Thatcherites reasoned, the all-powerful profit motive should be harnessed to ensure that crude was extracted and distributed efficiently.[1]

Under its newly private ownership and Horton's dynamic leadership, BP emerged, in Horton's own words, as "the most successful oil company in the world." Getting there, it turned out, mostly involved firing people.[2] With nearly 10 percent of the workforce gone, most found they were working in a largely unaltered bureaucracy, with approximately 10 percent more work to do. But at least BP was issuing 10 percent fewer paychecks, which helped its bottom line.

When Browne became CEO in 1995, he had the opportunity for a managerial do-over. Browne and Horton had sharply contrasting personalities. Horton had been full of blustery arrogance.

He once told a *Forbes* reporter, "Because I am blessed by my good brain, I tend to get to the right answer rather quicker and more often than most people." Browne was mild-mannered, circumspect, analytical. Yet Browne's objectives were the same as Horton's: a slimmer, more efficient BP that empowered managers to earn profits for shareholders and themselves. To get there, Browne would go beyond merely firing employees to working to get incentives right.

By the late 1990s, Browne had made good on his promises. BP went from losing nearly $1 billion in 1992 to seeing profits of nearly $5 billion by the end of 1997. The payroll had been cut to 53,000, down from the 129,000 people BP employed before Horton arrived. Yet the company managed to do more with less: the time required to drill a deepwater well was cut from a hundred days in 1995 to just forty-two by 1997. The staid culture of blindly following rules became one of risk taking and boundary pushing.[3] Browne's efforts transformed BP from an ossified and rusting quasigovernmental dinosaur into a profit-making machine, the darling of Wall Street investors and the subject of glowing business school case studies.

Browne himself achieved business guru status for his efforts, filling nineteen pages of a single issue of the *Harvard Business Review* with an exclusive interview on *how he did it*. Which was, it turned out, largely by following the basic principles of organizational economics as taught in MBA classrooms and described in the preceding chapters of this book. With government ownership in its rearview mirror, BP under Browne could worry less about reporting protocols and rules, and focus instead on hitting measurable cost and revenue targets. Local managers could be given responsibility for maximizing profits, and be rewarded based on their individual performance.

To the extent that a head office was necessary at all, it now facilitated the sharing of best practices among its far-flung operations, from Alaska to the Persian Gulf. BP was a "learning organization," unmediated by needless layers of central control. Each of ninety business units now reported directly to Browne and his team of nine top executives. This was the flattened org of the future.

It wasn't just that BP had swapped its government owners for private investors. The world had also changed around it. A network of interlinked databases and Web pages shared knowledge and information among management peers, and allowed Browne and his team to evaluate each group's performance based on the latest in performance metric design. "Balanced scorecards" weighed various aspects of performance from cost cutting to injury rates, to ensure maximum profits at minimum operating risk. Everything could be measured and evaluated, with rewards and punishments meted out accordingly. Bosses weren't necessarily told what to do, but they were certainly judged on how well they got things done.

But managing on the cutting edge of technology and incentive design proved no match for the enduring trade-offs faced by BP—nor indeed would it for any organization. BP's free lunch of higher profits with no apparent strings attached ended on March 23, 2005, with the explosion at BP's Texas City refinery, which killed 15 and injured more than 170 others. It stands as the worst industrial accident in U.S. history.

BP commissioned a panel headed by former secretary of state James Baker III to figure out what went wrong. The 374-page Baker Report faulted company leadership for encouraging corner cutting, cost cutting, and disregard for safety protocols in the name of profits. BP had inherited the Texas City operation with its takeover of Amoco in 2000. Even back then its director described it as being held together by little more than "Band-Aids and superglue." Yet BP leadership had demanded a further 25 percent cost reduction despite the pressing need for maintenance spending. Refinery management complied nonetheless, and had just about hit the target—their compensation depended on it.

BP's own report fingered, among other things, lax enforcement of safety rules and lack of awareness of basic safety protocols. It compensated victims richly, setting aside $1.6 billion to help families and survivors. But there wasn't any real acceptance of what might have underlain the disregard for safety and culture of negligence. The new and improved BP and its balanced scorecard leaned in favor of a short list of things that could be easily measured, such as injury rates, rather than focusing on whether the necessary bureaucratic processes were in place to prevent the occasional blowup. And management *still* had to trim 25 percent off the cost of running the refinery as part of Browne's turnaround.

Sometimes you get something for nothing—such as a 25 percent cost reduction as a reward for not being stupid and lazy—but not very often. It's now clear that BP wasn't quite so far from the profit-safety "frontier" when John Browne took over, despite proclamations to that effect in his 1997 *Harvard Business Review* interview.

BP and Browne spent $1 billion in safety upgrades after the Baker Report. Yet the Texas City incident was followed by a massive Prudhoe Bay leak in 2006, caused by corroded pipes that needed replacing, and the now-infamous Deepwater Horizon Well explosion in 2010, which leaked nearly five million gallons of oil into the Gulf of Mexico. The reason: skimping on safety to get the rig up on BP's tight schedule and at a lower cost.[4] BP needed more safety guardians, fewer profit-seeking stars.

By the time Deepwater exploded, it was painfully obvious that the BP leadership had made bad, and maybe even irreversible, choices. Problems persisted at Texas City and elsewhere in the BP oil empire. In 2009, BP received 760 citations from the Occupational Safety and Health Administration (OSHA) for safety violations. Sunoco had eight. Citgo had two. Exxon had one. But try telling that to shareholders at BP back in the 1990s, when John Browne was receiving his knighthood as BP's savior.

Disastrous Organization

John Browne's streamlining of BP was visionary and groundbreaking. Until things went wrong.

The results-focused approach of a turnaround artist such as Browne can make things appear to run pretty well by the numbers. Everything seemed fine from the distance of Browne's London office. It's only after the postmortems when we see the deadly effects of the relentless pressure to cut costs, coupled with the empowering freedom of decentralized control. BP paid Texas City management for cost cutting. So management cut costs. The balanced scorecard also rewarded lower injury rates, and minor workplace accidents fell accordingly. By 2004 the injury rates at Texas City had fallen to their lowest levels in the refinery's history, and were a third of the industry average.[5] Ironically, even encouraging steps to reduce mundane accidents might come at the cost of higher risk of one-time disaster, which almost by definition can't be benchmarked and rewarded. It's just a long string of zeros—i.e., nothing happens—followed by catastrophe.[6] You need to mess up only once. There are no second chances.

BP's recent history lays bare the difference between armchair theorizing on org design and the challenges faced by Browne and other would-be visionaries in changing their companies and perhaps the world: Is this going to be Lou Gerstner's storied turnaround of IBM ("The Man Who Rescued IBM from the Edge of Oblivion"), Lafley's successful makeover of P&G, or epic disaster at BP? It's often hard to say when the process is just getting under way. As we've emphasized from the beginning, an organization is an intricate creature with many moving parts that fit together in subtle and complicated ways. Decentralization can produce unprecedented innovation and efficiencies, result in death and carnage, or both. The BP story highlights the humility with which we should apply our theories and principles of org design, and the caution we might take in bringing about change. We never quite know what the collateral damage will be.

The grandfather of a friend of ours likes to give the example, likely apocryphal—or, as his grandmother puts it, and in Russian, "All this happened long ago and is not true either"—of a general in the czarist Russian Army who tried to combat the flea problem among his troops by offering a per-flea finder's fee. He anticipated, of course, that his enterprising troops would hunt down the parasites one by one. What he got was an even bigger infestation, as the hairiest, thickest-skinned soldiers cultivated armies of fleas to sell to their comrades, allowing everyone to profit from the flea bounty. (A modern managerial bug problem of another sort occurred at a Silicon Valley software firm that decided to reward its programmers for finding software bugs. The plan caused the same bug infestation as the czar's pay-per-flea program.)[7]

These cases merely reflect the unanticipated costs of a cost-benefit trade-off in incentive design. You pay for bugs, you get bugs. You pay for lower costs, you get lower costs, though sometimes with catastrophic consequences.

Performing well on all fronts is really very hard, which is why so few orgs actually do it well, and often end up doing at least one of their jobs very badly. It's the organizational equivalent of chewing gum and talking at the same time, or maybe drawing a picture with one hand while writing a letter with the other. This doesn't mean John Browne should have resigned himself to year after year of billion-dollar losses—change can be a good thing. But in his focus on measuring and streamlining BP, he failed to acknowledge the challenges of becoming a multipurpose org, which so often leads to frustration, disappointment, and even cataclysmic disaster.

Real Men Don't Type

There may be no organization more familiar with the pitfalls of competing objectives than the FBI. Orgs may end up with multiple goals by design (as in the cases of McDonald's, P&G, and BP), but just as often it's the result of historical accident. For the FBI, it was a combination of the two.

The FBI grew out of the Department of Justice, where, in 1908, the attorney general appointed thirty-four special agents to serve as a Bureau of Investigation, charged with investigating, catching, and prosecuting criminals. The new Bureau, made permanent the next year, helped to reduce the costs of catching crooks, and at the same time gave the AG unprecedented control over crime fighting in America. The Bureau soon set up field offices in nine major cities, with each one given authority and responsibility over crimes in its region. J. Edgar Hoover, who started as director in 1924 and never left (he died in 1972), enlarged the Bureau and professionalized it. He put in place performance evaluations, field offices inspections, and gave agents a bit of training before handing them a badge and a gun. (According to the FBI's own official history, in its early days the Bureau had consisted largely of poorly trained, poorly managed amateur crime fighters. One Philadelphia agent, for example, split his time between catching bad guys and tending to his cranberry bog.)[8] Hoover recognized the need to work with local cops, so he set up a National Academy to train city and state police as well.

The FBI's successes were glorified in news reports and cinematic accounts of its crime-fighting exploits. Little boys aspired to be special agents when they grew up. Hoover himself was a great PR booster, collaborating with radio networks in the 1930s to produce *Gang Busters* and *This Is Your FBI*, shows that provided adoring portraits of special agents doing what they did best: chasing down and cuffing bad guys.

But Hoover just couldn't stick to his knitting. He saw the rise of communism and fascism in the 1930s as an opportunity to expand the Bureau's mandate. With the blessing of President Franklin Roosevelt, the FBI, as it came to be called by the mid-1930s, got into the intelligence-gathering business, keeping tabs on the American Communist Party and other perceived risks to national security. It further diversified into counterintelligence in World War II, taking up the task of disrupting foreign spies operating inside the United States.

When the war came to an end, the FBI went back to its core business of finding criminals and locking them up. It's what it was created to do; it's what the FBI's culture had come to value;

it's what was rewarded with promotion and recognition within the Bureau. Intelligence work came from desk-bound employees tapping out memos and classified reports, with little outside visibility or sense of achievement. The pecking order was clear, embodied in well-worn Bureau maxims such as "real men don't type" and "the only things a real agent needs is a notebook, a pen, and a gun."

If there seemed limited grounds for bundling crime fighting with intelligence work, beyond satisfying Hoover's outsize ego, it may not have mattered much anyway. Most Americans felt that keeping criminals off the streets was mainly what they needed from the FBI, and the Bureau's intelligence objective was relegated accordingly to a secondary role. While the Cold War with the Soviet empire was playing out across the globe, this was mostly the domain of the Central Intelligence Agency, which was created after the Second World War to handle intelligence gathering on foreign soil.

This sense of complacency on national security matters, and their irrelevance within the FBI, changed on September 11, 2001, when two hijacked Boeing 767s crashed into the World Trade Center, each taking down one of the Twin Towers and leaving close to three thousand dead. Two separate teams of hijackers had commandeered planes and pointed them toward Washington, D.C. One crashed into the Pentagon; the other was headed for the Capitol but crashed en route, killing all aboard, when passengers attempted to take control of the cockpit.

All of a sudden, Hoover's crime-fighting FBI was going to have to get into the national security business.

Failed Intelligence

Could the 9/11 attacks been prevented by a better-designed national security apparatus? As the public outrage with Osama bin Laden and the hijackers themselves faded just a little, attention turned to the FBI and its intelligence partners, and their inability to thwart the attacks. The Bureau's failings spilled into public view when a thirteen-page memo sent from a Minneapolis agent to the FBI director's office was leaked to CNN in May 2002. The memo described some of the warning signs that were screaming "TERRORIST ALERT," had the Bureau taken any serious interest in them. Eventually, investigators turned up a dozen red flags that might have prevented the September 11 attacks.

Suspected Islamic radicals had enrolled in aviation courses in Phoenix, a fact that was noted with some alarm by FBI special agent Kenneth Williams. His memo, issued in the summer of 2001, recommended that there be a nationwide investigation of possible Al Qaeda enrollees in flight schools. It was largely ignored. A few weeks later another opportunity came and went, when the Minneapolis FBI office got a call from a trainer at the Pan Am International Flight School reporting that one Zacarias Moussaoui, with little prior flight training, had paid $6,800 in cash to learn to fly a 747 in "four or five days." The FBI determined that Moussaoui had jihadist beliefs, and had recently been to Pakistan. Yet the field office failed to get clearance from FBI headquarters in Washington to search Moussaoui's laptop and other belongings. In the now-infamous exchange that ensued, a Minneapolis FBI supervisor argued that he wanted to ensure that Moussaoui would not "take control of a plane and fly it into the World Trade Center." The agent in Washington replied, "That's not going to happen…You have a guy interested in this type of aircraft—that is it."

The 9/11 Commission created to investigate the attacks also faulted miscommunication among intelligence agencies. In one case, two of the hijackers were tracked by the CIA en route to a meeting of suspected terrorists in Malaysia in 1999. Agents obtained a copy of one of their passports and noted that the man held a valid U.S. visa. When the pair left the meeting headed for Thailand, word didn't get to CIA's Bangkok office in time, and the scent went cold. A little later the hijackers flew to L.A., breezing past Immigration and Customs officials unaware of the CIA's concerns.

Failure to communicate and respond to critical information on impending risks; head office bureaucrats quashing the well-meaning initiatives of front-line employees; sluggish responses to urgent circumstances; slowed or garbled communication across offices and branches—all standard fare in the realm of org satire.

The 9/11 Commission Report detailed these organizational failures, and also started the discussion of what to do to make sure another 9/11 wouldn't happen anytime soon.

Everyone could agree that the FBI was operating in a changed world, with different threats to American security, and the Bureau needed to change along with it. But the "right" way to reform the FBI and its national security brethren remains an active debate today. Reasonable people—much smarter and better informed than we—disagree on what the national security apparatus should look like.

And even if we could come to some consensus on what the future FBI *should* look like, is it possible for an old organization to learn new tricks?

Uncoordinated National Security

The FBI hadn't exactly been blindsided by Al Qaeda in 2001; there had been at least a couple of dress rehearsals in the decade prior that hinted at the emerging terrorist threat. A homegrown lunatic, Timothy McVeigh, had parked a truck full of explosives in front of the Alfred P. Murrah Federal Building in Oklahoma City in 1995 and lit the fuse, killing 168 and injuring hundreds of others. The FBI might also have learned something from the truck bomb detonated beneath the World Trade Center's North Tower in 1993 by Al Qaeda–trained radicals, who aimed to take down both towers by toppling the building into its twin to the south.

But these warning signs went unheeded. It's not that no one within the FBI saw it coming—one reason for the public's bewilderment at the lack of terrorism preparedness was the existence of internal Bureau reports that argued that a major terrorist attack was imminent. Still, it's hard to shift focus to a new job when the old one, fighting crime, is already stretching organizational resources so thin. For decades, the threats to American democracy had come more from the likes of Al Capone and his descendants than from Al Qaeda. And you can't turn a supertanker on a dime. Despite its stated two-handed mission, the FBI remained firmly focused on its original purpose of catching criminals. Little intelligence gathering emerged from the FBI's boxy, 1970s-era headquarters in Washington, and of that, only a tiny fraction focused on the growing threat of terrorism. In 2001 the FBI employed 28,000 people, the majority of whom were spread across 56 major field offices and 44 international outposts. By one estimate, only 200 of the FBI's 9,000 special agents focused on counterterrorism in 2001. In 1998 the agents produced 12,730 criminal convictions, the metric by which agents were evaluated. Thirty-seven were terrorism-related.

Shifting toward an intelligence focus wasn't simply a matter of reassigning field agents from organized crime to intelligence gathering. Just as the Methodists and Baptists developed new compensation, promotion, and monitoring practices to fit their reorganized churches, the FBI needed a whole set of changes to go along with its newly invigorated national security function. The new FBI would require distinct skills and incentives, would probably need to be housed within a differently structured organization, and would have to adjust its mind-set and culture to fit with these formal changes.

The old FBI was blessed with a purpose that lent itself to measuring performance and rewarding high achievers for their work. G-men solved criminal cases, and the justice system effectively provided them with the objective metrics they needed to identify top agents. Success was largely defined by headcounts of arrests, indictments, prosecutions, and convictions. The FBI's work was akin to that of homicide detectives, who were similarly evaluated and rewarded on the basis of solving cases.

What defines intelligence success? A deafening silence—no hijacked planes; no truck filled with explosives detonating in Midtown Manhattan; no American lives lost to terrorist attacks. In the words of Special Agent Charles Price, "A criminal case is all about figuring out what has happened. An intelligence case is all about figuring out what's going to happen"—then doing something to stop it. Intelligence officers were the FBI's equivalent of beat cops, played out with the immeasurably higher stakes of a terrorist attack.

The FBI's intelligence work had more in common with disaster prevention at BP than the FBI's traditional mission of closing criminal cases. If you do it well, catastrophes are averted, but the most visible indication of how you're doing is, almost by definition, something that hardly ever happens. What is an acceptable level of risk? One disaster per year? One per decade? None ever?

Suppose you *could* measure disaster risk—perhaps from near misses such as flammable leaks that luckily don't ignite, or failed alarm drills—you might end up making things even worse by motivating workers to cover up vulnerabilities that would provoke the boss's ire. For the communal task of intelligence gathering, it may be hard to provide any performance incentives at all. If national security is a jigsaw puzzle, how do you reward providers of each individual piece? If you do develop a system of pay-for-intelligence, holders of individual leads may be loath to share those leads with others, lest someone else get credit for their hard work.

Instead of measuring disaster "outputs" you could measure safety "inputs," such as hours devoted to safety drills or expenditures on equipment maintenance. The FBI tried evaluating analysts by measuring their productivity in generating intelligence reports, the inputs that collectively inform FBI leadership of emerging risks. After all, they had found that field offices producing the most reports were also doing the best intelligence work when evaluated by the Bureau leadership in Washington.

However, in trying to provide forceful incentives to intelligence officers, comparable to those working criminal cases, the FBI unwittingly invoked what economist Luis Garicano calls the Heisenberg Principle of incentive design: a performance metric is useful as a performance metric only as long as it isn't used as a performance metric. In 2007 the FBI started evaluating field offices based on pages of intelligence produced. By 2008 the positive relationship between reports produced and quality of intelligence work had disappeared—agents were simply filling their word-count quotas.

A similar tension existed for encouraging information sharing in a crime-fighting bureaucracy. Any one individual who had sifted through the phone calls and memos coming in from concerned agents around the country prior to the attacks of 9/11 might have put the country on a terrorist alert. (Indeed, some of the individual field agents were sufficiently concerned that they would have done so based solely on their piece of the overall puzzle.) Decentralization within the FBI and also across intelligence agencies made coordinated responses to border-crossing threats near impossible. It seems truly unbelievable that the CIA could, for example, maintain a separate list of suspects from the immigration officials who need to keep those suspects off American soil. Yet separate agencies naturally generate separate lists and databases.

This lack of coordination was fine back in the days when crime was mostly local. Bank robbers in Chicago stuck to stick-ups in the Windy City; drug dealers had their corners on the South Side. Each metropolitan area had its own separate Mob. The Scarfo family controlled the Philly Mafia, the Bufalinos ruled Scranton, and in New York, there was enough business to support five families. The criminal case tradition was well suited to the job, with each case owned by the field office that opened it. It would be pursued by local agents who had an established set of informants, relationships with local police, and an understanding of the local crime scene.

By and large, the FBI's staff in Washington kept their noses out of casework. Harvard Business School researchers who have closely followed the FBI and its reform quote a congressional staffer who described the special agents in charge (SACs) who headed each field office as "princes with their own little fiefdoms, and the [FBI] director like the king who doesn't necessarily have the power to rein them in." When a situation demanded national attention, the office that was first on the scene would take the lead in directing the investigation. This was true even for the mother of all terrorist cases: public enemy number one, Osama bin Laden, was first uncovered and indicted by the New York office, which then became a hub for all future investigations, with the headquarters' Counterterrorism Division playing only a supporting role.

This arrangement of loosely connected field offices worked for catching small-time crooks, but was ill-suited for taking stock of the big picture of emerging terrorist threats. Terrorist cells don't confine themselves to a single zip code, and seeing red flags appear across cities or countries can help to distinguish an eccentric Muslim who likes 747s from a terrorist determined to fly a plane into tall buildings.

The scattered hierarchy of the FBI was like the organization of national security in miniature. The FBI and CIA weren't really on speaking terms, and the various military intelligence ops kept to themselves. So when Thai officials told CIA agents in Bangkok that two suspected terrorists had boarded a flight to L.A., they never thought to inform the FBI. Partly as a result, the FBI missed an easy chance to collar the two men when they rented a room from an FBI informant in the spring of 2000, a year before they piloted American Airlines Flight 77 into the Pentagon as part of the 9/11 attacks. If FBI field offices competed for convictions, the various intelligence organizations competed for the good favor of Washington lawmakers, who divided the largely fixed pie of the intelligence budget among them. This was particularly true in the post–Cold War years, when the CIA was struggling to prove its continued relevance to a skeptical Congress always on the lookout for budget-trimming opportunities.

The dominance of gun-toting criminal agents over office-bound intelligence analysts was reflected in everything from career tracks—almost all FBI executive positions were filled by criminal agents—to computer systems. Even before the 9/11 attacks, the FBI had launched a technology upgrade, the Virtual Case File. It was canceled five years later, in 2005, a $170 million monument to the failure to change the FBI's pen-and-notebook culture. The criminal side didn't need an information-sharing system. They didn't *want* an information-sharing system. Little boys and girls don't dream of becoming G-men to do data entry. Agents saw only a downside to sharing and comparing notes anyway—particularly in an era of WikiLeaks and cyber-attacks, computer systems only increased the chances that their carefully constructed cases would fall into the wrong hands.

This all fed into what was, according to HBS professor Jan Rivkin, perhaps the FBI's greatest crime-fighting asset and also the greatest barrier to change: the culture and ethos of its agents. Agents didn't catch criminals just for a shot at a promotion. Many viewed a transfer off the streets and into management as a step down in the world. And it certainly wasn't just for more pay. Special agents could double their salaries simply by leaving for the private sector. FBI agents worked long hours solving crimes because it was what they had signed up to do. And they were damned if some bureaucrat in the nation's capital was going to make them do otherwise.

Organizing Counterterrorism

The Congress and the country could tolerate an embassy bombing here and there, or the occasional attack on U.S. military
installations. It was the cost of maintaining a global empire.
But the nearly three thousand killed on American soil elicited
a chorus of "Never forget, never again." Maintaining America's
nuclear arsenal had zero margin for error, and the U.S. military
had managed that job without incident.[9] Why couldn't the FBI
do the same?

Congressional hearings were held. Commissions were formed.
Reports were written. Academics and policy wonks weighed in
with their conclusions. Other academics and policy wonks
weighed in with opposite conclusions. Amidst it all, those inside
the FBI planned its reorganization.

The government's findings were presented in *The 9/11 Commission Report*. Its thirteenth and final chapter presented a set of
recommendations for national security reform. Of its five subsec-
tions, the titles of all but one began with the word *Unity*—"Unity
of Effort across the Foreign-Domestic Divide," "Unity of Effort
in Sharing Information," and so on. The splintered grouping
of intelligence agencies—and the splintered organization within
the FBI itself—was to blame for the failure to connect the dots.
The FBI's scattered national security efforts had resulted in catastrophe, just as BP's well-meaning decentralization had led to a
disastrous safety record. They both needed to become more like
the U.S. Army, with rule books and protocols to ensure collective
response to a common enemy.

Yet the loudest voice from the academic peanut gallery, coming from University of Chicago law professor Richard Posner,
argued that, if anything, a bit more splintering might be a good

thing. Posner hadn't had much interest in matters of national security until the *New York Times* asked him to look at *The 9/11 Commission Report* for its Sunday Book Review section. That anyone was asked to review a government report for the *Times*'s book pages was unusual to say the least. But 9/11 was an event that commanded so much public attention that the government contracted with publisher W. W. Norton for mass commercial distribution. (The report also turned out to be a page-turner—a National Book Award finalist, described by Posner as "riveting...an improbable literary triumph." The initial run of six hundred thousand flew off the shelves, and the report went on to sell well over a million copies.)

The *Journal of Legal Studies* lists Posner as the most cited legal scholar of the twentieth century. He has held forth on topics ranging from abortion to animal rights to antitrust—and that's just the first letter of the alphabet. Though he'd never thought much about national security, he agreed to write the review, later commenting, "There can be value in an outsider's perspective."

The report's authors had consulted with twelve hundred experts in ten countries, and pored over more than two million pages of intelligence-related documents. Yet after a couple of opening paragraphs complimenting the report's prose and narrative quality, Posner the outsider dismissed its findings as "unimpressive."

What started as a book review turned into a hobby. Others might spend their off-hours reading trashy novels, watching movies, or sitting in front of the TV. Posner writes faster than most Americans can read, and in just a few years his little sideline produced four book-length analyses of U.S. national intelligence.[10]

With regard to intelligence gathering, Posner was in the one-

handed rather than ambidextrous camp of organizational theorists. Everything about the FBI was set up to solve crimes,
he believed, so let them stick to their crime-fighting. It was
nothing more than Herbert Hoover's opportunistic expansion in
the 1930s that had burdened the Bureau with its divergent and
incompatible missions. Posner pointed to intelligence-gathering
operations outside the United States, in countries where rational
organization wasn't thrown off course by meddling from Hoover-
esque leadership. In the United Kingdom, criminal investigations
were managed by Scotland Yard, and domestic intelligence by
MI5. (James Bond worked for MI5's cousin, MI6, which handled foreign intelligence.) In Canada, these functions are split
between the Royal Canadian Mounted Police and the Security
Intelligence Service, which separated from the RCMP in 1984.

It wasn't only within the FBI that Posner went against the consensus view. The 9/11 Commission advocated the creation of a
national security czar, who would sit atop the vast pyramid of national security organizations. Such a position had existed, at least
on paper, since the 1947 National Security Act created the position of director of central intelligence (DCI), who would run the
CIA and oversee the wider community of intelligence agencies.
But this wider community, through a flurry of lobbying efforts,
saw to it that the DCI wasn't given any power outside his own
newly created agency.

The 9/11 Commission argued for revisiting this original principle of truly centralizing intelligence with the creation of yet
another position, director of national intelligence, who was of no
individual agency but had power over all agencies. Centralized
authority would help to harmonize information systems among
separate agencies, provide carrots and sticks for sharing critical information, and, it was hoped, prevent the sorts of lapses that had

allowed nineteen suicide bombers to enter the United States and plan their attacks largely unnoticed.

Posner, for his part, pointed to another epic lapse in intelligence gathering to make his case for the virtues of splintering. In the run-up to the U.S.-led invasion of Iraq in 2003, practically the entire intelligence apparatus of the United States held the mistaken belief that Saddam Hussein held biological, chemical, or nuclear capabilities—so-called weapons of mass destruction. (The United Kingdom's MI6 was similarly duped.) If the failure to prevent 9/11 had been not enough sharing or unity across intelligence branches, Posner believed, the faulty conclusion that Saddam possessed WMDs had been the result of *too much* shared information.

The challenge of intelligence analysis is to pick through scattered bits of information to distinguish useful clues from harmless distractions. From the perspective of a field agent trying to get ahead in the world, the tidbits with the most merit are the ones that will make his boss happy when reported up the chain of command. That's what yes-men do, and there's at least a bit of yes-man inside every one of us. If, for example, everyone knows the national intelligence director is already convinced that WMDs are being mass-produced inside Iraq, it's the brave-yet-foolish voice that tells him otherwise. Indeed, the government commission that investigated the WMD findings observed that intelligence managers punished those expressing WMD-contrarian views and rewarded those who dug up information supporting what the boss thought he already knew. A president, assuming he's not looking for intelligence yes-men himself, would want to set up truly autonomous intelligence-gathering units that would each give its honest and independent views on looming threats.

It's also the very nature of unified, pyramid-shaped organizations that they lose information as you get closer to the top: Agents on the front lines pass up whatever they uncover to their superiors—say, the SACs of each field office—who pick out what's most important from the tips they receive, do their analysis, and pass a report farther up the chain. This efficient information filtering is part of what managers do, but it also means that some ideas get lost amid the filters and higher-level judgments—after all, upper-level managers may be important, but they're not perfect. And, of course, the taller the pyramid, the longer it takes for front-line observations to make their way to the corner office at the top.

Does that mean that immense intelligence hierarchies are a bad thing? That depends on the intelligence problems you're trying to solve. Posner pointed to the product cycle of Procter & Gamble, where proposals go through forty to fifty approvals before getting an up or down decision from the CEO. That's just fine for the company. It's not like we're in the midst of a soap-and-detergent revolution where it's innovate or perish. And the company has plenty of existing brands that it wouldn't want to damage with untested "new and improved" formulations that end up causing cancer or killing babies.

The Cold War was the national security equivalent of P&G's stable and predictable business environment. The terrorism threats of today are closer to Silicon Valley: a constantly shifting landscape of networked and poorly understood orgs, where most clues lead nowhere, while the few great insights hold enormous value. Letting more ideas past the gatekeepers to the "product development" phase is a good thing.

This is particularly true given the stakes involved. When it comes to potential reformulations of Tide detergent, the cost of squelching ideas is modest, a rounding error for P&G profits perhaps. Sift out the finer details of intelligence too early, and you might miss the tip that prevents the next major disaster. When, in 2010, an Afghan-born Virginia resident claimed on Facebook that he knew how to build a pipe bomb to blow up the D.C. subway system, it was probably a psychotic delusion or a sick joke. And probably harmless. But there's a tiny chance that he'll back up his boasts with action, and the cost of a "false negative"—not responding when the threat is real—is death and carnage on the D.C. Metro.

Posner didn't see *only* a downside to centralizing intelligence gathering and analysis. But where the 9/11 Commission focused largely on past mistakes that would never have happened under a more unified intelligence service, Posner saw the inevitable trade-offs, and the future missteps (more yes-men, and critical clues left unnoticed) that would be a consequence of centralizing reforms.

On the Other Hand…

Well-informed insiders accepted much of Posner's critique. A book review of Posner's *Uncertain Shield* in the CIA's own *Studies in Intelligence* ("Journal of the American Intelligence Professional") largely goes along with his argument that when it comes to information sharing within a unified bureaucracy, it's possible to have too much of a good thing. (However, the review also argued that, as an outsider, Posner was clueless as to how decentralized the various intelligence agencies remained after supposed reforms following 9/11.)

Posner's argument that the FBI be split in two was met with more skepticism. The *Uncertain Shield* review was penned by Stanley Moskowitz, a CIA lifer experienced as an intelligence officer and liaison, with postings from Moscow to Jerusalem to Washington. Moskowitz turned the cost-benefit argument back on Posner, pointing out that in his forty-plus years working with intelligence agencies around the world, he found that agencies that carved up responsibilities, such as Scotland Yard and MI5, were often at one another's throats. There was no reason to expect that the FBI and a newly focused domestic intelligence agency would be any different. They each would be working similar turf in the same cities, trying to cultivate relationships with the same police departments, and often working different angles on the same case. This was true not just for counterterrorism cases. Heavily armed *narcotraficantes* were destabilizing the Mexican government just to the south. Catching drug smugglers and murderers was a law enforcement problem. But ensuring that the drug wars didn't spill over into Texas and California was a matter of national security. In practice, domestic security and crime fighting couldn't be as neatly split apart as the food and detergent divisions of a corporate conglomerate. Even in the corporate world, the most straightforward of no-fault divorces is complicated by the organizational equivalent of bickering over who gets the china.

And therein lies the question for all unhappy marriages, whether a union of two people or a pair of organizations. Every marriage is, after all, at least a little unhappy in its own way— the dirty socks strewn about; the occasional moodiness; the differences of opinion on schools, vacations, and everything else. But when do the costs of togetherness come to outweigh the joys of companionship and the economic efficiencies of staying together? And to torture the marriage metaphor, can the good parts be saved with a bit of counseling and mediation, or are the differences simply irreconcilable?

Posner saw the FBI as having two incompatible missions. Harvard Business School professor Jan Rivkin saw tension, but also an imperative for the intelligence and criminal parties of this organizational union to try to work out their differences. Rivkin, an accomplished management scholar and former consultant, turned his focus from corporate to national security strategy in 2005, when the opportunity arose to work with the FBI to analyze its management processes. Whereas Posner assessed the FBI with the objective detachment of an outsider, Rivkin followed the HBS tradition of doing his best to get inside the org, perhaps trading neutrality for a deeper sense of its strengths and challenges.

Rivkin, working with his colleagues Michael Roberto and Ranjay Gulati, spent the better part of six months talking to FBI insiders about reform. They got the perspectives of coffee-fetching gofers in satellite offices, senior managers in Washington (including FBI director Robert Mueller), and everyone in between. Perhaps they drank too much of the FBI-as-empire Kool-Aid in the process, but the three argued that the country would be better off if lawmakers ignored Posner's outsider wisdom and left the FBI intact. Over the course of half a dozen years, they produced a series of teaching case studies, a *Harvard Business Review* article, and an academic paper that, taken together, had a lower word count than a single volume by Judge Posner.

In Rivkin's view, the FBI had all the hallmarks of a marriage worth saving. Field agents were on a first-name basis with officers in local police departments around the country—it was the only way a force of eleven thousand FBI agents could uphold the law among three hundred million Americans—and these local connections were also crucial eyes and ears for intelligence gathering. Blowing stuff up can get expensive—the 9/11 attack was estimated to have cost nearly half a million dollars—so terrorists often have sidelines smuggling, dealing drugs, counterfeiting currency, and otherwise breaking the law to fund their operations. This may lead them to tip their hand to crime-fighting FBI agents who, if integrated with counterterrorism efforts, could pass on critical information to intelligence analysts. The threat of arrest could also be used to extract information needed to roll up entire terrorist cells, and actual arrests for lesser crimes could keep would-be terrorists off the streets, at least for a while. Such was the case for Zacarias Moussaoui, the "twentieth 9/11 hijacker," who was detained for an immigration violation, and kept from participating in the attack. Yet if the FBI is to prevent another 9/11, these benefits of remaining whole will have to move beyond a theoretical possibility. The Bureau will have to get past its days of being ruled by crime-fighting agents, and become a truly ambidextrous, dual-purpose org.

For BP, the dilemma of combining the "star" task of cutting costs with the "guardian" objective of drilling for oil safely seemed to have proven intractable by the summer of 2010—yet incoming CEO Robert Dudley still called for a doubling of exploration spending in years ahead, while claiming to make safety his top priority. Had Dudley uncovered the winning formula that had eluded Lord Browne, or was it another case of unrealistically aspiring to have his cake and eat it, too? Is it really possible for an organization to focus simultaneously on two distinct tasks, and do them both well?

An Ambidextrous FBI?

By September 12, 2001, it was clear that the FBI needed to reorder its priorities. This was formalized in May 2002 with a

statement from Director Mueller listing the Bureau's top ten objectives. "Protect the U.S. from terrorist attack" sat at the very
top; it has remained there since.

But bringing about actual reform remained, at the time of this
writing, a work-in-progress. In a rigidly controlled dictatorship—
such as the army—if the boss decrees a shift in priority from
fighting criminals to preventing terrorism, loyal foot soldiers
wake up the next morning and follow their new orders. But in its
pre-9/11 incarnation, the fiefdoms of FBI field offices couldn't be
coerced—they needed to be won over to the cause of counterterrorism. That was going to be a long, hard battle. When asked for
his view on the single greatest barrier to reform, Rivkin doesn't
point to antiquated computer systems, mismatched incentives,
or manpower constraints. He replies without hesitation: it's all
about culture. It would be hard to change *anything* at the FBI as
long as the Bureau remained an organization that celebrated what
could be accomplished with a badge and a gun over the cerebral
analytics of national security work. You can't herd unruly cats.

The country didn't have the time or patience for cat herding
in 2001. So, in the short run, Rivkin and his coauthors argue, the
FBI had little choice but to convert itself partway to a centralized
autocracy where the FBI director *could* lord over his field staff.
And that's what Director Mueller did, starting with the edict
that field offices follow up on *every* terrorist lead before devoting
time or effort to any other objective. With 180,000 leads coming
in between 2003 and 2010, special agents were inundated with
terrorism-related casework.

Shifts in staffing were also passed down from on high. Each
field office was given an intelligence group of ten analysts,
charged with figuring out what the FBI needed to know in each
locale to assess the gravest threats to national security. These

field-based teams weren't under local management but reported directly to a newly consolidated Office of Intelligence at FBI headquarters. The headquarters itself employed a growing number of Washington-based intelligence analysts to manage the information that came in from around the country. Intelligence analysts were also embedded in investigative squads, so relevant clues that turned up in law enforcement cases could be worked into security analysis—otherwise, what was the point in keeping the two functions together? Other agents were freed from casework to focus full time on cultivating informants and contacts to feed into national security assessment. And the office-of-origin system for assigning cases that allowed the New York office to preside over the Osama bin Laden file just because they found him first was replaced by centralized control over all counterterrorism casework.

While the Bureau diverted resources toward intelligence operations, Director Mueller struggled to ensure that they were well utilized. Prior to 9/11, the de facto job description of many intelligence analysts had been more gofer than national security expert—hardly a prescription for luring sharp-minded analysts away from D.C. think tanks. Despite claims of a new, improved analyst program, a 2005 report found that the Bureau was still having trouble filling these positions, partly because the job still required too much photocopying and not enough analysis.[11] Figuring out the metric for success, which is critical for developing an intelligence leadership pipeline, also proved a challenge. Rewarding the analyst with the highest word count in his monthly reports had undone the usefulness of report length as performance measure. Assessing intelligence agents on the number of informants they cultivated would similarly shift effort toward quantity and away from quality. Such are the challenges of any organization with "hard" tasks (hard to monitor, with multiple components, and executed in teams) such as intelligence analysis.

And then there was the continuing saga of efforts to computerize FBI case records—much valued by intelligence gatherers, and sometimes maligned by those in law enforcement. The $170 million Virtual Case File debacle had been followed by other abortive attempts at technology upgrades. In 2010, agents were still waiting for a new system to come online that would relieve them of clerical tasks, and thereby free up more time to do the jobs they were trained to do.

A glass-half-empty view of post-9/11 reforms might hold that trying to change an FBI set in its ways had satisfied no one and upset everyone. That would be at least half right. In the words of Director Mueller, the new FBI was to be "intelligence-led." Yet it still wasn't attracting the best and brightest to intelligence work, or fully taking advantage of the intelligence analysts it had. And the intelligence-led mission was threatening to the many law enforcement agents who had previously been the heroes of the FBI.

This presented a challenge to the longer-term plans Mueller had for his FBI. The whole point of leaving the FBI intact was that there were synergies from local connections and knowledge in the interrelated worlds of security threats and crime. And this was best accomplished by pushing decisions back down to field offices and individual agents, who could best adjudicate on which leads to pursue and which areas—whether drug cartels or Al Qaeda cells or something else entirely—represented the greatest threat to national security.

Over the past few years, greater autonomy over such decisions has been returned to field office managers, albeit with periodic monitoring and oversight from leadership in Washington to make sure that counterterrorism maintains its priority status.

Is everyone happy about the changes? Hardly.

Just as the New York field office was starting to shift its agent mix away from Mob surveillance and toward counterterrorism, we met with a prosecutor in the U.S. Attorney General's Office in Brooklyn. AG prosecutions lean heavily on evidence gathered by the FBI—this was the reason for the Bureau's creation just over a century ago. The prosecutor we spoke with was understandably upset about seeing these evidence-gathering resources getting cut. His particular focus was on organized crime, and the resource shift represented, from his perspective, a tragic weakening of efforts against the New York Mafia. The five field squads, one for each of the Five Families, were to be reduced to three. The FBI was going to be double-teamed by the Mob, a fact surely not lost on the families themselves. Years of crime-fighting work were about to be undone.

These personnel were to be shifted to counterterrorism. Did our friend the federal prosecutor think the new FBI's priorities were out of whack? Not necessarily. He fully understood that preventing the next big terrorist attack should be at the top of the FBI's agenda, to be balanced against the day-to-day work of wearing down the Mob.

His solution? Increase the FBI's budget to keep its war against the Mob intact while still supporting its new counterterrorism work. The Congressional Budget Committee might ask where all that money would come from. He'd thought of that, and immediately offered up the jobs of Justice Department lawyers whose approval he required for Mob wiretaps and other surveillance requests. Theirs were truly pointless positions, he argued, given the already onerous approval process in place in New York and at other field offices. He saw the extra layer of approval as an artifact of an earlier time that could be excised cost-free from the government balance sheet.

Indeed, sometimes there *is* a free lunch. But we would conjecture that the Washington-based Department of Justice lawyers working to prevent civil liberties abuses might see things differently.

If there's one message to take away from this book, it's that a glass half full may be the best you can hope for. If either intelligence gatherers or crime fighters had been fully satisfied, it would probably indicate that FBI leadership wasn't making the right trade-offs between the two. You can't please all the people all the time, nor should the director have such aspirations. You need to keep a lid on bank robberies, money launderers, and New York's Mafiosi, while also doing your best to prevent the next cataclysmic attack. As with the post-9/11 postmortem, the FBI will likely find that doing its best simply isn't good enough to prevent some loss of American lives. And once again, the organization will be blamed for failure by a public that refuses to acknowledge the imperfections of any org in a world full of trade-offs and compromise.

Conclusion

The Future Org

EVERY GENERATION HAS ITS UTOPIANS. So far, they've been wrong. Just ask the man who designed the cubicle.

When the office furniture design company Herman Miller introduced the Action Office in 1964, it was "the world's first open-plan office system of reconfigurable components and a bold departure from the era's fixed assumptions of what office furniture should be."[1] The flexible workspace, designed by a team led by Robert Propst, the company's head of research, was supposed to be efficient, equalizing, and liberating. Its designers aimed to revolutionize the way people worked, making them more productive by giving them more space than the "bullpen" design open floor plan that assigned one worker to one smallish desk. With more work spread out before them, more space for filing, the designers reasoned, individuals were bound to be more productive—hence the moniker "action office." The design—which included two desks, a couple of chairs, a small table, and some vertical filing stands—even accommodated working while standing up. It was revolutionary.

It was also a flop.

The Action Office accorded each employee a sprawling and uncontained collection of individual furniture units. It was too expensive and difficult to assemble, and the requisite square footage per employee made it poorly suited to large organizations. So Propst and the designers went back to the drawing board and in 1968 produced the Action Office II, which corrected the perceived deficiencies of the first version. Each employee got one desk, and the addition of low walls afforded some privacy. The compact design and walls also meant that more desks could be crammed closer together while still allowing neighbors to interact. Thus was the cubicle born. Sales took off, and many other office furniture manufacturers copied the design.

In the words of sociologist David Franz, the cubicle was rooted in the cybernetic-countercultural vision of "egalitarianism, communal networks, and democratic 'people power.'" It was more than efficient: it was moral. Proponents included Andy Grove, the CEO of Intel, who sat in a cubicle of his own on one side of the company's open-floor office. James Fallows, the normally hardheaded columnist for the *Atlantic*, pondered the spreading power of cubicle culture to the rest of the business world, "the tire companies, the machine tool makers, the color TV industry." The office everywhere was going to be super-groovy, boss-less, free. This was part of the vision of the office as Great Egalitarian White-Collar Workplace. Innovations such as the cubicle would flatten the org's hierarchy, freeing the minds of all the knowledge workers, empowering them to achieve something amazing.[2]

Media mogul/billionaire mayor of New York City and perhaps the most famous cubicle dweller of all, Michael Bloomberg, captured this spirit when he told the *New York Times*, "Walls are barriers, and my job is to remove them." Bloomberg's offices were meant to encompass the best of both worlds—low-paneled cubes that fostered open communication yet maintained personal space, with glassed-in meeting space for more private conversations. Matt Winkler, his number two man at Bloomberg News, said, "It's good to see the boss out there without any gatekeepers. It tells everyone that there are no secrets, that we're all in this together…It's like being in a boat."[3]

Remember that when you next log on to your workstation in your cube: it's like you're on Matt Winkler's boat.

George Nelson's evaluation of the cube is markedly different from Winkler's, and may ring truer. Nelson wrote, "One does not have to be an especially perceptive critic to realize that AO-II is definitely not a system which produces an environment gratifying for people in general. But it is admirable for planners looking for ways of cramming in a maximum number of bodies, for 'employees' (as against individuals), for 'personnel,' corporate zombies, the walking dead, the silent majority. A large market." Who was Nelson? One of the co-designers of the original Action Office. He left the project after its initial failure over arguments with Propst about the design's direction.

Even Propst, before he died in 2000, bemoaned his contribution to what he called "monolithic insanity."[4]

The Nature of the Org: A Reminder

Office reformers are pulled in two directions. They either follow Frederick Taylor (the father of scientific management) and the successive waves of management scientists who thought that with enough overhead cameras, spreadsheets, computing power, and analysis, they could "solve" the organization and its problems. Or they follow the dreamers of the 1970s and '80s, who, inspired by the cybernetic-counterculture movement, thought that by getting rid of that same organizational infrastructure, they could free workers to reach their full potential by embracing chaos, complexity, new technology, or all three. The Utopians assume that some combination of office furniture and computer chips, or lack thereof, will magically solve the problems of the org. They won't.

The org is not a problem. It's a solution—but one that comes with some messy realities, such as the continued need for human interaction to gather essential "soft" information; managers overwhelmed by too many spreadsheets and pulled in too many directions; complicated jobs that defy evaluation or incentives; and, sad to say, human nature, which requires red tape and bureaucratic oversight to keep us in line. These are the trade-offs of organizational life.

Ronald Coase's basic insight that started transaction cost economics back in 1937 remains true today. The boundaries of the org are defined by trading off the costs of making things in house versus transacting on the market. It's also still true, supercomputers and IT systems notwithstanding, that the costs of bureaucracy and management eventually go through the roof as organizations expand. Recognizing and understanding such immutable facts behind organizations can help us discern the things that can't or shouldn't be changed, those that can, and the difference between the two.

Another immutable fact of org life is that every change involves costs and benefits. Utopian visionaries seem blind to the costs. That's not how life works.

This isn't to say that orgs haven't changed. Of course they have, and in many ways for the better. It's easy to lose sight of these minor victories when the new new thing becomes the old and ridiculed standard. Pause for a moment and remember how offices worked before they were revolutionized by the Action Office—the very state of affairs that made Propst and his design team such inveterate if ultimately disappointed optimists. Consider *9 to 5*, a movie that hit theaters in 1980. It focuses on shifting gender roles in the office, as Dolly Parton, Lily Tomlin, and Jane Fonda kidnap their overbearing, misogynistic boss, played by Dabney Coleman, and take over the office.

Don't watch the movie for its dated, sexist dialogue and plot or early-'80s comedic star power but rather for a glimpse of the open-office bull pen—seemingly miles and miles of floor space uninterrupted by walls or partitions, populated by tiny desks laden with in- and out-boxes, typewriters, heavy black telephones, and not much else. (Even though the movie came out well after the Action Office hit the market, the cubicle took over office culture slowly, like dry rot.) Only bosses had offices, and those were spread around the floor's perimeter so that the managers could have windows—making the bull pen even more hellish for its harsh fluorescent lighting. How did anyone get anything done? Compared to this, the cubicle was like a mirage in the desert, promising privacy and productivity.

Utopia II: A Slow Evolution

Many such mirages have captured the Utopians' attention. One idea that persists despite constant evidence to the contrary is the "paperless office," a concept that started at Xerox's Palo Alto Research Center but gained real traction only as a marketing slogan, in this case for computer video terminals. But writers more visionary than copyboys at ad agencies soon got into the game. In

June 1975, *BusinessWeek* prophesied the end of paper in an article called "The Office of the Future," which looks eerily prescient in predicting the arrival of a PC on every desk but hopelessly Utopian in waving goodbye to paper.[5]

No doubt we've made dramatic changes in our relationship to paper. Just ask the U.S. Postal Service—on the verge of dissolution, as of this writing—which can testify to the decline in handwritten correspondence with the widespread adoption of e-mail and other electronic communication.

Despite advances in electronic data storage and communication, the paperless office remains a futuristic vision, as anyone who has ever printed out an e-mail for his files knows.[6] At Columbia University's Business School (where Ray enjoys life in a completely walled-off office), multiple paper copies of more than twenty thousand expense reports still float from desk to desk each year, printouts of electronic versions of the same documents that somehow never make it into the workflow.

You might think that going paperless would be easy, but the cost of change is high, a fact not lost on the head of accounts receivable at Columbia University who would oversee the process of digitizing expense reports. In weighing the costs and benefits of paperless expense reports, he envisions the morning after the change takes place, when all the unforeseen bugs in his carefully designed system make themselves apparent in an avalanche of e-mail complaints and calls for his head on a stick.[7] Offices have infrastructure and practices that are suited to paper—filing cabinets, for instance, filled with historical records that need to be reorganized and catalogued, and backed up in case of hardware failure.

Sometimes we even regret going digital. Lots of librarians still lament the loss of their beautiful, functional, historical card catalogues after they "went paperless." And it isn't pure nostalgia. Many library users feel that the sense of discovery—flipping through the catalogue for, say, a copy of *Bartleby the Scrivener*, by Herman Melville (one of the original org theorists), and stumbling upon *Benito Cereno*, Melville's lesser-known novella, on an adjacent card—disappeared as well.

Yet in 2007, *PC World* magazine was still trying to sell the idea, recommending the right hardware and software configurations and the essential steps (don't forget to "automate your scans" and "set up a workflow"). And a writer at *Forbes* recently focused on how tablet computing is slated to kill "big paper" and the "pax papyra."[8]

Information Technology and the Coffee Shop

Anticipation of the arrival of the paperless office grossly overestimates the impact of IT on org life. This same faith in the liberating power of technology also fuels the promise of the mobile office—a world of "digital nomads" freed from pointless commutes, cold institutional surroundings, and inflexible schedules to work more happily and efficiently from mountaintops and coffee shops.

Most plans for mobility are predicated on the idea that, with the proper technological infrastructure, we could work either from home or in a "third space" such as Starbucks. The third space itself was a breakthrough idea that Starbucks CEO Howard Schultz borrowed from sociologist Ray Oldenburg.[9] The basic concept was that Starbucks would create a unique customer experience focused not just on coffee but on patrons' desire to spend time in a welcoming atmosphere that approached the intimate: lines of sight to baristas handcrafting drinks, the smell of fresh-roasted beans, comfy chairs—what Schultz called "the warm feeling of a neighborhood store."

The idea of a third space was downright revolutionary, transforming how Americans interacted and mapped their neighborhoods and cities—and bought a cup of coffee. The first and second places of home and work now had a comfortable cognate out in the world: a place to sit, reflect, talk, read, write, and, yes, even work.

Starbucks spawned countless imitators—cafés with better coffee and comfier chairs; in many cases they actually were neighborhood stores. If the third space has moved on from Starbucks, it's alive and well in places such as Ritual Roasters in San Francisco, an ocean of laptops and iPads during business hours. According to a Silicon Valley investor quoted in a 2008 *New York Times* article, "when you go into Ritual, it seems they're either writing code or writing a blog or creating something with a widget that will make money." The third space mobile office is working for novelists, early-stage software start-ups, and freelance programmers looking to get out of the house without having to pay office rent.[10]

And it's also proving effective for many employees who enjoy some time out from the office now and then to work remotely from their neighborhood coffee shops. It's not that the Utopians had it completely wrong, but rather that they made giant leaps of logic to imagine that every org is somehow going to become a coffee shop. They see the advent of the third space and follow it to its beautiful but illogical end.

Realistically, though, we can expect that this mobile office revolution will come first, if at all, to solitary tasks with easily measured results. That is, it's just not going to work for the jobs that require face-to-face meetings or monitoring—perhaps the majority of what goes on in an org.

But for the right type of job—telemarketing, say—the advent of home computers and high-speed Internet connections could empower employees to work remotely full time, to their own benefit and also that of their employers. In fact, it already has. Nick Bloom, the Stanford economist who brought better management to Indian textile manufacturers in chapter 5, has also experimented with telecommuting telemarketers at an online travel agency in China.

Bloom and his Stanford coauthors teamed up with the founder of Ctrip, China's equivalent of sites such as Expedia and Travelocity, to equip the homes of half the customer service reps in Ctrip's airfare and hotels departments with everything they needed to do their jobs remotely. The service reps with birthdays on even-number days of the month got to telecommute four days a week, surrounded by the comforts of home. Those with odd-number birth dates continued their work lives as before, parked at a computer terminal in hangar-sized rooms lined with cubicles.[11]

Without supervisors keeping tabs on the frequency of smoking breaks or the courtesy paid to customers, it's possible to imagine the experiment in workplace flexibility going badly awry. The lure of the snack, or of the bright sunny day, or of the café, could be just too tempting. At the same time, it's also very easy to measure the weekly output of a service rep: the number of calls he takes and the rate at which calls are converted into orders for flight or hotel bookings.

In this case, flexibility did indeed win the day. Home-based workers took more calls than office-bound ones, and converted them into orders at about the same rate. More work got done amid the comforts of home. And perhaps a happy worker is a productive worker. Bloom and his coauthors also tracked the quit rates and frequency of absences by the two groups. The home workers were less likely to call in sick, and far less likely to leave their jobs than the ones who were forced to commute to an office.[12]

Flatter—but Bigger

The effects of IT are more far-reaching, complicated, and interesting than the Utopians imagined. The term *information technology* itself was tentatively coined in a 1958 *Harvard Business Review* article titled "Management in the 1980s." The authors, Harold Leavitt and Thomas Whisler, describe a "new technology that does not yet have a single established name," which they call information technology. The authors were visionary in their claim that IT would "move into the managerial scene rapidly, with definite and far-reaching impact on managerial organization." They were also at least partly correct in how they felt that this would reshape the org.

Like the office Utopians who followed, Leavitt and Whisler all but called for an end to middle management, which would be replaced by computer systems that promised "to eliminate the risk of less than adequate decisions arising from garbled communications, from misconceptions of goals and from unsatisfactory measurement of partial contributions on the part of dozens of line and staff specialists." The manager's function, in other words, was to be usurped by computer chips and algorithms. And as the mid-layers of org charts disappeared, companies would become less hierarchical—flatter.[13]

Clearly we're still stuck with middle management and garbled communications. But firms actually are flatter than they once were. In just the dozen years from 1986 through 1998, HBS professor Julie Wulf documented a decline of 25 percent in the layers of management separating CEOs from divisional heads in a sample of three hundred publicly traded companies. As companies flattened, they became "wider" as well, with more executives reporting directly to the CEO—an average of 8.2 in 1998, up from 4.4 in 1986. (This also means that in the org of the future, CEOs will spend even *more* time in meetings—Wulf found that the increase in direct reports from flattening translated directly into more time spent meeting with them.)[14]

Wulf and her coauthor, Raghuram Rajan, describe the 2002 reorganization of General Electric as a case in point. That year, the chairman of GE Capital resigned. Instead of replacing him, GE CEO Jeff Immelt simply made the four business unit heads report to him so that they would, in Immelt's words "interact directly with me, enabling faster decision making and execution."[15]

According to work by researchers at the London School of Economics, IT played at least some role in the Great Flattening of the last half century.[16] Companies that deployed information technology more intensively had more managers reporting directly to each supervisor. This flattening of the hierarchy was the result of greater autonomy given to lower-level employees. With more information at their fingertips, there's less need to consult supervisors for advice or expert opinion. If information is power, the spread of information technology has been empowering.

And yet, improved communication systems, as distinct from IT, actually push decisions back up the hierarchy. Imagine the owner of a small home heating oil delivery business who goes off to play tennis every Thursday afternoon. Inevitably, an employee will call to ask about a delivery—should such-and-such a customer get a credit extension? In an earlier era, the employee might have made the decision. But the owner has made himself available by cell phone, allowing him to pass expert judgment on such matters even while out of the office, even if he wishes he couldn't.

Technology has also altered the boundary of the org itself. And it isn't simply that we're all destined to be freelancers in Internet cafés. Paradoxically, it's caused a shift at least as much in the opposite direction. In 1980 the twenty-fourth-largest company on *Fortune*'s list of the five hundred biggest employers in America was Boeing, with a payroll of just under a hundred thousand. By 2011, the twenty-fourth-largest employer on the list was Lowe's, the home improvement mega chain, which employs nearly two hundred thousand.

What's driving this growth, at least in part, are the same technological forces that have flattened Boeing and others: more information. In fact, one contribution to Lowe's expanding payroll can be linked directly to the advent of onboard computers that allowed bosses to keep tabs on what a trucker working for the company did between leaving with his haul and arriving at his destination. In the days before trip recordings, the driver could, if he chose, take leisurely breaks at truck stops and make up the time by racing at eighty miles an hour down the highway, endangering himself, other motorists, and company profits.

Even worse, long-haul truckers would end up spending the night at truck stops, centers of prostitution, drug dealing, theft, and even murder. One borough in New Jersey with the worst crime record in its county blames it all on the truck stop.[17] It's bad enough when you have to send your employees to Vegas for a conference; sending them out on long trips in trucks can be much, much worse.

And so companies such as Lowe's used to hire freelance drivers who owned their rigs, making them responsible for the cost of wear and tear on the trucks and the consequences of reckless endangerment. Contractors such as these will drive more carefully and diligently knowing they're on the hook for damage or delays.[18]

The trip recorder altered the basic trade-off between in-house and outsourced trucking by providing a Big Brotherly presence to watch over drivers while they were out on the road. Now Lowe's can track and coordinate trucks and their shipments far more easily and reliably. So today, more trucks are company-owned and more truckers are company-employed than just a few decades ago—in part because of the same IT that helped make Starbucks a successful outpost of the modern office.

Networking at DEC

Solitary heroes, our comic book alter egos such as Batman, Superman, and the Lone Ranger, achieved greatness only by painting outside the lines, free of the org. (Villains, on the other hand, always seem to have henchmen waiting in the wings.) Batman wouldn't have had the time to keep Gotham City safe from evil if he had to spend his days in line at the DMV to register the Batmobile or file paperwork at police headquarters.

Becoming Batman may be the ultimate office fantasy. To shout, "I'm as mad as hell and I'm not going to take it anymore. Screw the paperwork! Forget reporting protocols! I see a job that needs doing for the good of the org, and together, we're going to get it done, damn it!"

While we celebrate the comic book successes of mavericks and freethinkers, they're often a recipe for disaster. As much of a downer as it might be, initiative and good intentions need to be kept in line by the rules of the org.

In teaching his students the perils of well-meaning employee initiative, Glenn Carroll, a professor at the Stanford Graduate School of Business, uses a case study of Digital Equipment Corporation (DEC), which tells of the company's well-meaning but ultimately ill-fated bid for a desperately needed contract.

In 1989, with the world mired in a recession, DEC had cut costs and downsized its payroll. At the same time, it knew that its main business, the mid-market minicomputer, was dying fast, trapped between mainframes and PCs that were quickly squeezing the mini market out of existence. A big win would provide a much-needed contribution to the bottom line, and perhaps, more important, a boost to morale.

Russ Gullotti, a DEC vice president in Enterprise Integration Systems, saw a contract to provide an internal communications network to Kodak as the Big Opportunity. For decades, DEC had provided Kodak with computing equipment. Kodak was now looking for a single company that would manage every aspect of its internal communications, from the sourcing of equipment to the management of its network. It was an opportunity worth tens of millions of dollars, with the potential to transform DEC into a provider of complete IT solutions to corporate clients—a direction in which DEC correctly anticipated the market was headed. If it lost the bid, it wouldn't merely lose out on new work—it expected to lose its current business with Kodak as well.

DEC had a small office in Kodak's hometown of Rochester, New York, to service the account. The Rochester team had no telecommunications experience, and were somewhat disconnected from the DEC headquarters in Maynard, Massachusetts.

DEC stood no chance against industry heavyweights such as IBM, AT&T, and Sprint if the job of putting together a proposal were left to the Kodak account team, and the contract was seen as important enough for the company's future that Gullotti was appointed godfather of the project.

With just a month to cobble together a bid, going through the standard channels of requisitioning staff time and resources simply wasn't possible. But that only played to DEC's strong suit. The company prided itself on a culture of initiative and innovation, and had a long history of leadership in computing technology. As with other incubators of innovation—HP, 3M, and the like—motivated individuals were encouraged to bring promising projects to life, provided they could get sufficient buy-in from superiors. With the buzz and excitement about the Kodak bid, Gullotti had the go-ahead to pull together whatever resources were needed to put in an aggressive bid on a very short time line.

Gullotti took full advantage of the opportunity. He had an unparalleled network within DEC and tremendous powers of persuasion: People from around the company uprooted their lives and moved to upstate New York to work around the clock, seven days a week. According to one employee involved in the project, "It was like the old DEC—'do what's right.' This was an opportunity to propel DEC into becoming a major telecommunications player. Some people moved to Rochester and gave their all for this project. They just canceled birthdays, anniversaries, canceled their life" for the project's duration. People just told their bosses, "They need us in Rochester."

The effort paid off. Kodak narrowed the field to IBM and DEC, before awarding DEC the contract. Gullotti and his impromptu team were the big winners.

After winning the contract to provide Kodak with a communications network, DEC still needed to hammer out the details on what services, exactly, it would provide. Gullotti had already returned to his life and job back in Maynard, as had the rest of the team that had flown out to Rochester. The task of actually servicing the contract was likely to fall to DEC's customer service division, which hadn't been involved in the process up to that point. The customer service people, in Gullotti's words, worked "straight from the book." Their involvement in the original bid for the contract would have been an encumbrance to the "technologists, creative types, mavericks" who had worked so hard, outside the normal chain of command, to put together the winning combination.

As the finance and customer service departments began to review the work they'd have to do to service the contract, these by-the-book, straitlaced creators of red tape discovered a significant financial miscalculation in the contract—and only hours before it was set to be signed. DEC's employees had put forth great effort, with the best of intentions, all to disastrous effect.

Flouting the rules of the org is great for getting things done. But sometimes, without sufficient checks and balances, they turn out not to be the *right* things. Much-maligned bean counters and compliance personnel exist to make sure this doesn't happen too often, even if it means that, some of the time, not much of anything gets done at all. Innovation and initiative have their place in any organization, but so do coordination and rules. The trick is knowing how much of each.

The dangers of networking in a big organization are clear: lack of accountability, lack of coordination, lack of oversight, lack of a clear definition of jobs and responsibilities—all the things that we have orgs for in the first place.

Sometimes we don't need Superman. Sometimes we need Clark Kent.

The Ultimate Org: Al Qaeda

When the terrorist organization Al Qaeda grabbed global headlines with its attack on the United States in 2001, many experts pointed to it as a triumph of the networked organization. Here was a group seemingly without a leader, without a bureaucracy, or much of a hierarchy. It had supremely devoted followers—ones willing to kill themselves in its service—who all were motivated by the same beliefs and were all aimed at the same objective. Could this be the organization of the future?

Once the United States invaded Iraq and encountered a successful insurgency that operated on the same networked principles, the answer seemed clear: the terrorist organization, a decentralized alliance of networks that was holding back the might of the U.S. military, surely held lessons for any organization looking to get stuff done.

But let's reflect on a memo, captured in 2008 but dating back to the 1990s, from Egyptian Al Qaeda leader Mohammed Atef to a subordinate. Atef, a former agricultural engineer, wrote:

> I was very upset by what you did. I obtained 75,000 rupees for you and your family's trip to Egypt. I learned that you did not submit the voucher to the accountant, and that you made reservations for 40,000 rupees and kept the remainder claiming you have a right to do so . . . Also with respect to the air-conditioning unit . . . furniture used by brothers in Al Qaeda is not considered private property . . . I would like to remind you and myself of the punishment for any violation.

That's right: Al Qaeda required a T&E report. Neither allegiance to a cause nor the threat of "punishment for any violation" was enough to keep the troops in line. Even Al Qaeda, the networked org of the future, succumbed to the weight of organizing.[19]

———

Max Weber, a nineteenth-century German philosopher who became one of the fathers of modern social science and one of the original org scholars, described the rise of bureaucracy as an "iron cage" that crushed free will and doomed us all to "the polar night of icy darkness." And yet, he wrote, "The decisive reason for the advance of bureaucratic organization has always been its purely technical superiority over any other form of organization."

This is not a pretty picture, and it's not the one we want you to leave with.[20]

We hope you see the message better summed up by the so-called Serenity Prayer, attributed to theologian Reinhold Niebuhr:

> *God, grant me the serenity to accept the things I cannot change,*
> *Courage to change the things I can,*
> *And wisdom to know the difference.*

We hope we've given you an appreciation of the trade-offs that organizations face as they grow and evolve, the serenity to accept the things about them that can't be changed, the courage to change the things you can, and the wisdom to know the difference.

ACKNOWLEDGMENTS

(Fisman)

I'd like to thank first and foremost my coauthor. Working on the book has been a case study in team production: the process was truly made greater than the sum of its parts through a very happy and productive collaboration.

I would also like to thank the many members of my family, nuclear and beyond, who have patiently listened to various half-baked ideas on the economics of organizations.

(Sullivan)

The old saw that you don't write a book alone is doubly true in this case. First, I'd like to thank Ray for his time, patience, expertise, and friendship.

I'd also like to thank my family, and especially my wife, Wendy, who has supported me—with good humor, graciousness, and insight—during the writing process even as I let my own end of the bargain slip.

———

Together, we'd like to thank the following people who read the manuscript, or parts of it, and offered comments, or who graciously agreed to be interviewed for or discuss the ideas in the book:

Nick Bloom, Glenn Carroll, David del Ser, Seth Ditchik, Stephen Dutton, Roz Engle, Todd Fitch, Carola Frydman, Joshua Gans, Luis Garicano, Karen Gennette, Bob Gibbons, Jimmy Guterman, Jay Hartzell, Tom Hubbard, Matt Kahn, Emir Kamenica, Jeff Kehoe, Scott Kominers, LTC David Lyle, Preston McAfee, Henry Mintzberg, Gardiner Morse, Peter Moskos, Chris Parsons, COL Jeffrey Peterson, Andrea Prat, Canice Prendergast, Jan Rivkin, Raffaella Sadun, LTC Reid Sawyer, Kendall Sullivan, Scot Sullivan, Scott Urban, John Van Reenen, Ted Weinstein, Ania Wieckowski, Julie Wulf, and participants at the Org Econ lunchtime seminar at MIT.

We'd like to thank Wouter Dessein in particular, for his generosity with his time and expertise in helping us navigate the enormous academic literature in the economics of organizations, and for his many fantastic ideas on how to connect theory to practical example. We've used so many of his ideas in this book that he probably deserves a 33 percent cut of our royalties.

Finally, we'd like to thank Jay Mandel, our agent, and Jonathan Karp, who originally showed interest in the proposal. Cary Goldstein, our editor and publisher, and his team at Twelve have performed beyond compare.

NOTES

Introduction: A Machine for Getting Stuff Done

1. On the hours spent at work, see the work and employment data from the U.S. Bureau of Labor Statistics American Time Use Survey. On the office spouse, see en.wikipedia.org/wiki/Work_spouse. The 65 percent figure is from a Captivate Office Pulse survey (officepulse.captivate.com/workspouse). For an overview of the idea of the work spouse, see Timothy Noah, "Prexy Sks Wrk Wf," *Slate*, November 17, 2004.

2. When economists tried to encapsulate the entire world in their simple black-box economy, the outputs were usually called things such as "corn" and "tractors"—that is, nourishment for labor and new capital for old and broken machines—to feed the agro-industrial complex that was those items' maker. The world was thus a virtous circle of production and consumption begetting yet more production.

3. You can read the whole sad saga at Curtis's website, www.dustincurtis .com/dear_american_airlines.html.

4. Stephen Meyer, "Efforts at Americanization in the Industrial Work-place, 1914–1921," in John Gjerde, ed., *Major Problems in American Immigration and Ethnic History* (New York: Houghton-Mifflin, 1998). Daniel Raff, "Wage Determination Theory and the Five-Dollar Day at Ford," *Journal of Economic History* 48, no. 2 (June 1988): 387–99. Raff argues that efficiency wages are an insufficient explanation, and that the real cause was Ford's fear of collective action by labor—that Ford was, in Raff's words, "buying the peace."

5. 3M, the company behind Post-it notes, seems to have been the first to offer this kind of deal, having introduced 15 percent time in 1948. See www.fastcodesign.com/1663137/how-3m-gave-everyone-days-off-and -created-an-innovation-dynamo. Tellingly, Google's big strategic move into social networking with Google+, an attempt to compete with sites such as Facebook, was a top-down initiative, not a bottom-up one.

6. The cycle continues. Now that Facebook is a billion-dollar publicly traded company, it is forced to defend its employees from the next round of start-ups promising options potentially worth untold riches, not to mention freedom from bureaucracy.

7. Michael Arrington at TechCrunch has done a series of articles on the poaching problem, including, "Google Making Extraordinary Counteroffers to Stop Flow of Employees to Facebook" (techcrunch.com/2010/09/01 /google-making-extraordinary-counteroffers-to-stop-flow-of-employees -to-facebook/, accessed July 15, 2012). The story of the former Apple engineer's firing from Google comes from Gawker (gawker.com/5696695/google -fired-an-apple-legend-for-leaking-internal-memo, accessed July 15, 2012). You can see a graphic of how Facebook seems to be winning the Silicon Valley talent wars at blog.topprospect.com/2011/06/the-biggest-talent-losers -and-winners/, accessed July 15, 2012.

Chapter 1: The Outsider

1. Urban charged $450 for basic frames when he started out and has increased his prices by about $100 a year. And in case you doubt that Urban Spectacles really are all that, we should note that Ray owns two pairs, which regularly attract adoring comments from beautiful twentysomethings in Manhattan.

2. It is perhaps poetic justice that when Ray visited the basement workshop, Urban's dog, Herb, took to chewing on Ray's newly purchased Barneys blazer.

3. That's not to say they always did everything well. In his autobiography, *The HP Way* (New York: HarperCollins, 1996), David Packard notes that

the price of their first product, a radio oscillator, was set so low that they initially lost money on each sale. We should note that the HP story has been told many times in many forums. We also draw on Michael Malone's *Bill and Dave: How Hewlett and Packard Built the World's Greatest Company* (New York: Portfolio/Penguin Group, 2007), among other accounts.

4. Peter Drucker, a management guru, introduced the term in 1954 in his book *The Practice of Management* (New York: Harper & Row, 1954).

5. Peter Burrows, "Hewlett & Packard: Architects of the Info Age," *BusinessWeek*, March 29, 2004 (www.businessweek.com/magazine/content /04_13/b3876054.htm, accessed July 14, 2012).

6. Andrew Pollack, "Hewlett's 'Consummate Strategist,'" *New York Times*, March 10, 1992 (www.nytimes.com/1992/03/10/business/hewlett -s-consummate-strategist.html?src=pm).

7. Alex Dobuzinskis, "Fiorina, Hurd: no practitioners of 'The HP Way'?" *Globe and Mail*, August 9, 2010 (theglobeandmail.com/news/technology /fiorina-hurd-no-practitioners-of-the-hp-way/article1666530/).

8. Bob Evans, "Global CIO: In Praise of Mark Hurd's 9,000 Layoffs at Hewlett-Packard," *Information Week*, June 2, 2010 (www.informationweek .com/news/global-cio/interviews/225300072).

9. According to Harold Demsetz in *Ownership, Control, and the Firm*, and quoted by Ronald Coase in his 1991 Nobel lecture, which you can read at www .nobelprize.org/nobel_prizes/economics/laureates/1991/coase-lecture.html.

10. In practice, most of those meeting at the Mercantile Exchange are traders speculating on future prices of copper, wheat, and pork bellies. Actual producers and consumers of raw materials have already signed "futures" contracts that lock in the prices they get for their output and pay for their inputs, passing the risk of future price fluctuations on to speculators who do nothing but trade without ever producing or consuming any tangible products.

11. Eric K. Clemons, Il-Horn Hann, and Lorin M. Hitt, "Price Dispersion and Differentiation in Online Travel: An Empirical Investigation," *Management Science* 48, no. 4 (April 2002): 534–49.

12. Organizations scholars, however, did pay heed to Coase's insights, and the work of Richard Cyert, James March, and Herbert Simon helped to set the stage for the next wave of organizational economics that we'll focus on throughout this book. We mean no disrespect to their contributions by ignoring them here. Book writing, too, involves a trade-off between brevity and completeness.

Chapter 2: Designing the Job

1. Moskos was following in the particular footsteps of MIT professor John Van Maanen, who in the 1960s followed Seattle police through their training and onto the streets.

2. Daniel resigned after just a few months, but as Moskos notes in *Cop in the Hood* (Princeton: Princeton University Press, 2008), on which, together with interviews of Moskos, we base much of this account, Moskos's ulterior motives were lost in the shuffle when Daniel's replacement came in.

3. In 2009, Baltimore had a murder rate that put it in the top five among American cities with more than 250,000 residents, much the same position it held when Moskos enrolled at the police academy.

4. On this point, see Steven Kerr's classic, and entertaining, article "On the Folly of Rewarding A while Hoping for B," *Academy of Management Journal* 18 (1975): 769–83.

5. More recently, the Baltimore City Police Department has both halved the arrest rate while simultaneously reducing the homicide rate—an impressive feat.

6. Jason Hibbs, "Firefighters Watch as Home Burns to the Ground," September 29, 2010, WPSD, local NBC affiliate in Tennessee (www.wpsdlocal6.com/news/local/Firefighters-watch-as-home-burns-to-the-ground-104052668.html).

7. Anonymous, "Factories: Disassembling the Line," *Time*, January 7, 1972 (www.time.com/time/magazine/article/0,9171,877659,00.html).

8. Team production also allows individual teams to self-manage and in-novate, coming up with their own solutions for arranging the team to maximize production. On an assembly line, each worker sees just one step in the production chain, so it's hard for him to think about how the overall process might be reconfigured to speed things up. As a result, assembly-line innovation is driven by top managers, who may be too far removed from the realities of the factory floor to see the best way of organizing.

9. Timothy Tyler, "Where the Auto Reigns Supreme," *Time*, April 3, 1972.

10. Brian Jacob, Lars Lefgren, and Enrico Moretti, "The Dynamics of Criminal Behavior: Evidence from Weather Shocks," NBER Working Paper No. 10739, September 2004 (www.nber.org/papers/w10739).

11. Gretchen Morgenson, "Was There a Loan It Didn't Like?" *New York Times*, November 1, 2008 (www.nytimes.com/2008/11/02/business/02gret .html?partner=rssuserland&emc=rss&pagewanted=all).

12. Pierre Thomas and Lauren Pearle, "WaMu Insiders Claim Execs Ig-nored Warnings, Encouraged Reckless Lending," Nightline/ABC News, October 13, 2008 (abcnews.go.com/TheLaw/story?id=6021608&page=1).

13. This is analogous to Home Depot execs donning orange aprons to work in company stores and warehouses, and to the premise of the *Under-cover Boss* reality show, which documents the travails of *Fortune* 500 CEOs forced to work on their companies' front lines. On Kayak, see "The Way I Work," as told to Liz Welch, *Inc.*, February 1, 2010 (www.inc.com/maga-zine/20100201/the-way-i-work-paul-english-of-kayak.html), and Robert Levine's "The Success of Kayak.com," *Fast Company*, September 1, 2008 (www.fastcompany.com/magazine/128/globe-trotter.html).

14. By 1997, *PC World* magazine was running articles arguing, "CD-ROM reference titles are so vastly superior to their printed counterparts that it almost makes you feel bad. Who's going to buy an $800, 500-pound, 12-volume bookshelf monster when you can get a $70, two-CD, unabridged multimedia title?" And then along came the Internet. Encyclopædia Britan-nica shuttered its print edition in the spring of 2012.

15. Lauren Dell, "The Perks of Working at Google, Facebook, Twitter and More," *Mashable*, October 17, 2011 (mashable.com/2011/10/17/google -facebook-twitter-linkedin-perks-infographic/).

16. Frances Frei and Corey Hajim, "Commerce Bank" (HBS Case 603-080) and "Four Things a Service Company Must Get Right," *Harvard Business Review*, April 2008.

17. Michael Spence won the 2001 Nobel Prize in economics for his work on signaling in job markets, which we describe here in its simplest form.

18. Tony Hsieh, *Delivering Happiness: A Path to Profits, Passion, and Purpose* (New York: Business Plus, 2010).

19. Even going back to the 1970s, when Joseph Wambaugh was writing lightly fictionalized, comically horrifying takes on policing in Los Angeles. See, for instance, *The Choirboys* (New York: Random House, 1975).

Chapter 3: Putting Together the Organizational Puzzle

1. The well-worn story that Luther nailed his theses to the cathedral door is sadly apocryphal.

2. The sale of indulgences had a long history in the church, falling under the doctrine of "good works" that the faithful had to perform. But even under more enlightened leadership, the sale of indulgences had fallen victim to the same kinds of problems that can beset any sales force. In 1215, for example, church leaders had issued a warning against pardoners staying in taverns or otherwise running up their expense tabs. But under Leo, the sales of indulgences were thoroughly corrupted. The chief publicist of the indulgences in Germany, a Dominican preacher named Johann Tetzer, came up with a sales pitch that historian Eamon Duffy translates as, "Place your penny on the drum / The pearly gates open and in strolls mum." *Ka-ching!*

3. United Methodist Church website, "Mission and Ministry" (www.umc .org/site/c.lwL4KnN1LtH/b.2295473/k.7034/Mission_and_Ministry.htm), accessed August 3, 2010.

4. Thanks to Jay Hartzell for the pointer.

5. Tammy never lost her faith or capitalist impulses, cashing in on her fame with a book deal and her own TV show, until her death in 2007. After a rocky road following the collapse of PTL, Jim continued his broadcasting career.

6. The quote is from the "Structure and Organization: Governance" section of the United Methodist Church's website: www.umc.org/site/c .lwL4KnN1LtH/b.1720699/k.528D/Structure__Organization_Governance .htm, last accessed July 8, 2012.

7. Chapter 258.2 of *The Book of Discipline of the United Methodist Church* (Nashville: Abingdon Press, 2009).

8. Ray is a collaborator on the first of these studies.

9. This was the well-meaning idea of the Church Growth Movement, first articulated by missionary Donald McGavran in the mid-1950s, according to William Chadwick, *Stealing Sheep* (Westmont, IL: InterVarsity Press, 2001).

10. Chadwick, *Stealing Sheep*.

11. Leonard Sayles, "Matrix Management: The Structure with a Future," *Organizational Dynamics* 5, no. 2 (Autumn 1976): 2.

Chapter 4: In Praise of Squelching Innovation

1. John Keegan, *A History of Warfare* (New York: Vintage, 1994).

2. Alfred D. Chandler, "The Railroads and the Beginnings of Modern Management," Harvard Business School case, 1995.

3. The misadventures of D-Day paratroopers were documented in detail in Stephen Ambrose's *Band of Brothers* (New York: Simon and Schuster, 2001), which is the source for the material we describe here.

4. This quote appears in a range of wordings. This version is from Stephen Ambrose's *D-Day* (New York: Simon and Schuster, 1994).

5. Colonel John T. Carney Jr., *No Room for Error: The Covert Operations of America's Special Tactics Units from Iran to Afghanistan* (New York: Ballantine, 2002).

6. The full story of the Black Hawk shooting is compellingly told by Scott Snook—a retired Army colonel and now a professor at the Harvard Business School—in *Friendly Fire: The Accidental Shootdown of U.S. Black Hawks over Northern Iraq* (Princeton: Princeton University Press, 2002).

7. John Love, *McDonald's: Behind the Arches* (New York: Bantam, 1986).

8. Best Global Brands 2011, Interbrand (www.interbrand.com/en/best -global-brands/best-global-brands-2008/best-global-brands-2011.aspx, accessed July 9, 2012).

9. We were not aware that there were any jokes in *The Hot Chick*, or, if there were, that they could possibly be consistent with Disney's image. Edward Jay Epstein, *The Big Picture: The New Logic of Power and Money in Hollywood* (New York: Random House, 2000).

10. Now that the operations are well established, McD's has finished selling off portions of its vertically integrated business. Andrew E. Kramer, "Russia's Evolution, Seen Through Golden Arches," *New York Times*, February 1, 2010 (www.nytimes.com/2010/02/02/business/global/02mcdonalds .html).

11. John Cloud, "In Defense of Applebee's," *Time*, July 25, 2006 (www .time.com/time/nation/article/0,8599,1218911,00.html).

12. The suggestion box does not always bear fruit: one item in the post–Operation Overlord suggestion box from the paratroopers was to force each pilot to jump out of a plane going 150 miles per hour to see what it was like.

13. For general background, see Love, *McDonald's: Behind the Arches.* Clayton Christensen, "Innovation: A Happy Meal for McDonald's," *Forbes*, October 26, 2007 (www.forbes.com/2007/08/31/christensen-innovation -mcdonalds-pf-guru_in_cc_0904christensen_inl.html).

14. Owing to depleted cod stocks, McDonald's switched to hoki in the 1990s, and more recently to Alaskan pollack with the decline in hoki populations.

15. Tim Hindle, "Survey: The Company: The New Organization," *Economist*, January 19, 2006.

16. It's a view that was endorsed by, among others, Joseph Schumpeter, an economist from the first half of the twentieth century who enjoys a cult-like status (at least among fellow economists) for his work on innovation. Schumpeter is best known for coining the phrase "creative destruction," used to describe the steady waves of entrepreneurial innovation that constantly supplant larger, older, profitable firms in a capitalist economy. Yet he also noted that much technological innovation came from precisely these overgrown dinosaurs, as they were the ones with the financial resources to spend on R&D, and would be driven to do so by fear of being displaced by upstart start-ups.

17. Stephen Ambrose, *Duty, Honor, Country: A History of West Point* (Baltimore: Johns Hopkins University Press, 1999).

18. David Cloud and Greg Jaffe, *The Fourth Star: Four Generals and the Epic Struggle for the Future of the United States Army* (New York: Crown, 2009).

19. At the time of printing, Sawyer was no longer at West Point. This discussion reflects conversations with Colonel Sawyer in March 2010.

20. As told to Wesley Morgan, a rising Princeton sophomore and ROTC cadet embedded with U.S. forces in Iraq during his summer break.

Chapter 5: What Management Is Good For

1. Perhaps unsurprisingly, McKinsey took a pass on participating in the study. What would it say to its clients about the value of its services if implementing McKinsey-style management had no effect, or even worse, if it reduced the cotton weavers' profits? It also may have balked at the cost. All of

the material for these studies can be found at www.worldmanagementsurvey
.org/. See Benn Eifert, David McKenzie, Aprajit Mahajan, and John Roberts,
"Does Management Matter: Evidence from India," Stanford University
Working Paper, 2012, for the India management study; and Nick Bloom
and John Van Reenen, "Measuring and Explaining Management Practices
Across Firms and Countries," *Quarterly Journal of Economics* 122, no. 4
(2007): 1351–408, for the original survey of management practices around
the world.

2. The remaining eight factories belonged to firms that owned some of
the first fourteen; the economists used them to see if "good" management
practices would spread to different factories owned by the same firm.

3. Some of these photos are reprinted in the study's back pages.

4. More recent work by researchers at MIT, Yale, and the World Bank
suggests that the payoff from better management is even higher at small organizations. In a 2012 study that provided $11,000 worth of management con-
sulting to small- and medium-size enterprises in Mexico (average number of
employees: fourteen), the authors found that the resulting increase in profits
was such that the consulting fees would pay for themselves within a single
month. Miriam Bruhn, Dean Karlan, and Antoinette Schoar, "The Impact of
Consulting Services on Small and Medium Enterprises: Evidence from a Randomized Trial in Mexico," Yale Economics Department Working Paper No.
100, Yale University Economic Growth Center Discussion Paper No. 1010.

5. The notion of the experience curve was developed in the late 1960s by
Bruce Henderson, founder of the Boston Consulting Group.

6. If he did catch the manager in the act of stealing, he would have little
legal recourse. As Bloom et al. point out, India's shortage of managers is out-
done by its extreme paucity of judges.

7. Alfred D. Chandler Jr., *The Visible Hand: The Managerial Revolution
in American Business* (Cambridge: Belknap Press of Harvard University Press,
1977). See also Steven W. Usselman, "Still Visible: Alfred D. Chandler's *The
Visible Hand*," *Technology and Culture* 47, no. 3 (July 2006), and the
Economist's obituary of Chandler, which ran in the May 17, 2007, edition.

8. The *D* in Alfred D. Chandler is for Du Pont. His family ties clearly gave him a leg up in documenting the practices of leading American businesses, not least GM which was owned in large part by the Du Pont family when Alfred Sloan was running it.

9. Michael Lewis, "The New Organization Man," *Slate*, October 30, 1997 (www.slate.com/articles/arts/millionerds/1997/10/the_new_organization _man.html, accessed July 11, 2012).

10. Roy Radner, "Hierarchy: The Economics of Managing," *Journal of Economic Literature* 30, no. 3 (September 1992): 1382–415.

11. While there was general agreement on the need for professional managers, it took several decades beyond the Harvard Business School's founding for the MBA really to take hold. And there was, and continues to be, much controversy over what constitutes professional management training, beyond bookkeeping, arithmetic, and penmanship. See Carter Daniel's *MBA: The First Century* (Lewisburg, PA: Bucknell University Press, 1998) for a thorough overview of the history of management education, including reference to the business school with separate penmanship departments.

12. Luis Garicano and Esteban Rossi-Hansberg, "Organization and Inequality in a Knowledge Economy," *Quarterly Journal of Economics* 121, no. 4 (November 2006): 1383–1485.

13. Guido Friebel and Michael Raith, "Abuse of Authority and Hierarchical Communication," *RAND Journal of Economics* 35, no. 2 (Summer 2004): 224–44.

14. Many companies have management rotation programs so would-be leaders can see if they're suited to leadership roles before being promoted.

15. Random promotions mean that you're unlikely to promote the best person from the lower level, which ensures continued efficiency (that is, the best person is unlikely to get promoted and will continue to do his or her job). Since there's no way to guess whether someone will be good at the new job, random chance is as good as any other method. Alessandro Pluchino, Andrea Rapisarda, and Cesare Garofalo, "The Peter Principle

Revisited: A Computational Study," *Physica A* 389, no. 3 (February 2010): 467–72.

16. For more on Project Oxygen, see Adam Bryant, "Google's Quest to Build a Better Boss," *New York Times*, March 12, 2011 (www.nytimes.com /2011/03/13/business/13hire.html, accessed July 11, 2012).

17. You can find Rands's series on why managers are not, in fact, evil at his website, www.randsinrepose.com/archives/2006/02/17/managers_are _not_evil_pt_1.html. Rands, aka Michael Lopp, also has a book, *Managing Humans: Biting and Humorous Tales of a Software Engineering Manager* (New York: Apress, 2007).

18. "Maker's schedule, manager's schedule," July 2009, at Graham's blog: www.paulgraham.com/makersschedule.html, accessed July 11, 2012.

19. IFC Advisory Services in East Asia and the Pacific, "Supervisory Skills Training in the Cambodian Garment Industry: A Randomized Impact Evaluation," IFC Working Paper, 2009 (www.betterfactories.org/content /documents/SST%20Randomization%20public%20report.pdf, accessed July 11, 2012).

20. It's not always someone else who's misbehaving. We just think it is. In *Predictably Irrational*, Duke psychologist Dan Ariely describes a lab experiment where subjects were paid based on the number of math questions they answered correctly. For the control group, the answers were graded by lab staff. For the other group, participants were allowed to self-report on how many questions they'd gotten right, providing a window for them to lie about their performance to increase their earnings. Not surprisingly, the self-report group reported getting more questions right. More intriguingly, subjects cheated much more when they were paid in tokens that were then converted into dollars, relative to when they were paid directly in dollars. Ariely suggests that this is a useful metaphor for the ease with which we all pocket pens and copy paper from the supply closet, even though many of us would never steal banknotes from the petty cash box.

Chapter 6: The View from the Corner Office

1. Rakesh Khurana, *Searching for a Corporate Savior: The Irrational Quest for Charismatic CEOs* (Princeton: Princeton University Press, 2002).

2. The "industrial" has long since been dropped from the name of MIT's management school, which now resides in an ultramodern Frank Gehry–designed $142 million facility overlooking the Charles River in Cambridge, Massachusetts.

3. Of course, given that these were longer meetings, they accounted for much more than 10 percent of the CEOs' total workdays.

4. Rosanne Badowski, with Roger Gittines, *Managing Up: How to Forge an Effective Relationship with Those Above You* (New York: Doubleday, 2003).

5. Which is why Mintzberg professes to dislike MBAs: he thinks they don't know which information is relevant.

6. The flow of information in a hierarchy has been studied extensively by, among others, leading organizational economist Luis Garicano in "Hierarchies and the Organization of Knowledge in Production," *Journal of Political Economy* 108, no. 5 (2000).

7. Michael E. Porter and Nitin Nohria, "The CEO's Role in Large, Complex Organizations," in Nitin Nohria and Rakesh Khurana, eds., *Handbook of Leadership Theory and Practice* (Boston: Harvard Business Review Press, 2010).

8. Both quotes taken from P&G CEO Robert McDonald's opening statement in the company's 2010 annual report.

9. Again echoing an earlier guru, HBS's Ted Levitt and his seminal article "Marketing Myopia," first published in the *Harvard Business Review* in 1960.

10. Adam Lashinsky, "How Apple Works: Inside the World's Biggest Startup," *Fortune*, May 23, 2011.

11. Marianne Bertrand and Antoinette Schoar, "Managing with Style: The Effect of Managers on Firm Policies," *Quarterly Journal of Economics* 118, no. 4 (2003): 1169–208.

12. £590,000 in salary, plus £1.04 million in bonus, and another £1.2 million in retention bonus.

13. By 2011, Mulally's annual salary was up to $34 million, as his leadership of Ford continued to produce record profits for the automaker. "EasyJet CEO: Because I'm Worth It," *Wall Street Journal*, "The Source," February 19, 2010 (blogs.wsj.com/source/2010/02/19/easyjet-ceo-because-im-worth -it/).

14. Card counting involves keeping track of the cards that have been dealt from the deck or decks in play, and using this information to tilt the odds of winning in favor of the counter. For example, in blackjack, where the objective is to accumulate cards as close in value to twenty-one without going over, it's an enormous advantage for a player holding a hand with nineteen to know how many twos have already been played. Vegas dealers use multiple decks at once and destroy the decks before all the cards have been dealt to limit the effectiveness of card counting.

15. Although casinos aren't as careful as you'd think they would be: see Andrew Rosenblum, "Why Baccarat, the Game of Princes and Spies, Has Become a Target for High-Tech Cheaters," *PopSci*, August 11, 2011 (www .popsci.com/technology/article/2011-08/baccarat-101-why-high-rolling -game-princes-and-spies-has-become-target-high-tech-cheaters, accessed July 11, 2012).

16. The immense profitability of card counting doesn't alone guarantee a high wage for card counters. If winning at the blackjack table were easy, the rivalry among card counters would compete away their share of the earnings, as they undercut one another to secure support from the relatively scarce financiers. If the best alternative for these players were, say, flipping burgers, they might not earn much above minimum wage. The fact that the McDonald's CEO earns about a thousand times his minimum-wage burger flippers implies that lots of people believe that the very best managers, capable of providing slightly higher profitability multiplied across a $1 billion operation,

are a scarce breed relative to the number of companies looking for people to lead them. In other words, there aren't enough superstar CEOs to go around. And that's certainly the implication of articles like this one in *Fortune*, praising McDonald's current superstar CEO: Beth Kowitt, "Why McDonald's Wins in Any Economy," *Fortune*, August 23, 2011 (management.fortune .cnn.com/2011/08/23/why-mcdonalds-wins-in-any-economy/, accessed July 11, 2012).

17. This is why, as reported in a 2012 study (Morten Bennedsen, Francisco Pérez-González, and Daniel Wolfenzon, "Evaluating the Impact of The Boss: Evidence from CEO Hospitalization Events," available at www .stanford.edu/~fperezg/valueboss.pdf), CEO hospitalizations harm company profits, while the hospitalizations of other senior executives have no measurable effect on the bottom line.

18. Sherwin Rosen, "The Economics of Superstars," *American Economic Review* 71, no. 5 (December 1981): 845–58. Even in cases where CEOs *are* in fact worth it, superstars are at risk of taking their eye off the bigger picture—distracted by the many opportunities that come with fame and media attention, such as writing books and sitting on more corporate boards. Or so say finance professors Ulrike Malmendier of Berkeley and Geoff Tate of UCLA, who have written extensively on what happens to superstar CEOs who start to believe a little too much in their own infallibility. Malmendier and Tate examined executives' records after they got awards such as "CEO of the Year" from magazines including *Forbes*, *Chief Executive*, and *Business-Week*. They find that being CEO of the Year is good for the CEO—the pay of award-winning leaders rises faster than that of other execs in their companies, who presumably should also have gotten some credit for improving corporate performance. But relative to runner-up CEOs, profits decline at the companies of prize-winning CEOs in the years following the award. "Superstar CEOs," *Quarterly Journal of Economics* 124, no. 4 (November 2009): 1593–638.

19. Quote is from David Buik, BCG Partners, quoted in Graeme Wearden, "BP Credit Rating Downgraded after Tony Hayward's Grilling by Congress," *Guardian* (UK), June 18, 2010 (www.guardian.co.uk/business /2010/jun/18/bp-credit-rating-downgraded-oil-spill-hayward).

20. W. Bruce Johnson, Robert P. Magee, Nandu J. Nagarajan, and Harry A. Newman, "An Analysis of the Stock Price Reaction to Executive Deaths: Implications for the Managerial Labor Market," *Journal of Accounting and Economics* 7, nos. 1–3 (1985): 151–74.

21. "Inherited Control and Firm Performance," *American Economic Review* 96, no. 5 (December 2006): 1559–88. In related work using data from Denmark, Pérez-González shows that companies led by CEOs who have male first-borns have lower performance when those CEOs retire. The reason, he suggests, is that companies are more likely to keep leadership in the family if there is a male heir-apparent. Since the first-born's gender is truly random, it's hard to argue that the performance difference is the result of different management styles at companies that choose to keep management all in the family.

22. Though having such influential shareholders isn't without its problems—the Walton family could use its might on the board to appoint a feeble-minded Walton cousin as CEO, just so he has something to occupy his time; or lobby to have company funds diverted to Walton family charities; or insist that stores be built by Walton-owned construction companies at inflated prices.

23. Louis Lavelle, "The Best and Worst Boards," *BusinessWeek*, October 7, 2002 (www.businessweek.com/magazine/content/02_40/b3802001.htm), and John A. Byrne, "The Best and Worst Corporate Boards," *BusinessWeek*, January 24, 2000 (www.businessweek.com/2000/00_04/b3665022.htm).

24. David Matsa and Amalia Miller found that only 7.6 percent of corporate board members at large U.S. corporations were women in 1997. By 2009 it was up to 14.8 percent. Still pretty gentlemanly. "Chipping Away at the Glass Ceiling: Gender Spillovers in Corporate Leadership," *American Economic Review P&P* 101, no. 2 (May 2011): 635–39.

25. Kevin Hallock, "Reciprocally Interlocking Boards of Directors and Executive Compensation," *Journal of Financial and Quantitative Analysis* 32 (1997): 331–44. A 2003 analysis performed by The Corporate Library found that in 2002, more than 1,000 in-demand directors were on four or more

boards; 235 of these were on six or more. ("US Board and Director Inter-locks in 2003," The Corporate Library).

26. Brian Bell and John Van Reenen, "Firm Performance and Wages: Evidence from across the Corporate Hierarchy," CEP Discussion Paper No. 1088, May 2012 (cep.lse.ac.uk/pubs/download/dp1088.pdf).

27. This isn't to say there haven't been flagrant exceptions to this. In justifying Dick Grasso's enormous compensation package at the New York Stock Exchange, a nonprofit, the peer lists included such financial goliaths as Citigroup and Wells Fargo, but no other stock exchange or nonprofit organizations. Michael Faulkender and Jun Yang, "Inside the Black Box: The Role and Composition of Compensation Peer Groups," *Journal of Financial Economics* 96 (2010): 257–70, and "Is Disclosure an Effective Cleansing Mechanism? The Dynamics of Compensation Peer Benchmarking" (unpublished working paper).

28. Thomas A. DiPrete, Gregory M. Eirich, and Matthew Pittinsky, "Compensation Benchmarking, Leapfrogs, and the Surge in Executive Pay," *American Journal of Sociology* 115, no. 6 (May 2010): 1671–712.

29. At the same time, with so many hostile raiders on the hunt for takeover targets—which generally involved a lot of turnover at the top—it no longer seemed as worthwhile for CEOs to devote themselves to learning the intimate ins and outs of their companies.

30. It's worth noting that Jensen has since changed his mind.

31. Jesse Edgerton, "Agency Problems in Public Firms: Evidence from Corporate Jets in Leveraged Buyouts," *Journal of Finance*, forthcoming. Raghuram G. Rajan and Julie Wulf, "Are Perks Purely Managerial Excess?" *Journal of Financial Economics* 79 (2006): 1–33.

32. A few of the more successful ones were profiled by Michael Lewis in *The Big Short: Inside the Doomsday Machine* (New York: W. W. Norton, 2010).

Chapter 7: The Economics of Org Culture

1. The quotes come from Anonymous, "Traffic Change Drives Samoa into Turmoil," *Television New Zealand,* March 25, 2009 (http://tvnz.co .nz/world-news/traffic-change-drives-samoa-into-turmoil-2587483), and David Whitley, "Samoa Provokes Fury by Switching Sides of the Road," *Telegraph* (London), July 3, 2009 (http://www.telegraph.co.uk/motoring /news/5732906/Samoa-provokes-fury-by-switching-sides-of-the-road.html).

2. Organizational culture is, in more formal terms, "general shared social understanding, resulting in commonly held assumptions and views of the world among organizational members." This definition is from Roberto A. Weber and Colin F. Camerer, "Cultural Conflict and Merger Failure: An Experimental Approach," *Management Science* 49, no. 4 (April 2003): 400–15.

3. Weber and Camerer, "Cultural Conflict and Merger Failure."

4. Www.straightdope.com/columns/read/634/why-do-the-british-drive -on-the-left. See also books.google.com.au/books?id=lyoDAAAAMBAJ&lpg =PA11&pg=PA37#v=onepage&q&f=false. A less credible explanation suggests that most of Europe became right-sided because of the French Revolution. Before the revolution, the story goes, sword-wielding (and left-riding) aristocrats in France forced peasants off to the right. So when the revolution came, a right-handed norm had already developed among the formerly downtrodden, who were now in charge. The aristocrats who hadn't yet been guillotined just wanted to lie low and blend in—so they traveled on the right as well. Napoleon took care of the rest, spreading the right-handed norm through his conquest of Europe, including Germany, which then passed it on to Samoa. At least the last part of the story is about right.

The definitive guide to the history of driving rules seems to be Peter Kincaid's *The Rule of the Road: An International Guide to History and Practice* (Westport, CT: Greenwood Press, 1986).

5. It also has been much applied to strategy in actual games. The poker star Chris Ferguson—later indicted in the Full Tilt Poker fraud scandal of 2011—took thirteen years to finish a PhD in computer science in part because of his growing sideline as a cardsharp.

6. Robert Sutton, *The No Asshole Rule: Building a Civilized Workplace and Surviving One that Isn't* (New York: Business Plus, 2007). See also Sutton's blog post: bobsutton.typepad.com/my_weblog/2006/06/the_no_asshole_ .html.

7. Ernst Fehr and Simon Gächter, "Cooperation and Punishment in Public Goods Experiments," *American Economic Review* 90, no. 4 (September 2000): 980–94. In a recent study, researchers from Harvard and the Stockholm School of Economics demonstrated that allowing subjects to reward others for good behavior promotes cooperation just as much as punishments do. See D. Rand, A. Dreber, T. Ellingsen, D. Fudenberg, and M. Nowak, "Positive Interactions Promote Public Cooperation," *Science* 325 (2009): 1272–75.

8. In this sense, Mahatma Gandhi wasn't quite right in saying that an eye for an eye only ends up making the whole world blind—if everyone knows the consequences of harming others, no one loses an eye in the first place.

9. You can read the *New York Times* coverage of the company and the disaster here: topics.nytimes.com/top/news/business/companies/massey -energy-company/index.html. The report is available at library.corporate -ir.net/library/10/102/102864/items/305025/Massey_CSR_sm.pdf, accessed September 26, 2011.

10. See this post from the website Investors' Hub: Naureen S. Malik, "The Best Value in Coal Country" (investorshub.advfn.com/boards/ read_msg.aspx?message_id=23351598).

11. Once again, however, the threat of punishment is a useful complement to altruism. In a variant on the dictator game, the anonymous recipient gets to decide whether the dictator's split is fair. If the receiver decides it isn't, both sides get nothing. The prospect of retaliation (which harms both parties) helps a lot more dictators to decide that it's in their interest to play fair.

12. The classic paper is H. Tajfel, M. Billig, R. Bundy, and C. Flament, "Social Categorization and Intergroup Behaviour." *European Journal of Social Psychology* 1 (1971): 149–77. But Tajfel did many such experiments.

13. Articles 89 through 91 of the Uniform Code of Military Justice out-line the infractions and maximum punishments.

14. It's much less straightforward for suicide bombers, whose families are well compensated financially for successful attacks and who genuinely believe they'll be handsomely rewarded for martyrdom in the afterlife. John Easter-brook, "Salaries for Suicide Bombers," CBS News, February 11, 2009 (www.cbsnews.com/stories/2002/04/03/world/main505316.shtml, accessed July 11, 2012).

15. See Robert Gibbons and Rebecca Henderson, "Relational Contracts and Organizational Capabilities," *Organization Science* (Articles in Advance), December 22, 2011. Available at http://orgsci.journal.informs.org/content/early/2011/12/22/orsc.1110.0715.abstract, accessed July 11, 2012.

16. Such stories may not be true, but that's not the point. For instance, see this debunking of the Nordstrom story at the website Snopes.com: www.snopes.com/business/consumer/nordstrom.asp, accessed July 11, 2012.

17. Bob Sutton, "Places That Don't Tolerate Assholes: Updated Honor Roll," *Management Matters* blog, July 22, 2007 (bobsutton.typepad.com/my_weblog/2007/07/places-that-don-1.html, accessed July 11, 2012).

Chapter 8: Disaster and Change

1. A similar logic prompted governments around the world to sell their oil companies, power concessions, water utilities, and other state-run orgs that might be suited to private management and incentives.

2. Horton's efforts at slimming down BP bureaucracy were preceded by a memo to employees promising to offer them all a "challenging career"—which was followed in his short, unhappy two years by massive job cuts that, many employees would surely agree, presented career challenges to say the least.

3. See, for example, Joel Podolny, John Roberts, and Andris Berzins, "British Petroleum: Focus on Learning," Stanford GSB Case Study, S-IB-16A, 1998.

4. The Prudhoe Bay leak was followed in 2008 by "Operations Academy (OA)—founded…through the MIT Professional Education Program and the Sloan Executive Education office," a joint venture between BP and MIT. It was designed "to enhance the culture of continuous improvement at BP"— essentially an effort to put into effect the results of the Texas City refinery disaster report. For MIT's announcement of the venture, see web.mit.edu /newsoffice/2008/bp-mit-0410.html. See also Mattathias Schwartz, "How Fast Can He Cook a Chicken," a review of two recent BP books in the *London Review of Books* 33, no. 19 (October 6, 2011): 25–26 (www.lrb.co.uk/v33 /n19/mattathias-schwartz/how-fast-can-he-cook-a-chicken).

5. Chemical Safety Board, "CSB Investigation of BP Texas City Refinery Disaster Continues as Organizational Issues Are Probed," October 30, 2006 (www.csb.gov/newsroom/detail.aspx?nid=215, accessed July 11, 2012).

6. This is not quite the case. You can imagine tracking and rewarding near-misses. But that may simply encourage management to bury any record of close calls.

7. Scott Adams, "The Dilbert Principle," *Wall Street Journal*, May 22, 1995 (available online at voxmagister.ifsociety.org/dilbert_principle.htm, accessed July 11, 2012).

8. The FBI's version of its history is available on its website: www.fbi.gov /philadelphia/about-us/history, accessed July 11, 2012. On the rise of the FBI in the face of kidnappings and other cross-state-border crimes, see Brian Burrough, *Public Enemies: America's Greatest Crime Wave and the Birth of the FBI, 1933–34* (New York: Penguin Press, 2004).

9. How much of this could be chalked up to luck is an unanswerable question. A handy website titled "20 Mishaps That Might Have Started Accidental Nuclear War"—half of them during the five days of the Cuban Missile Crisis—recounts the case of the faulty computer chip and other chilling tales of how the world nearly came to an end. See www.wagingpeace.org/articles /1998/01/00_phillips_20-mishaps.php.

10. During the same three-year stretch, he completed two other books, a few dozen academic articles, kept up an active blog with Nobel Prize–winning

economist Gary Becker, and served as a judge on the Chicago Seventh Circuit Court of Appeals. "I work pretty continuously," he says. "I don't have hobbies. [Unless you count national security analysis.] I don't watch television or sports." Quoted in Eric Herman, "Posner the Pragmatic," *American Bar Association Journal* (September 1990): 100.

11. Melanie W. Sisson, "The FBI's 2nd-Class Citizens," *Washington Post*, op-ed, Saturday, December 31, 2005 (www.washingtonpost.com/wp-dyn /content/article/2005/12/30/AR2005123000994.html, accessed July 11, 2012).

Conclusion: The Future Org

1. Or so says Herman Miller on its corporate website: www.hermanmiller .com/designers/propst.html.

2. David Franz, "The Moral Life of Cubicles," *New Atlantis* 19 (Winter 2008). On the history of the Action Office, see Jerryll Habegger, *Sourcebook of Modern Furniture*, 3rd ed. (New York: W. W. Norton, 2005), and Leslie Pina, *Classic Herman Miller* (Atglen, PA: Schiffer Publishing, 1998).

3. Although, frankly, this doesn't sound like any boat we've been on. Maybe it's a reflection of life in Hyannis Port aboard the Winkler family yacht. The quotes are from John Tierney, "The Big City; By the Cubicle, The Dilberting of City Hall," *New York Times*, January 4, 2002.

4. On Nelson: Stanley Abercrombie, *George Nelson: The Design of Modern Design* (Cambridge: MIT Press, 1995). The Propst quote comes from Julie Schlosser, "Cubicles: The Great Mistake," *Fortune*, March 22, 2006 (money.cnn.com/2006/03/09/magazines/fortune/cubicle_howiwork _fortune/).

5. Abigail J. Sellen and Richard H. R. Harper, *The Myth of the Paperless Office* (Cambridge: MIT Press, 2001); see also Anonymous, "The Office of the Future," *BusinessWeek*, June 30, 1975 (www.businessweek.com/print /technology/content/may2008/tc20080526_547942.htm).

6. In fact, in *The Myth of the Paperless Office*, Abigail Sellen and Richard Harper report that e-mail adoption led companies to increase paper consumption by 40 percent on average.

7. We'll soon find out how it goes. Columbia is planning to go paperless with its expense reports as this manuscript goes to press.

8. Venkatesh Rao, "The End of Pax Papyra and the Fall of Big Paper," *Forbes* blog March 13, 2012 (www.forbes.com/sites/venkateshrao/2012/03 /13/the-end-of-pax-papyra-and-the-fall-of-big-paper/).

9. The subtitle of Oldenburg's book, *The Great Good Place*, gives you a sense of the thrust of his argument: *Cafés, Coffee Shops, Community Centers, Beauty Parlors, General Stores, Bars, Hangouts, and How They Get You through the Day* (New York: Paragon, 1989).

10. Gregory Dicum, "Hipster Hunting Ground," *New York Times*, July 13, 2008 (www.nytimes.com/2008/07/15/travel/15iht-13surfacing .14498817.html, accessed July 11, 2012). In Schultz's words, as a result of aggressive expansion, Starbucks has "diluted the customer experience" at its stores. In customers' words, Starbucks kind of sucks. Try convincing someone under the age of twenty that when the business started it was considered "fancy." The Schultz quote is from a memo leaked to the *Starbucks Gossip* blog, "Starbucks Chairman Warns of 'the Commoditization of the Starbucks Experience'" (starbucksgossip.typepad.com/_/2007/02/starbucks_chair_2 .html).

11. Nicholas Bloom, James Liang, John Roberts, and Zichung Jenny Ying, "Does Working from Home Work? Evidence from a Corporate Experiment," Stanford University working paper, 2012.

12. Bloom observed the same dynamic at JetBlue, which hired moms who fitted their work between getting kids ready for school and other daily errands and tasks (private communication).

13. In making grand predictions for the future, Leavitt and Whisler inevitably got a few things wrong. Most notably, they predicted that computers would also consolidate power in the C-Suite, whereas many see organizations headed in the opposite direction.

14. Oriana Bandiera, Andrea Prat, Raffaella Sadun, and Julie Wulf, "Span of Control and Span of Activity," Harvard Business School working paper 12-053.

15. Leavitt and Whisler were also at least partly right in foretelling the replacement of middle management by spreadsheets and other IT systems. Labor economists blame at least some of the recent stagnation in wages among the relatively educated bottom 99 percent on the substitution of lower-level white-collar jobs by IT systems.

16. Nicholas Bloom, Luis Garicano, Raffaella Sadun, and and John Van Reenen, "The distinct effects of information technology and communication technology on firm organization," Center for Economic Performance Discussion Paper, 2009.

17. Teresa Fasanello, "Bloomsbury Has Highest Crime Rate but It's Blamed on the Truck Stop," *Hunterdon County Democrat*, November 24, 2010 (www.nj.com/hunterdon-county-democrat/index.ssf/2010/11 /bloomsbury_has_high_crime_rate.html).

18. Hiring freelance truckers wasn't without consequences of its own. A company such as Lowe's relied on truckers to help out with filling and unloading plywood and two-by-fours at either end of the trip—hard, time-consuming work, potentially also involving delays at the loading dock while the trucker waits around for goods to arrive. It's a classic "multitask-ing" problem—as when policemen divide their time between solving murders and writing parking tickets. If Lowe's tried to contract with an independent driver, he could end up cutting corners, busting power tools, and otherwise cutting into the bottom line. George P. Baker and Thomas N. Hubbard, "Empirical Strategies in Contract Economics: Information and the Boundary of the Firm," *American Economic Review* 91, no. 2 (2001): 189–94; Thomas N. Hubbard, "Information, Decisions, and Productivity: On Board Computers and Capacity Utilization in Trucking," *American Economic Review* 93, no. 4 (2003): 1328–53; and George Baker and Thomas N. Hubbard, "Make Versus Buy in Trucking: Asset Ownership, Job Design, and Information," *American Economic Review* 93, no. 3 (2003): 551–72.

19. Sebastian Rotella, "Al Qaeda crosses the Ts in 'terrorist,'" *Los Angeles Times*, April 16, 2008.

20. Weber did suggest that charismatic leaders—warriors, prophets, and other visionaries, including politicians—could escape the iron cage.

INDEX

Browne, John, 217–22, 223, 224, 243
bureaucracy:
  coordination and, 103–4
  information and, 162, 240
  innovation and, 110–12, 113, 114, 117, 118, 119–21, 124, 125
  management and, 129, 147
  organizational structure and, 69, 70, 86, 88, 89, 97
  Weber on, 266
Burrows, Peter, 17–18
Bush, George W., 148

Caffarelli, Paul, 191
Camerer, Colin, 194–95, 197–98, 199
capitalism, 94, 137, 140, 192, 277n16
card counting, 170–71, 282n14, 282n16
Carnegie Mellon University, 194, 199
Carroll, Glenn, 262
Catholic Church, 67–71, 74, 274n2
cell phones, 28, 29, 114, 161, 168, 172, 260
Central Intelligence Agency, 226, 228, 232, 233–34, 237, 240
CEOs:
  autonomy of middle management and, 145
  compensation of, 169–72, 176, 179–85, 189–90, 282n12, 282n13, 282–83n16, 283n18, 285n27

corporate jets and, 188
daily tasks of, 157–62
decisions and, 22, 162, 168, 239
effect of hospitalizations, 283n17
golden parachutes and, 185–88, 190
hostile takeovers and, 285n29
incentives and, 78, 181, 187–88
information and, 160, 161, 162–66, 281n5
layoffs and, 19, 20
leadership of, 59, 166–68, 173
management style of, 168–72
market value of, 172–76
meetings and, 159–66, 188, 189, 215–16, 259, 281n3
merger opportunities and, 186–87
message of, 165–66
organizational structure and, 69, 84, 259
owners and, 176–79, 284n21
principal-agent problem and, 7
reputation of, 156–57
as superstars, 171–72, 283n18
Chadwick, William, 79–80, 275n9
Chandler, Alfred D., Jr., 137–42, 147, 279n8
change, 213–16, 223, 224, 244, 252
Chevron, 176–77, 183
Chicago Mercantile Exchange, 28, 271n10
Christensen, Clayton, 111
Chrysler, 140, 170
Citigroup, 169, 190
Clinton, Bill, 34, 165, 216
Cloud, John, 109

From Byron, Austen and Darwin

to some of the most acclaimed and original
contemporary writing, John Murray takes pride in
bringing you powerful, prizewinning, absorbing
and provocative books that will entertain you
today and become the classics of tomorrow.

We put a lot of time and passion into what we
publish and how we publish it, and we'd like to
hear what you think.

Be part of John Murray – share your views with us at:

www.johnmurray.co.uk

 johnmurraybooks

 @johnmurrays

johnmurraybooks

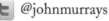
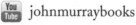